Democracy's Literature

Democracy's Literature

Politics and Fiction in America

EDITED BY
PATRICK J. DENEEN
AND
JOSEPH ROMANCE

ROWMAN & LITTLEFIELD PUBLISHERS, INC.
Lanham • Boulder • New York • Toronto • Oxford

ROWMAN & LITTLEFIELD PUBLISHERS, INC.

Published in the United States of America
by Rowman & Littlefield Publishers, Inc.
A wholly owned subsidiary of The Rowman & Littlefield Publishing Group, Inc.
4501 Forbes Boulevard, Suite 200, Lanham, Maryland 20706
www.rowmanlittlefield.com

PO Box 317
Oxford
OX2 9RU, UK

British Library Cataloguing in Publication Information Available

Library of Congress Cataloging-in-Publication Data

Democracy's literature : politics and fiction in America / edited by Patrick J. Deneen and Joseph Romance.

p. cm.

Includes bibliographical references and index.

ISBN 0-7425-3258-5 (alk. paper) — ISBN 0-7425-3259-3 (pbk. : alk. paper)

1. Political fiction, American—History and criticism. 2. American fiction—History and criticism. 3. Politics and literature—United States. 4. Democracy in literature. I. Deneen, Patrick J., 1964– II. Romance, Joseph, 1966– III. Title.

PS374.P6D46 2005

813.009'358—dc22 2005003647

Printed in the United States of America

∞™ The paper used in this publication meets the minimum requirements of American National Standard for Information Sciences—Permanence of Paper for Printed Library Materials, ANSI/NISO Z.39.48-1992.

Contents

Introduction

The Art of Democratic Literature

Patrick J. Deneen and Joseph Romance

In 2002, due to their disapproval of the president's policy with the war on terror, several prominent scholars of American literature initially refused to attend a White House gathering in honor of eminent American authors. First Lady Laura Bush responded to this threatened boycott with the following riposte: "There's nothing political about American literature."[1]

As the essays in this volume attest, nothing could be further from the truth: American literature is profoundly, almost inescapably, political. Indeed, it is hard to imagine such a democratic society not producing a literature that is decidedly political. However, the way in which American literature is political resists two prominent contemporary usages of the word "political." First, in contrast to the first lady's meaning, American literature is not political in the word's narrow, partisan connotation. This is not to say that American authors cannot be, or have not been, partisan and deeply political in this sense: indeed, many have been and will continue to be engaged in daily, partisan politics. But in the most important sense, one would be hard pressed to identify anything resembling a party platform in the great literary works of the American tradition. The political lessons our great writers teach are of a more profoundly philosophic nature.

Second, and perhaps more relevant for our age, American literature is not narrowly "political" in the sense often used by members of the professorate, namely, containing an assemblage of unconscious "isms": racism, sexism, colonialism, imperialism, capitalism, heterosexualism, and so forth. According to this meaning of "political," contemporary critics understand the works of authors better than they did themselves, exposing their unconscious prejudices and inoculating contemporary readers against any such narrowness. Contemporary readers are taught to approach classic literary texts from a position of assumed superiority, rejecting out of hand the possibility that they might contain a teaching or even offer a corrective to our own contemporary shortsightedness.

According to both of these inadequate definitions of politics, to be political is to be wholly subject to the limitations of one's own time. If, according to the first definition of "political," actors are so overly engaged in the reigning controversies of their day as to be rendered incapable of seeing deeper to the most fundamental and enduring aspects of politics, according to the latter definition, they are unconscious representatives of the narrow ideologies of their respective eras—ones from which today's enlightened critics have freed themselves. Both these distinct but equally limiting understandings of "politics"—one as narrow partisanship, the other as unreflective prejudice—miss the most important and fundamental sense in which America's great literary works are political. The essays in this volume point to this more fundamental and expansive understanding of politics.

Politics, by this understanding, consists of the active engagement by imperfect humans to forge a stable and vibrant political community in which citizens are at once individually distinctive yet also members of and participants in a larger political whole.[2] In America, the challenge of politics has been particularly daunting: as a democracy, the balance between communal cohesion and individual autonomy has been difficult to achieve and to maintain. Much of American political thought has consisted of this effort to find the proper balance between the rights of individuals and the demands of citizenship. Often this attempt unfolds as a kind of philosophic partisanship, notably in recent years in the form of debates pitting the claims of "communitarians" against "liberals." Stated with oversimplicity, these countervailing perspectives assume at their base a distinct human anthropology: for the former, humans are conceived as "situated selves" according to which individuality is constituted by and through our bonds and relationships with other humans; for the latter, humans are most fundamentally possessors of individual rights that allow and encourage resistance to encroachments on individual liberty in the form of political or communal membership. Debates have raged since America's founding—indeed, since the dawn of human consciousness, truth be told—over the proper relationship of the parts to the whole, of the many to the one. Mottos such as "E pluribus unum" ("out of many, one") point to the insoluble puzzle of democracy.

America's founders forged institutional structures designed at once to allow and contain this democratic struggle between the individual and the community. Yet, as the Declaration of Independence points out, this struggle is inevitable: in order to secure the inviolable rights of individuals, "governments are established" of necessity. Such governments cannot consist of public functionaries who work on behalf of private-regarding individuals: even liberal governments necessarily rely upon a sufficiently robust public spirit among rights-bearing individuals. The formal necessity of government—instituted, in the liberal tradition, in order to secure individual rights—nevertheless simultaneously requires a high degree of public spirit and even willingness to sacrifice the full measure of those rights. While the Declaration of Independence, on the one hand, claims that the rights of life, liberty, and the pursuit of happiness are inalienable, nonetheless its peroration attests to the willingness of its signers to pledge their "lives, fortunes, and sacred honor" in the effort to secure those rights. In order to secure the right to life, those who would enjoy it must be willing to sacrifice it.

The founders realized that a rights-based regime could not rely upon institutions alone to secure those rights: Madison wrote in *Federalist* 55, "as there is a degree of depravity in mankind which requires a certain degree of circumspection and distrust, so there are other qualities in human nature which justify a certain portion of esteem and confidence. Republican government presupposes the existence of these qualities in a higher degree than any other form . . . [otherwise] the inference would be, that there is not sufficient virtue among men for self-government."[3] Nevertheless, the Constitution did not itself seek positively to inculcate the civic virtues that a liberal regime necessarily requires: the framers left this work to the private realm where an instruction in virtue would take place in families, in churches, in local schools, and within the context of small communities.

While these local institutions had, and still retain, the bulk of responsibility in the cultivation of civic virtue, as America became increasingly a *national* system, particularly during the nineteenth century and especially in the wake of the Civil War, many of its thoughtful citizens grew concerned that such haphazard, local forms of civic education were insufficient for the increasingly complex task of equipping people for citizenship in a vast and complex nation-state. Some—such as Horace Mann, and later, John Dewey—sought to establish a more standardized system of education that emphasized national identity and civic competence. Others, echoing a sentiment Lincoln articulated with succinct force in his Gettysburg Address, sought to invest the nation with a form of "civic religion," a political belief that would effectively forge a national consciousness and identity akin to the devotion of religious faith.[4]

What these undertakings point to more generally is an effort by thoughtful Americans to inculcate a *philosophic* disposition that would encourage individual and collective efforts to balance the necessary devotion to nation and the core belief in individual autonomy. Such a balance could not be achieved automatically as a result of one's easy identification with one's locality and an appreciation for its contribution to one's individuality. Because of the continental expanse of the American system, such identification with the whole increasingly required a philosophic frame of mind. Devotion was not to "land" or place as such, but to the *idea* of America.[5] We were a people devoted to a *proposition*, according to Lincoln, not to a particular piece of land in which generations of our ancestors were buried. America presented a unique challenge: how to cultivate a generalized philosophic disposition in the citizenry of such a sprawling and "abstract" nation. For much of the world's history, there was the assumption that the heights of philosophy were only available to the privileged few. America was faced with the challenge—seemingly insurmountable—of making philosophy sufficiently accessible and broad yet sufficiently profound to forge a democratic citizenry on a mass scale.

America has had its philosophers—Dewey, James, Peirce, and in recent years, Rawls, Rorty, and any number of academic philosophers—but largely their most rigorous work has been, and increasingly is being, undertaken in universities, intended for a tiny circle of fellow academics. If one were to search for any philosophic texts that have made a deep and widespread impression on the American democratic psyche, one would be hard pressed to name a single volume. Nothing would come close to the influence of the Bible, then or now. On the other hand, observers as early as Alexis de Tocqueville noted that Americans are avid readers—of newspapers, certainly—but, surprisingly, of novels as well.[6] America—populated with a practical and pragmatic people—has nonetheless long been a nation of readers of fiction. America's most thoughtful authors long ago realized that it was through the novel, the novella, and the story that the philosophic education of America's citizens would best be undertaken. While many commentators have long suggested that America's contributions to political philosophy offer only slim pickings, it is only because often they have been looking in the wrong places. A vast political and philosophical corpus exists in America, but much of it is to be found on the fiction shelves, not necessarily or exclusively in the philosophy section.

American philosophy is thus "pragmatic" in a broader sense than is commonly conceived: in its literary guise, it is a philosophy intended to be *public, political*, and *accessible*. It is a philosophy intended to have an effect upon its readers in concrete ways: to foster thoughtfulness and reflection among citizens, to inculcate a set of civic dispositions such as liberality, magnanimity, and generosity, to cultivate an expansive democratic sensibility. Democratic philosophy, unlike that of an aristocratic regime, must necessarily seek to touch and influence the broadest range of potential citizens. And unlike aristocratic literature, a democratic philosophy must necessarily be infused with not only a spirit of egalitarianism, but also an outlook that retains a devotion to individual distinctiveness. It is a philosophy that must at once stress the general and the specific, that which makes democratic citizens fundamentally similar amid their uniqueness.

Indeed, this inescapable feature of democratic literature points us to the recognition that the literary form of American public philosophy is not epiphenomenal or merely an entertaining format for popular consumption, but rather an inherent feature of its pedagogy. A democratic philosophy—as Walt Whitman so evocatively argued in *Democratic Vistas*—is drawn to the literary form. While it is foolish to attempt to reduce the multiplicity of literary voices to a single overarching philosophical theme, it is perhaps not inaccurate to suggest that at its broadest and most comprehensive level, the American public philosophy advanced in its greatest literary works attempts to teach a form of what Hannah Arendt has called "enlarged mentality" through "representational thinking."[7] By drawing us into the thoughts, the consciousness, the sensations of fictional characters, democratic literature seeks, on the one hand, to expand the vision of democratic individuals beyond the dangerous shoals of what Tocqueville called "individualism."[8] On the other hand, by allowing us, in turn, to think with and closely experience the consciousness of *specific* characters, democratic literature prevents us from being drawn too closely to the other opposite hazard, which Tocqueville described as another danger to democracy, namely, the resistance to draw distinctions between individuals, between man and nature, between man and God, that is, "pantheism."[9] Literature, in this sense, represents a democratic reformulation of the truth of Philip Sidney's sixteenth-century "Defence of Poetry," in which he defends the pedagogical superiority of literature over that of history and philosophy. History, on the one hand, immerses us in hearsay and facts and does not cultivate the ability to think more generally about the implications or even applications of such specifics to our own lives and times. Philosophy, on the other hand, engages in analysis at the level of pure abstraction, divorced from the real and material considerations of actual human beings.[10] Literature—like democracy—requires us to remain at the midpoint between the specific and the general, drawing from the truths of each without falling prey to their respective excesses. Democracy and literature are natural partners, a relationship that America's greatest authors have long realized in their subtle efforts to craft a democratic public philosophy.

★ ★ ★ ★ ★

The essays collected in this volume all implicitly reflect an acknowledgment of this close relationship between democracy and literature, as well as an understanding that the greatest American literary works are also works of profound philosophical insight. For all their variety, these essays all begin with the assumption that thoughtful authors in a democracy have a teaching. This is not to say that such a teaching is akin to a rote classroom lesson: rather, these works seek to challenge and deepen unreflective American self-understanding. Furthermore, the depth and subtlety of literary teachings serve as an important corrective to the more sterile nature of some traditional political science. In many ways, these essays capture the depth and complexity that is democratic practice in America. Above all, these works point to the *art* and *artfulness* of democratic literature. There is a craft to writing works of such philosophical subtlety, but equally, there is an extraordinary craft to *reading* such texts. If democracy needs supremely gifted and thoughtful authors to articulate an accessible yet serious democratic teaching, democracy equally needs discerning guides who foster the reflective disposition and interpretive skills that such works—and indeed, a democratic setting itself—require.

The authors of the literary works examined in these pages pay their readers the supreme compliment of making their teachings *difficult*. The subtlety of these *readings* of the various crafty literary works shows that the teaching of the respective authors is most often not obvious or superficial. The sophistication of the teachings in these literary works at once reveals the exceedingly high standards and expectations that these diverse authors set for their readers while also pointing to the high regard of these authors for the capacities of their democratic reading audiences. These are not teachings intended to be reserved only for those with extensive philosophical training; rather, they suggest that a central feature of America's great literature consists of a shared effort to ennoble democracy by setting the bar of equality high rather than, as has been feared by many of democracy's critics, attempting to appeal to the lowest common denominator. These works point citizens to the best angels of their nature, even as they warn against the aspiration to make a heaven of earth. As Ralph Ellison argued, it is through fiction that democracies can bring the ideal and the real into closest proximity: "even if true political equality eludes us in reality—as it continues to do—there is still available that fictional vision of an ideal democracy in which the actual combines with the ideal and gives us representations of a state of things in which the highly placed and the lowly, the black and the white, the Northerner and the Southerner, the native-born and the immigrant combine to tell us transcendent truths and possibilities."[11]

The artfulness of the authors of these works—and the craft of their readers in this volume—point finally to the truth of Mark Twain's great acknowledgment of the compatibility of democratic equality and excellence: "we all have music and poetry in our souls; some of us simply are able to get it out better than others."[12] The authors of the essays in this volume help us all hear that music a bit more clearly.

Notes

1. Elisabeth Bumiller, "Laura Bush and Her Off-the-Page Guests," *International Herald Tribune*, October 8, 2002, available at www.iht.com/articles/73054.html.

2. On this recurrent aspect of politics generally, and American democratic politics particularly, see James A. Block, *A Nation of Agents: The American Path to a Modern Self and Society* (Cambridge, MA: Harvard University Press, 2003).

3. Alexander Hamilton, James Madison, and John Jay, "Federalist Paper 55: The Total Number of the House of Representatives," in *The Federalist Papers*, ed. Isaac Kramnick (New York: Penguin Books, 1987), 339.

4. See Eldon J. Eisenach, *The Next Religious Establishment: National Identity and Political Theology in Post-Protestant America* (New York: Rowman & Littlefield, 2000).

5. See John Schaar, "The Case for Patriotism," *American Review* 17 (May 1973): 59–99, for an excellent clarification of the distinction between "natural" and "covenantal" patriotism.

6. Alexis de Tocqueville, "On the Relation between Associations and Newspapers," in *Democracy in America*, trans. Harvey C. Mansfield and Delba Winthrop (Chicago: University of Chicago Press, 2000), II.ii.6; hereafter cited as *DA*. See also *DA*, "The Literary Face of Democratic Centuries," II.i.12. There, Tocqueville contrasts the shared literate and educated aristocratic formalism of literature with the rough and easily consumed (and quickly forgotten) democratic form of literature. While Tocqueville is undoubtedly right in predicting the rise of what we now call "best-selling" fiction, he also noted that "writers will be encountered now and then who will want to take another path, and if they have superior merit, they will succeed in getting themselves read in spite of their defects and their [good] qualities; but these exceptions will be rare, and these very ones who have departed in this way from common usage in the entirety of their works will always return to it in some details" (449).

7. Hannah Arendt, "Truth and Politics," in *Between Past and Future: Eight Exercises in Political Thought* (New York: Penguin Books, 1956), 241.

8. Tocqueville, *DA*, "Of Individualism in Democratic Countries," II.ii.2.

9. Tocqueville, *DA*, "What Makes the Mind of Democratic Peoples Lean toward Pantheism," II.i.7.

10. Philip Sidney, *A Defence of Poetry* (Oxford, U.K.: Oxford University Press, 1966), 32, 38.

11. Ralph Ellison, "Introduction to *Invisible Man*," in *The Collected Essays of Ralph Ellison*, ed. John F. Callahan (New York: Modern Library, 1995), 482.

12. Notebook 42, June 1897–March 1950, Mark Twain Papers, Bancroft Library, University of California, Berkeley.

1

Billy Budd and the Politics of Prudence

Dan Sabia

Among the many themes dramatized in Herman Melville's *Billy Budd, Sailor*, political and philosophical divisions between proponents of revolution, equality, and popular liberty and government, on the one hand, and defenders of law and order, hierarchy, and elite privilege and power, on the other, have a prominent place. Although the relevance of these oppositions for political and social life was hardly unique to Melville's nineteenth-century America, nevertheless they were of great significance in that often violent time and place, just as they had been in the preceding revolutionary and founding period of American history. In that earlier time, the oppositions had been ably represented, or at least well illuminated, by Burke and Paine, in the historic debate that remained a matter of public interest and commentary in the United States even while Melville was working on the manuscript of *Billy Budd* nearly a century later.[1] Hence, it is not surprising, particularly in light of Melville's well-known philosophical and political interests, that many of the presuppositions and claims present in that famous debate have a prominent, if not, indeed, central place, in his equally famous story.[2] Readers of the tale are in effect informed of this fact in the very first chapter, when they are told by the narrator that the merchant ship on which Billy was serving, and from which he was being taken after being impressed into the British navy, was named the *Rights-of-Man*. "That was the merchant ship's name. . . . The hardheaded Dundee owner [of the vessel] was a staunch admirer of Thomas Paine, whose book in rejoinder to Burke's arraignment of the French Revolution had then been published for some time and had gone everywhere" (297).[3]

Within the broad context of Burke's condemnation and Paine's defense of popular revolution and government, attention was paid by both thinkers to the nature of and conditions for political prudence, or wise judgment in politics. On Burke's account, political prudence was one of the great goods sacrificed on the altar of democratic politics, whereas for Paine, democratic practices alone guaranteed political wisdom. The claim of this essay is that *Billy Budd* speaks to this disagreement and sheds light on it. At the center of the drama is a series of difficult, potentially explosive decisions made by Captain Vere regarding the proper treatment of Billy Budd. Budd serves in the story as a symbol of natural innocence, while Vere is easily and often taken as the embodiment of political virtue or prudence par excellence, typically in a Burkean mode.[4] I argue initially that Vere's character and the decisions he makes do embody and reflect a Burkean, or what might be termed an "aristocratic," prudence. But I then argue that the text invites readers to question both the attractiveness of Vere's character and the wisdom of his decisions. By throwing doubt on Vere's prudence, the text can be read as questioning the association of good judgment with superior men and elitist political practices and as entertaining the possibility, and possible superiority, of what might be termed a "democratic" prudence. Although this suggestion is no more original in our time than it was in Melville's, attention to his provocative and insightful text is warranted in light of current disagreements over the substance of political prudence and its place in our politics.[5]

Despite disagreements, many scholars agree that political prudence names both a kind of virtue, or excellence, and a kind, or faculty, of judgment. Until the rise of what used to be called the democratic age, prudence so conceived was most often associated with monarchical and aristocratic politics; in conservative quarters, the association persists to the present day.[6] Prudent men—until recently, of course, always men—were thought, by birth and training aristocratic or elite, superior in intellect and virtue when compared to the common folk or the many or multitude. Given the great demands, dangers, and temptations of political life, communities were accordingly thought to do best by entrusting such men with authority and power, permitting them to dominate, if not wholly control, key political processes such as lawmaking. Something like this was the view of most Greek and Roman theorists, for instance Aristotle and Cicero, of medieval and Renaissance thinkers like Aquinas and Thomas More, and, in different guises, of many modern writers, especially of conservative and cautious thinkers like Burke, Madison, and Weber.

The superiority of the prudent, the reasons given for why they make the best legislators or founders, kings or princes, leaders or statesmen, of course varies across thinkers and over time. Yet, there is perhaps a certain family resemblance that is not so hard to discern. It looks, I think, something like this: unlike most people, the prudent have access to philosophical or theoretical knowledge, so they are particularly good at fashioning and evaluating moral and political principles and ends, as well as particular laws and institutions, policies and actions; in addition, and again unlike most people, they are well-educated, keen observers of the human condition, with much experience and thus considerable worldly knowledge, so they are not likely to chart for the ship of state a foolish or dangerous course; and, finally, unlike most people, they have an ensemble of certain character traits—self-knowledge and self-control, foresight and flexibility, circumspection, decisiveness, courage, empathy—which make them especially trustworthy and successful as rulers. They are, accordingly, the kind of men most likely to aim at and to secure policies and laws that are the best they can be—*prudent* policies and laws that actually work and yet are morally or ethically the best they can be, given the typically constraining, complex, and contingent circumstances in and under which political decisions have to be made.

Captain Vere is, or certainly seems to be, an exemplar of this family portrait. True it is that Vere captains a warship and not a ship of state, but this fact arguably serves only to underscore how crucial prudent leadership is, since the business of warships is so very important. The fact does not, in any case, affect my interest in exploring the connection between prudence and political forms, since the aristocratic Captain Vere appears to be an exceptionally able leader ruling a decidedly undemocratic ship in a decidedly undemocratic manner. There is no doubt that he would reject out of hand any scheme that sought to democratize his ship, because he regarded schemes to do precisely that to political communities as being "at war with the peace of the world and the true welfare of mankind" (312). Why did he feel that way? And, more importantly, was he right? Is prudence a rare gift, or talent, or can democratic citizens—or democratic polities—be prudent? In the following section, I begin addressing these questions by making the case for Vere's prudence.

I

"Captain the Honorable Edward Fairfax Vere . . . was a bachelor of forty or thereabouts, a sailor of distinction even in a time of renowned seamen" (309). The time referenced is 1797, when the warship captained by Vere is in hostile Mediterranean waters. The date (and also the place, as we shall later see) play an important role in the story, for it is not only a time of war with revolutionary France but, as well, follows by only a few months various rebellions by British seamen, the most exceptional of which was known as the "Great Mutiny" at Nore on the Thames. Protesting their inhumane and oppressive treatment, including the ongoing practice of impressment, the mutineers were "more menacing to England than the contemporary manifestoes and conquering and proselyting armies of the French Directory. To the British Empire the Nore Mutiny was what a strike in the fire brigade would be to London threatened by general arson" (303). During the mutiny, thousands of rebels ran up the red flag at Nore, challenging not merely the authorities but authority itself: "Reasonable discontent growing out of practical grievances in the fleet had been ignited into irrational combustion as by live cinders blown across the Channel from France in flames" (303).

Although ultimately suppressed, the discontent that spawned the Great Mutiny "lurkingly survived. . . . Hence it was not unreasonable to apprehend some return of trouble sporadic or general" (308). In fact, when on "short notice" a naval engagement began, "the lieutenants assigned to batteries felt it incumbent on them, in some instances, to stand with drawn swords behind the men working the guns" (308). Such behavior was not necessary, however, on Captain Vere's ship because of his leadership skills and "exceptional character" (311; also 309). Aristocratic by birth, Vere's successful advancement in the navy reflected more his talents than his class connections (309). "He had seen much service, been in various engagements, always acquitting himself as an officer mindful of the welfare of his men" (309). He was, of course, "thoroughly versed in the science of his profession" and had more than once proved his gallantry; regarding the latter, he was in fact "intrepid to the verge of temerity, though never injudiciously so" (309). A somber and "undemonstrative" man, Vere's "unaffected modesty" and "resolute nature" reflected his aristocratic background and temper (310).

Besides his "sterling qualities" as a naval officer, Vere "had a marked leaning toward everything intellectual" (311). Engaged as he was in one "of the world's more heroic activities" (310), the captain's reading habits aimed at uncovering information and insights useful to a man with his responsibilities:

> He loved books, never going to sea without a newly replenished library, compact but of the best. . . . [H]is bias was toward those books to which every serious mind of superior order occupying any active post of authority in the world naturally inclines: books treating of actual men and events no matter of what era—history, biography, and unconventional writers like Montaigne, who, free from cant and conviction, honestly and in the sprit of common sense philosophize upon realities. (311)

This selective reading served to clarify and confirm Captain Vere's "more reserved thoughts . . . touching most fundamental topics" (311). And because they could be neither challenged nor affirmed "in social converse" among the inferiors he dealt with at sea, Vere's ideas about topics "fundamental" grew into quite steadfast convictions.

> In view of the troubled period in which his lot was cast, this was well for him. His settled convictions were as a dike against those invading waters of novel opinion, social, political, and otherwise, which carried away as in a torrent no few minds in those days. . . . While other members of that aristocracy to which by birth he belonged were incensed at the innovators mainly because their theories were inimical to the privileged classes, Captain Vere

> disinterestedly opposed them not alone because they seemed to him insusceptible of embodiment in lasting institutions, but at war with the peace of the world and the true welfare of mankind. (312)

Aristocratic, well-educated, and well-read, superior in intellect, experienced, courageous and resolute, Vere was, perhaps as a result of these characteristics, a discerning and empathic man as well. He could, for instance, easily read and understand a person's feelings, motives, even character. Referring early on to the "moral phenomenon" represented by Billy Budd (i.e., Billy's "primitive" goodness and innocence), the narrator opines that few besides Vere were "intellectually capable of adequately appreciating [this fact]" (328).[7] Such "insight" is also referenced when readers are informed that "something exceptional in the moral quality of Captain Vere" enabled him on most occasions to discern another "man's essential nature" and again when it is said that he could "immediately divine" from the actions of others their likely motives or states of mind (346–47, 349).

All of Vere's talents are put into play after Billy Budd strikes and kills the "depraved" master-at-arms, Claggart. This bizarre incident occurs when the warship is alone in hostile waters, separated from the fleet. It had been sent out on a scouting mission and had moved yet further from the fleet in failed pursuit of an enemy ship. Vere's warship had been chosen for this task "not alone because of her sailing qualities . . . but quite as much, probably, that the character of her commander, it was thought, specially adapted him for any duty where under unforeseen difficulties a prompt initiative might have to be taken in some manner demanding knowledge and ability in addition to those qualities implied in good seamanship" (340). Hence, the incident could "not have happened at a worse juncture" (353). The ship is isolated in dangerous waters. And what was worse, the event occurs "close on the heel of the suppressed insurrections, an aftertime very critical to naval authority, demanding from every English sea commander two qualities not readily interfusable—prudence and rigor" (353).

Prudence is always discerning and, therefore, sometimes flexible. Circumstances change, cases are always to some degree unique. The tension between flexibility and rigor is in *Billy Budd* reflected in the extraordinary incident at its center, recognized by Vere as "a moral dilemma involving aught of the tragic" (356). For the captain knows that, though the evil Claggart had intrigued against the innocent Billy Budd, Billy's behavior meant that

> innocence and guilt personified in Claggart and Budd [had] in effect changed places. . . . Yet more. The essential right and wrong involved in the matter, the clearer that might be, so much the worse for the responsibility of a loyal sea commander, inasmuch as he was not authorized to determine the matter on that primitive basis. (354)

Pressed by the perilous circumstances represented by his ship's isolation in hostile waters with a potentially hostile crew, Vere decides to call a drumhead court to deal with the incident. To his subordinate officers, this decision seems unwise, even "mad." The "thing to do," they think when told of the incident, is "to place Billy Budd in confinement, and in a way dictated by usage, and postpone further action . . . to such time as they should rejoin the squadron, and then refer it to the admiral" (352). The officers are not cognizant of the dangers seen, nor are they mindful of the possible dangers foreseen, by the captain. Vere, in fact, wishes he could follow "usage" by locking Billy up and deferring the matter to the admiral later in time (354–55). But precisely time is not, in the circumstances, available. Decisive action is required, for "unless quick action was taken on it, the deed of [Billy], so soon as it should be known on the gun decks, would tend to awaken any slumbering embers of the Nore among the crew" (355). The same consideration, we shall see, enters into the decision of the court regarding Billy's ultimate fate.

Since Vere's authority is absolute, and time is dear, it is not at first clear why he bothers with the court-martial proceeding. The narrator provides the following explanation:

> [T]hough a conscientious disciplinarian, he was no lover of authority for mere authority's sake. Very far was he from embracing opportunities for monopolizing to himself the perils of moral responsibility, none at least that could properly be referred to an official superior or shared with him by his official equals or even subordinates. So thinking, he was glad it would not be at variance to turn the matter over to a summary court of his own officers, reserving to himself, as the one on whom the ultimate accountability would rest, the right of maintaining a supervision of it, or formally or informally interposing at need. Accordingly a drumhead court was summarily convened. (355)

Sensitive to the "perils of moral responsibility," Vere apparently calls for the court, then, because he wants to think through his options and test his intuitions, most especially his virtually immediate judgment, made when Billy kills Claggart, that Billy "must hang" (352). Vere does this despite knowing that his subordinate officers are not his equals, that they are "not intellectually mature" (360). Although he goes out of his way to include on the court his best officers, he feels that none are really up to the task; the most "judicious" and "thoughtful" of the three he selects was not likely to "prove altogether reliable in a moral dilemma involving aught of the tragic," while the "intelligence" of the other two "was mostly confined to the matter of active seamanship and the fighting demands of their profession" (355–56).

Throughout the proceeding, Vere's assessment of his officers seems accurate; they have to be guided throughout by their prudent captain. He has to remind them of the distinction, so critical to the military code, between motive and action (358). He must articulate for them the central dilemma presented by the strange case: that it seems to present "a clash of military duty with moral scruple—scruple vitalized by compassion" (361). In a striking passage, Vere instructs the men to "challenge" their scruples, to "make them advance and declare themselves," so that they can be examined and evaluated (361). Reminding them of their duties, he distinguishes between "natural justice" and what the military code and the king demand (361). Admitting that he too feels compassion for Billy, that Billy's plight moves his heart as well as theirs, he warns them not to let "warm hearts betray heads that should be cool" (362). As they must not allow their personal feelings to cloud their reason, he continues, so too must they resist "private conscience," since their authority to judge (to "officially proceed") derives from the military code and not from private or natural right (362).

Perhaps most important, Vere has to return to the distinction between intention and action, explaining to the officers why, since Billy in fact intended "neither mutiny nor homicide," his guilt is nonetheless certain and cannot be extenuated. The reason, he explains, is because "we proceed under the law of the Mutiny Act . . . [which] resembles in spirit the thing from which it derives—War" (363). In "this ship"—in a warship under dangerous and pressing circumstances—actions alone are what count. Men at war must take their bearings by the things people do and not by the reasons they may have for doing them; nor can they postpone action because of "anxieties" or moral discomfort, since at any time an "enemy may be sighted and an engagement result" (363).

Concluding, then, that "we must do [i.e., act immediately]," Vere's officers nonetheless wonder aloud whether they might "convict and yet mitigate the penalty" (363). Thus, Vere must again explain to them the need to "consider [the circumstances and] the consequences" of their actions, in this case "the consequences of such clemency" (364).

> The people [meaning the ship's company] have native sense; most of them are familiar with our naval usage and tradition; and how would they take it? Even could you explain to them—which official position forbids—they, long molded by arbitrary discipline, have not that kind of intelligent responsiveness that might qualify them to comprehend and discriminate. No, to the people [Billy's] deed, however it be worded in the announcement, will be plain homicide committed in a flagrant act of mutiny. What penalty for that should follow, they know. But it does not follow. *Why?* they will ruminate. You know what sailors are. Will they not revert to the recent outbreak at Nore? Ay . . . [and so they will] think that we flinch, that we are afraid of them—afraid of practicing a lawful rigor singularly demanded at this juncture, lest it should provoke new troubles. What shame to us such a conjecture on their part, and how deadly to discipline. (364)

The maintenance of discipline, so essential to the order, safety, and military readiness of the ship and its crew, explains the need in this case for a rigorous application of the military code, just as those same ends justify the code itself. Although Vere "feels for the boy," although he "suffers" from his decision, his prudence carries the day (364, 367). Wholly committed to the good of the ship, he can see what that requires, and he can meet its demands. The situation he confronts is one of "military necessity," an emergency "involving considerations both practical and moral, and [in which] it is imperative promptly to act" (364, 365). Unlike the lowly sailors on his ship—"in character a juvenile race" (337)—Vere knows why the code takes the form it does, and why, in this case, it must be rigorously and immediately applied. Unlike his officers, who can to some degree share in this knowledge only when guided by their captain, Vere's intelligence and foresight help him locate the best decision, his self-control enables him to resist the pull of private feeling and conscience, and his courage allows him to act decisively. He is a superior man, theoretically informed, practically wise, with an exceptional character. He is, in brief, a prudent ruler, and it is good that his rule is absolute. "God bless Captain Vere!" are Billy's last words; "God bless Captain Vere!" echo "the ship's populace" when Billy is put to death (375).

II

Captain Vere's ship, it seems fair to conclude, models a form of politics in which the superior man, the kind of man reminiscent of Aristotle's *phronimos*, is sovereign. The story suggests that this form of politics is desirable because of the nature of both politics and humankind: politics is too important to individual and collective well-being, too difficult, given the dangers and uncertainties of political action, and too demanding, given the temptations and intellectual and moral challenges of political office, to be left to the juvenile and intellectually immature, which describes most of humanity. Ideally, intellectual and moral superiority or excellence should alone mark a person deserving of rule. Because (as Burke put it) prudence is "the first of all virtues," or because (as Aristotle expressed it) "the only virtue special to a ruler is *phronesis*," prudence should be the primary, if not the sole determinant of the distribution of political authority.[8]

As we have seen, Captain Vere certainly appears to be such a ruler. He is portrayed as well-intentioned and reflective, discerning and insightful, impartial and self-controlled, always in command of his passions, a good, smart, sensitive leader with a cool head. He is inegalitarian in outlook and no friend of democracy, correlating deserved political status with intellectual capacity and moral merit or maturity. He guides his officers and disciplines his crew, but only for the good of his ship. His judgment is clearly informed by theoretical as well as experiential knowledge; he has a sophisticated grasp of morality and political ethics, as reflected in his comments about the limits of "natural" and "perfect" justice and the demands of law, duty, and circumstance. Although committed to the law, he exercises reflection and foresight before applying it in unusual cases. And he recognizes—one might well say the story emphasizes—how caution and a tolerance for imperfection and even evil are necessary qualities in an impure, inadequate, and dangerous world.

There are many examples and indications in *Billy Budd* of how an array of human and natural forces, imperfections, inadequacies, and obstacles constrain choice and recommend both moderation and accommodation to the necessary and the inevitable. One especially pertinent example concerns the practice of impressment. The reader is told early on that impressment was "not practicable to give up in those years," even though the passage goes on to suggest that the practice had become a political and moral embarrassment, as well as a festering source of discontent and mutiny (308). The problem was an imbalance of demand and supply: the demand for men to hoist "innumerable sails" and shoot "thousands of cannon" was "multiplying" because of "contingencies present and to come of the convulsed Continent" (308). Hence, the "abrogation [of the practice] would have crippled the indispensable fleet" (308). During the court proceeding, Vere seems to endorse both judgments—that impressment is an evil, but a necessary one—when he asserts, "In his Majesty's service—in this ship, indeed—there are Englishmen forced to fight for the King against their wills" (363). Another example is not much more than a passing remark, made about "men of the world," who develop a "ruled undemonstrative distrustfulness" in their dealings with other human beings, the suggestion being that a degree of feigning, and of wariness and distrust of others, deserves cultivating in a world short on saints and long on sinners (337). Many more examples could be cited.

But all the examples, even the necessary evil of impressment, pale in comparison to what is said to be the necessary but less than ideal treatment of Billy Budd. It is not just that the law applicable to Billy, the naval code, appears to require his execution despite his innocent intentions, nor even that the good of the ship appears to require that he be sacrificed. There is the larger if less obvious point that Billy's primitive goodness and moral innocence renders him seemingly unfit for the civilized world: "Billy in many respects was little more than a sort of upright barbarian, much such perhaps as Adam presumably might have been ere the urbane Serpent wriggled himself into his company" (301). Billy is naive, illiterate, inexperienced, and unknowing and a danger for all these reasons; unable to defend himself in a civilized manner when falsely accused by Claggart, he can only "gesture and gurgle" and then strike out in violence (349, 350). This is, on one reading of the novel, the underlying reason Billy has to die. People like Captain Vere, whose job it is to bring a degree of security and justice to the world, know their duty in such a situation. Just as they will not tolerate pure evil, so too will they not tolerate the wholly or naturally good, at least not when it runs amok (as it inevitably will once it intrudes into the political arena); and so they negotiate the very large space between the two poles.[9]

But is Billy's death really a tragic necessity? Is Vere's decision in this matter truly prudent? Was it, in the circumstances, politically and morally the best possible course of action? On the reading presented so far, the decision to execute Billy is the last in a series of prudent decisions made by a prudent leader in an imperfect and dangerous world, decisions that reflect the need for an informed and well-intentioned posture of "circumspection and caution" and accommodation to "necessity" (the words are Burke's).[10] The ship's predicament, the requirements of law and institutional duty, and Billy's unfitness all require his execution, however disconcerting or sad we find this to be. Support for this interpretation is provided not only by the dying words of acclamation by Billy and their echo by the crew, but also by the facts that Billy's death is described as perhaps "a species of euthanasia" and that, on his own deathbed some weeks later, Vere remains clearly troubled by the Budd case yet free of "remorse" (377, 382).

Yet, the related contentions that Billy's death is a tragic or lamentable but justified event, and the captain's character and decision making prudent, are open to question. In fact, the narrator at least twice invites, and many times seems to encourage, scrutiny of both Vere's character and his decisions. The first explicit occasion arises after the captain summons the ship's surgeon to his cabin, the place where Billy struck and killed Claggart moments after the incident occurred, in order to confirm that Claggart is indeed dead. Also described as a "prudent" man, the surgeon wonders to himself whether the captain has come "unhinged," not literally "mad," but suffering a "degree of aberration." His wonderment is aroused by "the excited manner [displayed by Vere in the cabin, and which] he had never before observed in the . . . captain," as well as by Vere's "passionate" outbursts (proclaiming "Struck dead by an angel of God! Yet the angel must hang!") and then by his surprising call for an immediate and secret drumhead court proceeding, all of which conduct certainly calls into question Vere's presumed self-control, if not his sanity (351–52). The narrator, after remarking that the line between "sanity and insanity" can in certain instances be hard to draw, invites the reader to "determine for himself" whether the surgeon's assessment of the captain is justified (353).

The narrator also openly questions, as did the surgeon, the captain's felt need for secrecy. After Claggart accuses Billy of threatening mutiny, the captain, who suspects Claggart of lying, decides to have him confront Billy in the privacy of his own cabin. Ordinarily, such a serious charge would warrant an immediate investigation, but Vere hopes to avoid making the matter public because that "might undesirably affect the ship's company" (347). He likewise decides to keep secret the disastrous result of that confrontation, then, too, the drumhead trial, again in both instances in order to avoid potential trouble from the crew. The narrator wonders about this penchant for secrecy, saying that the captain's decision "to guard as much as possible against publicity" may have been mistaken, that in this regard "he may or may not have erred" (354).

In addition to these explicit statements inviting readers to question Vere's character and judgments, it turns out that the text destabilizes in many other ways the image of Vere as an exceptional man and prudent leader. Despite his aristocratic lineage, "philosophical" education, and wide experience and despite his asserted talents and skills, Vere appears on closer inspection to be less than perfect, to be flawed and limited at best and actually imprudent at worst. As we shall see, this revelation in turn raises broader questions about the nature of prudence and about the political conditions under which its appearance is likely.

III

Unlike the extraordinary characters of Billy, Claggart, and Vere, the political character of the "great warship" on which they play out their mingled fates is not very different from that of others in the British navy at the close of the eighteenth century. That character is best termed authoritarian. Power and authority were distributed in a quite rigid hierarchy, with most of the power and virtually all of the authority concentrated at the top, Captain Vere being in a "supreme position aboard his own ship" (368). By contrast, the "people of [the] great warship," that is, the crew, were wholly excluded from politics, without any authority and with few if any rights, as Billy's forced departure from the *Rights-of-Man* symbolizes (368). Decision making was accordingly carried on by a tiny fraction of the ship's population behind closed doors, sometimes in secret. Absolute obedience to authority was expected—from the crew to the officers, from the officers to the captain, and, as Billy discovers, from the captain to the authority of "the law" and "the King" (361). And, finally, obedience was, "when necessary," enforced by "harsh," "rigorous," even "arbitrary" discipline and punishment, as, for instance, a flogging witnessed by Billy (318) and Billy's own punishment dramatize.

Captain Vere freely serves, clearly benefits from, and, on the whole, embraces this authoritarian, repressive political culture. Is it a culture likely to nourish and cultivate prudent men (as distinct from men born into the aristocracy)? And is it likely to promote prudent decision making (as distinct from efficient decision making)? By subverting at times the positive image of Vere as a prudent leader, the text encourages consideration of possible connections between his character and this undesirable political culture and, in turn, between that political culture and his decisions. In this section, I make these connections explicit by reexamining, first, the portrait of Vere presented in the text and then, second, the decisions Vere makes regarding Billy Budd.

Careful readers will actually wonder about Vere's character very early in the story, long before the narrator raises his own questions. One reason for this concerns the narrator's digressions, in chapters 4 and 5, focused in part on the brilliant career and charismatic personality of Admiral Horatio Nelson of Trafalgar fame. This effusive account of Nelson occurs immediately before the account, in chapters 6 and 7, of Captain Vere, an arrangement that seems to invite a comparison between the two men. Especially pertinent here is that the extraordinary admiral is praised as a true military man because he threw "personal prudence" aside for "love of glory" and because he was an officer so inspiring that he was widely thought able, "by force of his mere presence and heroic personality," to win the allegiance of every sailor in the British navy, including, in particular and explicitly, the discontented, would-be mutineers of the sort so much on Captain Vere's mind (307–8). So, when in the next two chapters readers are introduced to Captain Vere, it is hard not to draw a comparison between the two men and hard not to see that Vere is no Nelson.[11] I know I have reported, and faithfully so, that Vere's many qualities are described in these chapters as "sterling," but I have neglected to disclose what the narrator actually says in chapter 6, that "whatever his sterling qualities [Vere] was without any brilliant ones" (310). This striking qualification, made so soon after the tribute to the truly brilliant Nelson, at best reduces Vere to human proportions and, thereby, puts the reader on notice that he may well have his flaws. Let us see.

If, as I have maintained, flexibility is a key trait of the prudent, there are definite indications that Captain Vere is on this count deficient. Perhaps this should be expected, given the association between authoritarianism, rigidity, and the captain's occupation, but the fact, in any event, is that there is much evidence of Vere's inflexibility. There is, for one thing, the matter of his "settled convictions," which, as we have observed, serve Vere as a kind of "dike" against the novel political theories of his day (311). The narrator emphasizes the rigidity of these convictions by claiming that Vere believes they will remain "essentially unmodified" for the rest of his life, and the narrator then opines that, in light of "the troubled times . . . this was well *for him*" (311, 312, emphasis added). Knowing what these convictions are, readers may doubt that they are well for others. For example, the captain is convinced of the inferiority of everyone around him and of the childlike behavior of common seamen, and these beliefs, which surely help account for his conservative political opinions and confidence in the legitimacy of his own claims to authority and obedience, perhaps also help explain why he expects so much trouble from his crew and why he stands always prepared to impose on them "necessary" disciplines and punishments.

Vere's temperament in many respects seems to reflect and perhaps contribute to the rigidity of his convictions. Never one for "tolerating an infraction of discipline," in fact a "military disciplinarian" without much "humour," often "remote" and "grave in his bearing," Vere has as well "a queer streak of the pedantic running through him" (309, 350, 312). These traits help explain his decided fondness for formal rules and clearly defined duties, as well as for stability, order, and control. Vere's commitment to his official duties is at one point compared to that of a monk's commitment to "his vows of monastic obedience," and if these duties are for him, as they are for monks, plain and absolute, then there is little, if any, room for flexibility in their discharge (355). This opens up the possibility that Billy's execution is required, not by the ship's predicament or circumstances, as the captain ultimately emphasizes, but only by what he says are the plain and absolutely binding duties he and his officers have to law and king (361).

Relatedly, it might be the case that Vere's assessment of the potential for mutiny on his ship is magnified by his need for order and control or by his fear of disorder, powerlessness, and vulnerability.[12] Certainly, the captain's everyday conduct and demeanor lead at least "some" people to deem him "a martinet," and he clearly universalizes his own need for order and discipline to everyone else: "'With mankind,' he would say, 'forms, measured forms, are everything.' . . . And this he once applied to the disruption of forms going on across the Channel and the consequences thereof" (380). Regarding this need for control, certainly required by his office if not also by a rigid personality, Vere's reactions to the events in his cabin are perhaps telling. He becomes, as we noted, "excited," "vehement," and "passionate"; and while this temporary loss of composure, which so worried the surgeon, might be considered normal, given the abnormal circumstances—even for a prudent man who keeps a cool head and maintains self-control—alternative interpretations of his behavior are possible. There is the obvious possibility that, in striking Claggart, Billy strikes at the very base of the order on which Vere's authority and position, and perhaps also his emotional balance, or "sanity," depends, because Claggart is the master-at-arms whose job is described as "a sort of chief of police charged among other matters with the duty of preserving order on the [ship]" (313).[13] Another possibility is that what most upsets Vere about the violence that unfolded in his cabin is the fact that he is its architect. Fearing trouble from the crew and loss of control over his ship, the captain repairs to the privacy of his cabin precisely in order to remain wholly in control of the situation; instead, by *his* design in *his* cabin, *he* loses control of the situation and indirectly threatens the very disorder he fears.

This incident is also instructive because it obviously conflicts with the presumption about Vere's foresight, another essential characteristic of the prudent. I have argued that the text provides evidence to the effect that Vere seems to possess this great gift, but there is also textual evidence to the contrary. Doubts about the clarity of the captain's foresight are initially raised by the disaster that results from his decision to have the scheming Claggart directly confront the innocent Billy Budd in his cabin. The violence of that encounter clashes with what is said to be Vere's expectation, viz., that the encounter will proceed "in a quiet, undemonstrative way" (347)! After observing this rather dramatic failure, only a very dull reader would fail to examine Vere's foresight with respect to the most important matter in the story, the likelihood of mutiny on the part of the ship's crew. Vere contends that it is the possibility of revolt that most necessitates and justifies Billy's trial and execution; in fact, fear of rebellion plays a key role in every decision the captain makes: to have Claggart confront Billy in the privacy of his cabin, to try Billy immediately, to convict him, to execute him, and to maintain secrecy throughout. But is his fear warranted? Indeed, are either of the reasons cited for Budd's treatment—the likelihood of insurrection and the requirements of the law—convincing? I am going to press the possibility that they are not and to press also the possibility that Vere's reasons for thinking them convincing have as much to do with the political context within which he judges and acts as they do with his personal deficiencies. In order to see this, we need to revisit the drumhead court proceeding.

During that proceeding, Vere identifies different standards of justice or forms of just treatment that might be applicable to Billy: the kind appropriate in a military court; the kind appropriate in "a court less arbitrary and more merciful than a martial one," where Billy's innocent intentions would "largely extenuate"; and the kind appropriate to the last judgment, or in an ideal world ("at the Last Assizes," says Vere), where Billy's innocence would "acquit" (363). This analysis is not, however, definitive, and it is not convincing. As we have seen, the code under which Billy must be tried seemingly allows room for at least some discretion—probably not acquittal, but perhaps something short of execution (as the officers suggest), or perhaps a finding of guilt with a punishment of execution recommended but not applied until the ship returns to the fleet and the case can be reviewed by the admiral. These options are partly ignored and partly dismissed by the captain on the highly dubious grounds that the law is in this matter clear-cut, absolutely binding, and therefore unforgiving. These contentions appear to reveal more about Vere's inner need for clarity and closure and his obsession with discipline and order than they do about the legalities of the situation. But they also illuminate how the demands of Vere's political position require that he transform a difficult, ambiguous situation into a fixed decision that serves the ship's (supposed) need for discipline and order.[14]

A related understanding of Vere's thinking is that he implicitly recognizes that he does have considerable latitude with respect to what the law requires, but he rejects all options that fall short of execution on the basis of his expectation that failing to execute the innocent boy will put the safety of the ship in danger. On this reading, it is this expectation alone that explains and justifies, from Vere's point of view, both the verdict and the punishment.[15] But the plausibility of this expectation depends on Vere's foresight and knowledge of the crew. How trustworthy is that foresight, and how dependable that knowledge?

On the one hand, Vere's expectation can be defended by citing the recent discontent and mutinies in the British navy and by the fact that at least some of the conditions (impressment, harsh discipline) that sparked those troubles and revolts persist on his ship. On the other hand, there are a number of reasons for thinking Vere's expectation either mistaken or exaggerated and, to some degree, rationalized. There is, first of all and most importantly, the fact that under Vere's sterling leadership, his crew is seemingly satisfied and loyal, rather than discontented and mutinous. There is no need on his ship, we are told, for "lieutenants assigned to batteries . . . to stand with drawn swords behind the men working the guns" (308). And Vere, it is important to note, is aware of this; this is one reason why he "did not permit himself to be unduly disturbed" by Claggart's fabrication that "some sort of [subversive] movement" among the crew is being instigated by Billy (344, 342).

A second reason for thinking the expectation unwarranted is that it hinges on an inconsistent (and convoluted) argument regarding the reasoning capacities of the crew. Recall that Vere makes the following argument: the crew's initial reaction to an official announcement that Billy had killed Claggart but would not be executed would be one of surprise and disbelief, for like children the crew expect the law to be uniformly applied as custom requires; if an attempt were made to *explain* to the crew why Billy was treated in an exceptional manner, they, being so immature, could not "comprehend and discriminate" such an explanation; but while the crew would be too dumb to comprehend that explanation, they *would* be smart enough to come up with an alternative on their own, namely, that the decision not to execute Billy, and the attempt to explain it, must reflect fear and weakness on the part of the ship's captain and officers.

Nor is that all. The claim made about the crew's immaturity and stupidity forgets the existence, among the crew, of mature, even "prudent" old veterans like Dansker, a minor character in the story. It forgets, too, that the crew, however limited, certainly knew both Billy and Claggart, and they might be able, as a result, to comprehend an official explanation that points to Billy's innocence and Claggart's machinations. This surmise gains considerable credibility when, at the very end of the story, we are told that the sailors "instinctively felt that Billy was a sort of man as incapable of mutiny as of willful murder" (384). It also gains credibility in light of the reaction of the crew, first to the captain's announcement of Billy's trial and execution and then to the execution itself, moments after they echo Billy's dying words blessing the captain. In both cases, there are faint but unmistakable hints of anger, "a confused murmur" in the initial instance, in the second, sounds of "murmurous indistinctness" that resembled sounds "mobs ashore are liable to" (in both cases the threat is "suppressed" by ordering the men back to their stations) (369, 378). The anger expressed by the crew does not indicate that they believe Billy's "deed" to have been "plain homicide committed in a flagrant act of mutiny," as the captain had predicted (364). It indicates instead that they feel his treatment to be unjust. Thus, whereas Vere believes Billy's harsh treatment will serve to avoid mutiny, there is instead evidence that it risks precipitating it. Had the captain liberated Billy, one suspects that there would have been a celebration, not a revolution.[16]

Reconsider in this light Vere's decision to call for the drumhead court. It indicates that he knows that his initial intuition, that Billy must die, is debatable, that it needs more careful consideration and reflection. Yet, the narration of the court proceeding demonstrates that Vere never puts that intuition and its supporting assumptions to anything resembling a debate, nor to any kind of empirical test. The only evidence on which Vere draws to support his fears about the crew is really quite abstract, the facts that there have been mutinies and that some of the causes of those mutinies concerned practices present on his ship. As to actual, concrete evidence that his crew might be disloyal or likely to rebel, there is none; ironically, the only clearly treacherous person on the ship is Claggart, the man, recall, "charged among other matters with the duty of preserving order" (313). Vere, in fact, knows very little about the men under his command, and so, his foresight must rely on his abstract knowledge and "settled convictions."

The captain's ignorance and to some degree his prejudices are rooted in the political structure and culture of his ship. His position, not just his beliefs and temperament, isolate him from the crew and even from his officers. This isolation is perhaps best exemplified when Vere claims that his "official position" prevents him even from explaining his decisions to his crew—the presumption being, of course, that providing explanations might be misconstrued as an acknowledgment that the crew have a right to explanations. The extraordinary separation between the holders and the subjects of authority on the ship help sustain and intensify Vere's prejudices regarding the capacities and characters of his subordinate officers and crew, and it feeds his fears of disorder and loss of control. Because the captain is so alienated from the crew and the crew so excluded from deliberations concerning the functioning and welfare of the ship, it is impossible for him to reassure himself about the crew's loyalty and what he admits is their "native sense," to learn that some of them at least are actually prudent, and to discover their "instinctive" feelings about Billy. And so, he must rely on his abstract knowledge, his settled convictions, and the deliberations he has with his officers.

But there are no deliberations to speak of, no genuine discussion or debate, in the drumhead court proceeding. Instead, Captain Vere wholly controls the proceeding and dominates his officers, who meekly defer to everything he says: he acts out his character and prejudices and exercises the prerogatives of his office, while they act out their roles as subordinates in the hierarchical institution called a British warship. A mere "glance" from the captain, for instance, is enough to control what they say and whether they say anything at all (359). And while the officers are not in the end wholly uninfluenced by the substance of what Vere has to say, "at bottom they dissented from some points Captain Vere had put to them"; still, they are not about to question a man "not less their superior in mind than in naval rank" (364). "Loyal lieges," the officers in truth pronounce a verdict for which the captain alone has argued and which he alone favors (364).

IV

The excessive deference, muted voices, and passivity displayed by Vere's officers in the court proceeding are costs of authoritarianism referenced elsewhere in the text. When, for instance, Claggart approaches the captain, mention is made of the fact that he has to stand in "the place allotted to men of lesser grades" hoping to speak with superiors (341). And when an audience is granted by the captain and Claggart merely alludes to mutiny, as he does at first, the captain is both "angry" and "indignant" that a mere petty officer would broach such a sensitive topic with him (343). Similarly, when the "prudent" surgeon is alarmed by the captain's behavior in the cabin and thinks the captain's call for immediate action unwise, the narrator describes the surgeon's position as "trying" since there is nothing he can do but blindly obey; to "argue [with the captain] would be insolence," says the narrator, and to "resist him would be mutiny" (352–53). Within the inegalitarian and repressive culture of Vere's ship, initiative and communication, and very likely then prudence too, suffer.

Another "prudent" man, the veteran named Dansker, also reflects the costs of authoritarianism. Described as an experienced and exceptionally wise old man whose "leading characteristic" is his "cynicism," Dansker befriends Billy Budd and quickly discerns that Claggart is obsessed with destroying him. Yet, beyond a general warning, Dansker does nothing to help Billy because his years of living "subordinated . . . to the will of superiors" has rendered him both fatalistic and passive (321). "Long experience had very likely brought this old man to that bitter prudence which never interferes in aught and never gives advice" (336). Even Billy—no prudent man, he—is instructive here. A powerless actor in the drama on Vere's ship, at least until he strikes out in violence, Billy plays a quite different part on the *Rights-of-Man*. There, he is a great "peacemaker," who, by force of personal beauty and sugary virtue, turns a quarrelsome ship into a "happy family" (295–96). The stark contrast must be explained by the differences in the two ships, the one captained by Captain Vere, policed by Claggart, and staffed by impressed tars and deferential officers, the other headed by a Captain Graveling, a man also of "much prudence," informally policed by Billy, and staffed by free sailors in a much more egalitarian and fraternal atmosphere. Apparently, on a democratic ship even Billy Budd is appreciated, and his unique talents put to good, political use (294).

The large number of characters said to be prudent in *Billy Budd* is quite surprising considering how few characters there are. What might we conclude from this? Perhaps, as Thomas Paine liked to believe, every person has, if not the extraordinary prudence of the sort of statesman dreamed of by Burke, at least some modicum of good or common sense. And if so, then democratic ships of the sort on which Billy initially sailed may do much better at producing "the wisest laws, by collecting wisdom where it can be found."[17] One might do well, in fact, to envision ships and societies as like "an assemblage of practical knowledge, which no one individual can possess" but which democratic or republican processes and governments can organize and articulate (142). If prudent decisions and policies require, among other things, an unbiased, critically informed, and factual grasp of circumstances and likelihoods, the authoritarian structure and culture characteristic of Captain Vere's warship seems poorly designed to achieve them. Widespread participation by free and equal citizens is much more likely to expose in the glare of public debate prejudice and partiality, as well as errors of fact and logic, and to bring to bear on decision making a great diversity of talents and skills, experiences and information, knowledge and perspective.

Like the questioning of Captain Vere, the large cast of modest, imperfectly prudent men in *Billy Budd* can help us see that the beguiling portrait of the aristocratic or superior leader, who alone on his watch knows best how to govern because of his possession of extraordinary prudence, is extraordinarily imprudent. It is imprudent because it is an image that too easily lends itself to the legitimation of the claims of the privileged and to all forms of elite politics. It is also imprudent because it ignores the fact that even well-educated and well-intentioned men like Captain Vere have their all-too-human limits and flaws. And it is imprudent because it forgets or masks the fact that prudence in the service of politics is prudence in the service of power. Vere must make decisions morally difficult and practically portentous, but he must make them as a captain. As a result, one can be certain that the responsible exercise of Vere's practical judgment concerning what morality permits and politics requires will be deemed eminently reasonable by the British navy; equally certain is that the vast majority of those who serve the navy are likely to have a different view. Near the very end of the tale, the narrator describes how a wildly inaccurate account of the events on the warship was later published in "an authorized weekly publication of the British navy," according to which Billy was the "depraved" "ringleader" of likely mutineers and Claggart a "respectable" officer "vindictively stabbed to the heart" in the course of heroically performing his duties (382). The account concludes that "the promptitude of [Billy's] punishment has proved salutary" since "nothing amiss is now apprehended aboard [the warship]" (383).

Notes

1. With respect to public interest in Paine and Burke in the United States during the 1870s and 1880s, see R. B. Browne, "*Billy Budd*: Gospel of Democracy," *Nineteenth-Century Fiction* 17 (1963): 321–37; also see note 2 below. The *Billy Budd, Sailor* manuscript, never quite completed and published long after Melville's death, was being developed and repeatedly revised in the mid-1880s and early 1890s (Melville died in September, 1891; a version of the short novel was first published in 1924). For the definitive "genetic" account of the revisions, see H. Hayford and M. M. Sealts Jr., *Billy Budd, Sailor* (Chicago: University of Chicago Press, 1962).

2. That issues raised in and by the debate, and by the French Revolution as a watershed event in modern history, are central to *Billy Budd* is widely recognized and often emphasized. Among political theorists, perhaps the most widely known interpretations premised on this understanding are those by H. Arendt, *On Revolution* (New York: Viking, 1963), and C. H. Zuckert, *Natural Right and the American Imagination* (Savage, MD: Rowman & Littlefield, 1990), ch. 5. Zuckert's comment is characteristic: Melville "tells the story in the context of the debate between the revolutionary ideology of Thomas Paine and the conservative outlook of Edmund Burke" (113).

Browne ("*Billy Budd*") documented American public interest in both Burke and Paine and their debate while Melville was working on the manuscript, although the inferences he drew regarding Melville's beliefs and intentions on the basis of that evidence were dubious, as critics quickly pointed out; see, e.g., B. Suits, "Billy Budd and Historical Evidence," *Nineteenth-Century Fiction* 18 (1963): 288–91. But concerning the significance of the debate for Melville there is no doubt. Particularly in his work from the 1870s onward, Melville often referred and alluded to both writers and their debate, and he often explored the theoretical and practical significance and implications of the French Revolution as noted, for example, by H. Parker, *Reading Billy Budd* (Evanston, IL: Northwestern University Press, 1990), 17–22. Indeed, the first French Revolution has been called Melville's "lifelong obsession" by L. J. Reynolds, *European Revolutions and the American Literary Renaissance* (New Haven: Yale University Press, 1988), xiii.

As Reynolds and others have pointed out, the European revolutions of the mid-nineteenth century were also a source of great interest for Americans, including Melville, signifying for them, and for him, the ongoing struggles between progressive and conservative, republican and absolutist, ideas and forces. Of course, struggles in nineteenth-century America, for instance over suffrage, slavery, and working-class radicalism, reflected similar ideological and practical tensions and divisions. See, e.g., M. P. Rogin, *Subversive Genealogy: The Politics and Art of Herman Melville* (New York: Alfred A. Knopf, 1983); L. Ziff, *Literary Democracy* (New York: Viking, 1981); and N. Fredericks, *Melville's Art of Democracy* (Athens: University of Georgia Press, 1995).

Authoritarian and democratic ideals and ideas were also played out in the public arena in the United States over the *Somers* naval affair in the 1840s. This curious, high-profile case involving a suspected mutiny and the swift execution of perhaps innocent sailors aboard a U.S. Navy warship became a rallying cry for conservatives and progressives alike, the former defending the need for discipline and order, the latter objecting to the perversion of justice by establishment forces. The case is often seen as bearing directly on *Billy Budd*, since it not only shares certain resemblances to the story but because we know Melville was well aware of it (indeed, a cousin of his was directly involved) and because he explicitly cites the case in the story (as well as in another novel). Regarding this case and its possible importance for understanding *Billy Budd*, see both E. Homberger, "Melville, Lt. Guert Gansevoort and Authority: An Essay in Biography," in *New Perspectives on Melville*, ed. F. Pullin (Edinburgh: University of Edinburgh Press, 1978), 255–74; and Rogin, *Subversive Genealogy*, ch 9.

3. The page reference in parentheses is to the Penguin Classic text, H. Melville, *Billy Budd and Other Stories* (New York: Penguin, 1986). I shall throughout follow this form of placing page references to this text in parentheses rather than employing endnotes.

4. Among political theorists, Arendt's extremely positive assessment of Vere in *On Revolution* is probably best known. For a spirited critique, see K. Widmer, *The Ways of Nihilism: A Study of Herman Melville's Short Novels* (Los Angeles: University of California Press, 1970), ch 2. Vere has in truth been called everything from "pathetic" by M. Bowen, *Self and Experience in the Writings of Herman Melville* (Chicago: University of Chicago Press, 1960), 217, to "vicious" by Widmer, *The Ways of Nihilism*, 9, to Aristotle's magnanimous or "great-souled man" by W. Berthoff, "'Certain Phenomenal Men': The Example of Billy Budd," in *Herman Melville's Billy Budd, Benito Cereno, Bartleby the Scrivener, and Other Tales*, ed. H. Bloom (New York: Chelsea House, 1987), 39. Readers familiar with the extensive secondary literature on *Billy Budd* know that Vere is often warmly praised and just as often condemned and that these evaluations are typically connected to presuppositions and assertions about Melville's (or the older Melville's) philosophical and ideological leanings. Readers may also know that Melville's late revisions to the manuscript often were focused on Vere, revisions that served to make him a more complex and arguably a less attractive character. Widely cited—see, e.g., Rogin, *Subversive Genealogy*, 295; B. Johnson, "Melville's Fist: The Execution of Billy Budd," in Bloom, *Herman Melville's Billy Budd*, 72; and Parker, *Reading Billy Budd*, 37–38, 136f.—this historical fact should not, however, be taken as proof that Melville in fact sought to indict Vere and all the things he may or may not signify. For what Melville intended

is in fact unclear. Nor is it at issue in this chapter. Like those of all great artists, Melville's characters are typically complex and often embrace inconsistent tendencies, habits, and beliefs. As Ziff argues in *Literary Democracy*, Melville throughout his career recognized the contradictions that permeate human existence and the inconsistencies that mark most human beings, and he almost surely sought to illuminate, not resolve, the world's problems and the mysteries of human beings. D. Kirby, *Herman Melville* (New York: Continuum, 1993), 13, makes the same (by no means uncommon) point, observing that all of Melville's great works are "shot through with ambivalence and outright contradictions."

5. See, e.g., R. Beiner, *Political Judgment* (Chicago: University of Chicago Press, 1983); P. Steinberger, *The Concept of Political Judgment* (Chicago: University of Chicago Press, 1993); and, in particular, R. S. Ruderman, "Aristotle and the Recovery of Political Judgment," *American Political Science Review* 91 (June 1997): 409–20, who criticizes these and other writers such as B. Barber in both *Strong Democracy* (Berkeley: University of California Press, 1984) and in *The Conquest of Politics* (Princeton, NJ: Princeton University Press, 1988) for aiming in one fashion or another to reconcile democratic politics with conceptions of prudence often reminiscently Aristotelian in character.

6. For example, Ruderman, "Aristotle."

7. The passage actually refers to the capacity of Claggart to do this—Vere is indirectly referenced as being the "one [other] person" on the ship who could do the same. This is one of a number of similarities between Claggart and Vere, similarities often emphasized by interpreters who draw a negative assessment of Vere and who apparently believe that by linking the evil Claggart to the more complex and ambiguous Vere, their case against Vere can be strengthened (see, e.g., Widmer, *The Ways of Nihilism*, 29–30, and C. N. Manlove, "An Organic Hesitancy: Theme and Style in *Billy Budd*," in Pullin, *New Perspectives*, 281). However, while both Claggart and Vere can quickly discern the character or inner nature of people, and while both are in this and other ways "prudent," there is a very important difference between the two: Claggart is said to possess an "uncommon prudence" (329), defined as the ability to "direct a cool judgment sagacious and sound" regarding means when aiming at his evil ends (326). Claggart's brand of prudence, in other words, seems to be precisely what Aristotle (in *Nicomachean Ethics*, VI, 12, 1144a24–36) called cleverness and which he distinguished from genuine prudence. In contrast to Claggart, Vere never *deliberately* aims at evil ends.

An additional point regarding this passage perhaps deserves brief mention: Zuckert, *Natural Right*, 117, says that it is Dansker, not Vere, who shares with Claggart the insight about Billy's true nature. (Dansker is a veteran sailor who befriends Billy and who, as I will later note, is also said to be "prudent.") Zuckert's inference, though at odds with mine, is not necessarily mistaken. The story in fact makes rather clear that *both* Vere and Dansker (in addition to Claggart) understand the "moral phenomenon" that Billy represents. Hence, the "mistake" lies with Melville; it is surely one of a number of such minor errors that would have been rectified had Melville ever finished the manuscript and prepared it for publication.

8. E. Burke, *Reflections on the Revolution in France*, ed. J. G. A. Pocock (Indianapolis, IN: Hackett, 1987), 54; Aristotle, *Politics*, III, 4, 1277b25, and see III, 13, 1284a3–b34. Aristotle's position on democratic processes and forms is, of course, greatly disputed, and while I recognize that his position is complex and not wholly

negative, he does in my view embrace a generally critical attitude toward democracy and a favorable one toward aristocratic government (and the aristocracy). For an overview of recent developments and debates regarding these (and related) issues, see G. Mara, "The Logos of the Wise in the Politeia of the Many," *Political Theory* 12 (December 2000), 835–60, and also R. Mulgan, "Was Aristotle an 'Aristotelian Social Democrat'?" *Ethics* 111 (October 2000), 70–101. I should perhaps add that I am aware that Burke, too, is not wholly opposed to democratic practices; nor is he blind to the weaknesses of aristocrats and of forms of elite rule.

9. Arendt, *On Revolution*, adopts essentially this position. For a thoughtful consideration of this and related interpretations, see Johnson, "Melville's Fist," ch. 8.

10. Burke, *Reflections on the Revolution in France*, 148.

11. Parker, *Reading Billy Budd*, 110–13, 144, 174, discusses the Nelson material at length, pointing out that some, though not all, of that material was removed from the manuscript by Melville in 1888; it is not clear, however, whether he intended to keep it out. Those who, like Parker, believe the material essentially forces a negative view of Vere include Bowen, *Self and Experience*, 229–30, and Widmer, *The Ways of Nihilism*, 31.

12. Bowen, *Self and Experience*, contends that "control is perhaps [Vere's] most marked characteristic," 221.

13. C. Davis, *After the Whale* (Tuscaloosa: University of Alabama Press, 1995), 193, is one of a number of scholars who have made this interpretation.

14. Rogin, *Subversive Genealogy*, 299, presses something like this interpretation in part by comparing Vere's reasoning to that used by the captain in the *Somers* case. The real captain of the *Somers*, Rogin points out, admitted that he had no legal right to execute the suspected mutineers, whereas Captain Vere believes he "relied on the stern necessities of the law." The notion that Vere's need for what I have termed "closure" is not only psychological but political is asserted by Johnson, "Melville's Fist," 76, when she suggests that Vere's political function, and indeed the function of political judgment, is "to convert an ambiguous situation into a decidable one."

15. Manlove, "An Organic Hesitancy," 277, infers on this basis that the legal arguments to which Vere appeals are accordingly but "a mask for self-preservation."

16. Zuckert, *Natural Right*, 118–19, argues that, had Billy cried out his innocence (instead of his benediction), Vere would have caused the very revolt he feared.

17. T. Paine, *Rights of Man*, ed. G. Claeys (Indianapolis, IN: Hackett, 1992), 138, 142.

2

Yankee Go Home

Twain's Postcolonial Romance

Paul A. Cantor

> This kind of humor, the American kind, the kind employed in the service of democracy, of humanity, began with us a long time ago; in fact Franklin may be said to have torn it with the lightning from the skies.
>
> —William Dean Howells

> I believe the people of the United States have offered to the world more valuable information during the last forty years, than all Europe put together.
>
> —John Bright

> We Americans worship the almighty dollar. Well, it is a worthier God than Hereditary Privilege.
>
> —Mark Twain

I

Postcolonial studies has become one of the most prominent fields of contemporary literary criticism. In search of new material, critics have turned to the rich and complex body of imaginative writing that has emerged in areas formerly under European rule. In Africa, the Indian subcontinent, Latin America, the Caribbean, and other regions, authors have struggled to come to terms with a profoundly ambiguous cultural heritage from the colonial era. Often writing in countries that have in recent memory battled to become independent of Europe, these postcolonial authors have fought their own wars on the literary front to overcome years of cultural domination. They view the cultural forms of Europe—the artistic traditions, the literary genres, sometimes the very European languages themselves—as forms of domination and labor in their works to free themselves from what they regard as alien ideologies imposed on them by cultural means. For some postcolonial authors, merely to continue to write in one of the European languages—English, French, or Spanish—is to prolong colonial domination in its most insidious and invidious form—the imposition of a foreign worldview in linguistic terms.[1]

And yet, when they are honest with themselves, postcolonial authors must admit that their cultural heritage from Europe is not purely negative. Often educated in Europe or in European-style university programs, many of these authors find themselves deeply indebted to European culture for their training in their craft. Often, they first encountered literature in European forms, and hence, their very awakening to writing as a way of life was sparked by European models. Postcolonial authors are thus placed in a deeply paradoxical situation—they may wish to rebel against European ideologies, but they seem forced to do so in European forms, which are in many respects saturated with those ideologies because they were, after all, originally developed to express them. Can one, for example, write a novel to call into question European values, when for centuries the novel has been precisely the preeminent cultural form in which Europeans learned to embody those values? If, as many critics have supposed, form and content are linked in literature, expressing non-European or anti-European content in European forms should be problematic, if not impossible.

Thus, postcolonial authors have had to become very resourceful, and, much like the wily slaves in Nietzsche's dialectic, they have learned how to turn the tables on their erstwhile masters. In a mode of writing that has come to be known as "The Empire Strikes Back" or "The Empire Writes Back," many postcolonial authors have figured out how to turn their cultural debt into an asset.[2] Openly acknowledging that they are working within a European tradition, they have found a way of inserting themselves into the tradition that actually works to reverse its values and subvert it. An early example of this mode is the 1966 novel *Wide Sargasso Sea* by Jean Rhys, an author from the small Caribbean island of Dominica, who went on to make a literary career for herself in Europe but decided to return to her Caribbean roots in what turned out to be her last major work. Coming from the Caribbean, Rhys from an early age found fault with one of the classics of English literature, Charlotte Brontë's *Jane Eyre*, for the way it portrays the Creole plantation owner's daughter, Bertha Mason. Although famous for its sympathetic (and, hence, protofeminist) portrayal of its titular heroine, *Jane Eyre* gives a very unsympathetic portrayal of the one Caribbean woman in the story. As the first wife of the novel's male protagonist, Mr. Rochester (he had been tricked into marrying without knowledge of the strain of madness in her family), Bertha threatens to ruin his life and, in particular, stands in the way of his finding true love and marriage with Jane. Brontë portrays Bertha as virtually subhuman and animal-like in her mad captivity and never allows her to tell her side of the story. Her main contribution to the plot is to burn down Rochester's country house and blind him in the process. To Rhys, therefore, *Jane Eyre* is a perfect example of the Old World's bias against the New. In its negative portrayal of the one Creole woman in the story, this classic of English literature denigrates the world Rhys comes from and tries to teach her a lesson in European superiority. In *Wide Sargasso Sea*, Rhys is determined to have her literary revenge and right the wrongs Brontë had perpetrated against Caribbean womanhood.[3]

Rhys' strategy is to write what Hollywood would call a prequel to *Jane Eyre*. She narrates the events that led up to the story Brontë tells in her novel, in particular recounting in detail the circumstances of Rochester's marriage to Bertha Mason, bringing into the light of day the key events that Brontë left in the shadows in her version of the tale. The result of allowing Bertha to tell her side of the story is inevitably to make her a more sympathetic character and, above all, to demonstrate that she is a victim of colonial injustice (an arranged marriage to recoup the fortunes of her family). Rhys finds all sorts of ways, in terms of imagery and narrative point of view, to redress the imbalance in the story—to expose Brontë's pro-European bias and to create sympathy for her Caribbean characters. Moreover, her narrative strategy allows her to deal with her indebtedness to the European literary tradition. Rhys' problem is that Charlotte Brontë got there first and was in effect able to set the terms of the literary contest. But by writing a prequel to *Jane Eyre*, Rhys manages to outflank her European predecessor. She is writing at a later date than Brontë, but she is dealing with an earlier part of the story. Thus, in the terms of Harold Bloom, she manages to turn her belatedness into an earliness, making it seem as if Brontë inherited the story from her and is following in Rhys' footsteps.[4] This is, of course, an illusion, but in a strange way, it works. No one who has read *Wide Sargasso Sea* can ever read *Jane Eyre* the same way again, and that is what it means to say that Rhys has turned the tables on Brontë and cut her down a notch or two. Rhys' counternarrative has permanently stamped Brontë's story as limited in perspective and made us aware of its European biases. The Caribbean author has not quietly accepted a position subordinate to her English predecessor in the literary tradition; rather, she has muscled her way into literary history in a manner that expresses her antagonism to Brontë and all she stands for in terms of European values.

Rhys' solution to the postcolonial problem—finding a way to work within a literary tradition while overturning its basic presuppositions—has been duplicated all over the world. One could cite the many postcolonial reworkings of Shakespeare's *The Tempest*, in which the villainous Caliban is remade into the hero of the story or shown successfully rebelling against Prospero's rule.[5] Salman Rushdie has throughout his career struggled with precursor texts by Rudyard Kipling; in particular, his *Midnight's Children* can be viewed as an attempt to rewrite *Kim* from an Indian perspective. The Kenyan novelist Ngugi Wa Thiong'o based the plot of his *Grain of Wheat* on Joseph Conrad's *Under Western Eyes* and created a revisionary version of the European classic in the process. Perhaps the most pointed and concentrated postcolonial rewriting of a European novel is *Foe* by the South African author J. M. Coetzee. In this retelling of a classic colonialist text, *Robinson Crusoe*, Coetzee posits that the real author, Daniel Defoe, stole the story from a fictional character named Susan Barton. Moreover, we learn that Crusoe's native sidekick, Friday, was literally silenced—his master may have ripped his tongue out. Coetzee thus uncovers a double bias—against women and against natives—in European colonial discourse, an imbalance he tries to redress in his version of the story. By the end of the twentieth century, the postcolonial rewriting of a classic European text had become a minor literary genre unto itself. In a variant of the "if you can't beat 'em, join 'em" strategy, postcolonial authors decided that if they were somehow locked into the European literary tradition, they would accept their artistic fate and make the most of it—working within that tradition but finding ways to stand it on its head.

But I want to go back to the nineteenth century and offer what may be the first example of a postcolonial rewriting of a European classic, Mark Twain's *A Connecticut Yankee in King Arthur's Court*. It may at first seem odd to group Mark Twain with postcolonial authors like Salman Rushdie. But, as many critics have begun to realize, American literature is the first postcolonial literature, and we can profitably use the approaches developed to analyze African, Caribbean, and other contemporary literatures to help us understand what was going on in nineteenth-century literature in the United States. The colonies that became the United States were, after all, the first to break away from a European mother country and assert their political independence. Now that the United States has become the most powerful nation on earth, it is difficult to realize that there was ever anything dubious about its independence. But throughout the nineteenth century, England, not the United States, was the most powerful nation on earth and, in particular, the only one capable of projecting its power globally (by virtue of its unchallenged naval superiority). Although the United States had achieved political independence from England, it remained economically and culturally dependent on its former colonial master throughout the nineteenth century. England was the largest foreign investor in the United States; for example, much of the capital used to finance the American railroad system was raised in Britain, and, of course, the railroad itself was a British invention—a good reminder that in many of its most important economic developments in the nineteenth century, the United States was simply following the lead of the British.

America's cultural dependence on England in the nineteenth century was even greater than its economic. Americans had, of course, continued to use the language of their former rulers, and one might argue that there was something culturally self-defeating about a Declaration of Independence from the King of England that was itself written in the King's English. In all the arts, including painting, music, and architecture, Americans tended to follow British models. In literature, they worked within the genres they inherited from the British, and British authors continued to be popular in the United States throughout the nineteenth century, Charles Dickens being the most notable example. Nineteenth-century Americans were thus understandably worried about their cultural independence and, indeed, wondered whether the United States could ever stake its claim to having a distinctive culture worthy to stand comparison with the great cultures of Europe.[6] Even European admirers of the political independence of the United States, such as Alexis de Tocqueville, had their doubts as to whether America would ever have much to contribute to the fine arts.[7] One of the greatest cultural achievements of nineteenth-century America, Noah Webster's *An American Dictionary of the English Language* (1828), was explicitly devoted to documenting the emergence of a distinctively American language. American authors were similarly concerned with establishing their cultural autonomy, seeking out distinctively American subject matter and a distinctively American voice (often rooted in a distinctively American dialect). But at the same time, they kept one eye fixed on the British market for literature and actively courted it. They naturally coveted the financial returns possible in London—the world's center for publishing in the nineteenth century. But, perhaps more importantly, American authors such as Nathaniel Hawthorne and Henry James dreamed of being accepted as great writers by the British reading public—as the only true validation of their literary status. In a pattern typical of postcolonials, James tried in many respects to be more English than the English in his novels and became obsessed with the theme of people caught between the worlds of America and Europe.

Thus, American authors in the nineteenth century found themselves in exactly the postcolonial predicament we have analyzed in the twentieth. On the one hand, they were driven by the nationalist feelings characteristic of any newly independent country and wished to assert a distinctively American identity as authors. This spirit was evident in the United States' earliest moments as a new nation, as shown in 1787 by James Wilson in one of his speeches in defense of the ratification of the Constitution:

> As we shall become a nation, I trust that we shall also form a national character, and that this character will be adapted to the principles and genius of our system of government; as yet we possess none; our language, manners, customs, habits, and dress, depend too much upon those of other countries. Every nation in these respects, should possess originality; there are not, on any part of the globe, finer qualities for forming a national character, than those possessed by the children of America. . . . I think there is strong reason to believe that America may take the lead in literary improvements and national importance. . . . That language, sir, which shall become most generally known in the civilized world, will impart great importance over the nation

> that shall use it. The language of the United States will, in future times, be diffused over a greater extent of country than any other that we know. . . . Besides the freedom of our country, the great improvements she has made, and will make, in the science of government, will induce the patriots and *literati* of every nation to read and understand our writings on that subject; and hence it is not improbable that she will take the lead in political knowledge.[8]

Wilson reveals how American cultural self-confidence was ultimately based on political self-confidence. Nineteenth-century authors were often proud of the great American experiment in democratic government and sought to champion its cause against the various forms of autocracy that they associated with European culture.

On the other hand, American authors tended to look to the British for their literary standards. And the artistic forms the Americans inherited and worked in were overwhelmingly European in nature, raising doubts about their ability to establish any true cultural independence from Europe. This is the context in which I wish to discuss Mark Twain and the challenge he took on in *A Connecticut Yankee in King Arthur's Court*. In a remarkable anticipation of twentieth-century writers such as Rhys, Rushdie, and Coetzee, Twain set out to rewrite a European classic with what we would call a postcolonial twist. His choice of precursor text is particularly significant. In his initial inspiration—based on a dream according to Twain[9]—he merely intended to burlesque one of his favorite books, Thomas Malory's *Le Morte D'Arthur*. Twain originally had in mind simply generating all the humor he could out of the incongruity of placing a modern man in a medieval setting. But as Twain worked up the material, elements of Walter Scott's *Ivanhoe* and Alfred Tennyson's *Idylls of the King* found their way into his mix, until he turned out to be dealing with the larger significance of the King Arthur story in the British imagination.[10] And that significance was as a symbol of British imperialist aspirations. Indeed, at important moments in the history of the British Empire, British authors have turned to the King Arthur story to embody their hopes and fears for their nation's imperial destiny. At the very beginning of British efforts to colonize the New World, Edmund Spenser drew upon Arthurian legends to shape his epic *The Faerie Queene* and its vision of a British empire to rival Rome's. In Twain's day, the poet laureate of England, Tennyson, had once again revived the story of Arthur in his *Idylls of the King* in order to celebrate the peak of the British Empire in the nineteenth century (although his story contains dark forebodings about what might happen to that empire if it did not remain true to its core values as Tennyson saw them).

Thus, Twain's choice of the story of King Arthur for his burlesque turned out to have more artistic repercussions than he at first realized. As he evidently sensed, by the nineteenth century the story of King Arthur had come to serve as the foundational myth of the British Empire. The image of chivalrous knights riding out to save the world, basing their claims to rule on their nobility and higher ideals, had become the self-image of the British as imperialist masters. Hence, the best way for Twain as an author to challenge the British Empire was to take on the myth of King Arthur and subvert it. Indeed, in striking at the legend of Camelot, he was striking at the heart of Britain's self-idealization and its claim to rule its empire.[11] In a stroke of genius, Twain came up with the idea of showing a typical American—a Connecticut Yankee—striding right into the imaginative center of British power—Camelot—and taking over by virtue of his good old Yankee ingenuity. Twain could not have come up with a better means of symbolizing the way America was beginning to displace Britain as the world's great power by the end of the nineteenth century. In *Connecticut Yankee*, Twain foresees the coming of the American century. But, although American power—and that means largely economic and technological power—figures prominently in Twain's story, the American challenge to Britain he portrays goes deeper. His Yankee has a lesson to teach the British, a lesson in the value of democracy and, hence, a critique of British monarchy and aristocracy.[12] Thus, Twain as American author truly turns the tables on his British precursors in *Connecticut Yankee*. Far from being merely derivative from the British, American culture can teach Britain an important political lesson, and, if Britain were to take instruction in democracy from the United States, British culture might paradoxically be said to be derivative from America.

As part of this imaginative reversal, Twain, in the best postcolonial fashion, can resituate himself in literary history. Using his time traveling Yankee, Twain inserts himself at an earlier point in literary history, indeed in some sense at the earliest point—the sixth century AD—the archetypal beginning of British literary history, the age of King Arthur and, hence, the fountainhead of all British fable. As the Yankee himself puts it, mirroring his author's concern for origins and originality, "I stood here, at the very spring and source of the great period of the world's history."[13] By the time Twain is finished, his model, Thomas Malory, turns out to be imitating him, copying long passages into his *Le Morte D'Arthur* from newspaper articles the Yankee's staff originally composed. In the imaginary universe of *Connecticut Yankee*, everything is turned upside down, and, as far as we can tell, the classic legends of King Arthur, which we had thought formed the very core of British myth, were in fact invented by the American Mark Twain.[14]

II

Connecticut Yankee thus constitutes a remarkably perceptive act of literary criticism on Twain's part, one that anticipates contemporary ideas about the way nineteenth-century literature was complicit in the European imperialist project. On some level, Twain intuited that in Britain the literary form of the Arthurian romance had become the bearer of imperialist values and the monarchic/aristocratic ethos that was bound up with the British Empire. To understand how fully Twain turned the British literary tradition on its head, together with the imperialist self-image it embodied, it is necessary to examine the form of imperialist romance in detail. For this purpose, an excellent choice is H. Rider Haggard's *King Solomon's Mines*, which came out in 1885 (just as Twain was conceiving *Connecticut Yankee*), modestly advertised as "the most amazing book ever written."[15] I have been unable to locate hard evidence that Twain was familiar with this book, but one prominent Twain scholar, Louis Budd, claims that he "most probably knew about" it.[16] Indeed, given the way Twain paid careful attention to the book market in both England and the United States, it is difficult to believe that he was not aware of one of the great publishing phenomena of the 1880s. "In England alone *King Solomon's Mines* sold 31,000 copies during the first twelve months . . . while in the United States of America at least thirteen different editions appeared before the year was out."[17] As we shall see, just from reading the text, it seems likely that Twain was directly responding to *King Solomon's Mines* in *Connecticut Yankee*. In any event, Rider Haggard's novel perfectly embodies the kind of British imperialist myth Twain set out to debunk in *Connecticut Yankee*.

Rider Haggard's peculiar act of genius was to take the Arthurian romance and transpose it to the imperial frontier. Although set in nineteenth-century Africa, *King Solomon's Mines* draws upon the age-old formulas of romance and, in particular, follows conventions established in the romantic novels of Walter Scott, especially *Ivanhoe*. Rider Haggard's heroes are modern explorers and big-game hunters, but they are clearly patterned on knights in shining armor and go off to Africa on what amounts to a chivalric quest. Rider Haggard presents his Sir Henry Curtis as a kind of poster boy for the Anglo-Saxon race and, indeed, pictures him as stepping right out of the pages of medieval romance: "if one only let his hair grow a bit, put one of those chain shirts on to those great shoulders of his, and gave him a big battle-axe and a horn mug" (11). *King Solomon's Mines* thus provides a good example of how the Arthurian myth served to undergird British imperialist ideology and provided a justification for British rule over supposedly inferior natives all around the globe. In their quest to find Curtis's lost brother, Rider Haggard's heroes come upon a hidden African kingdom. They, in effect, conquer it, install a new ruler, and remake its laws and customs, bringing them more in line with British ideas of justice. Rider Haggard presents them as entitled to do so because they are morally and intellectually superior to the Africans. With their nobility and higher ideals, they represent for Rider Haggard the cause of civilization triumphing over barbarism.

In particular, Rider Haggard portrays the British superiority over the African natives as technological in nature. His heroes are able to awe the

Africans into submission with the power of their modern rifles—weapons able to kill at a distance and, thus, to terrify the natives, who have never seen such a thing before. In the central symbolic pattern of the book, the British are associated with science, technology, and rationality, while the Africans are associated with superstition, magic, and irrationality. The rationality of the British both entitles and enables them to rule over the Africans. In a key scene, which seems to have a special relevance for Twain, the British are able to maintain their godlike status in the eyes of the African natives by successfully predicting an eclipse. As Europeans, the British believe in a rational, scientific world order, in which events follow the laws of physics and, hence, are mathematically predictable, while the superstitious Africans regard all natural phenomena as, in fact, supernaturally ordained and subject to human control by magical means. The scientific rationality of the British is related to their respect for law and order in the political sphere. Their aim is to replace the capricious rule of priests and witches in Africa with something approaching the regularity of the British rule of law.

In an effort to maintain a sharp line between European civilization and African barbarism, Rider Haggard denies any cultural achievements to the natives in the story. Although the explorers come across a variety of impressive structures in the African kingdom—a well-made road, colossal statues, and, of course, the mines—they automatically assume that no African could be responsible for such achievements.[18] Rather, they speculate that people from the more familiar world of the Mediterranean must have migrated south to bequeath such constructions to the African natives. As Curtis says, "Perhaps the colossi were designed by some Phoenician official who managed the mines" (259). Rider Haggard thus works to deny the Africans their own history—they cannot take credit for anything admirable in their midst. This conceit is built into the very notion of King Solomon's mines. The local treasure is not really local—if one goes back far enough into the past, it belongs to a figure out of the Old Testament and, hence, closely associated with European civilization. Thus, if the European explorers were to appropriate the treasure, they would merely be reclaiming what is already theirs by ancestral right. In the terms of *King Solomon's Mines*, history is always European history, thereby providing another justification for European rule over non-European peoples.

King Solomon's Mines thus provides the background for more fully understanding what Twain is doing in *Connecticut Yankee*. One can derive the formula for Twain's novel by simply inverting the pattern of British imperialist romance. Twain's American is to the British as the British are to the non-European natives in novels such as *King Solomon's Mines*. By using a time traveler to take his story deep into the British past, Twain is able to portray Britain as what we would call a Third World nation. It is no accident that time travel began to be explored as a literary possibility in the late nineteenth century, just when the imperialist romance was flourishing. The journey to the imperial frontier was often presented as a form of time travel, a journey into the deep past. In *King Solomon's Mines*, for example, Rider Haggard's explorers have to leave the modern world behind them and enter a more primitive land. At the beginning of the story, they say farewell to parliamentary government and humanitarian concerns and go on to confront forms of autocracy and savagery in Africa that in Europe could be found only in the ancestral past (or on the fringes of Europe, such as the Transylvania of *Dracula*). Imperialist encounters are often portrayed as a clash of two time periods, with the Europeans living in the present and the non-Europeans living in the past. The jumps in time[19] that were presented in geographic journeys in imperialist romance eventually suggested the idea of time travel, as is clear in the first full-fledged time travel story, H. G. Wells's *The Time Machine* (1895).[20] Wells modeled his time travel story on an imperialist romance. His hero jumps to the future only to encounter exactly the kinds of "tribes" an imperial explorer routinely encountered in nineteenth-century romance: a peaceful, docile, childish tribe (the Eloi) and a hostile, savage, cannibalistic tribe (the Morlocks). His time traveler establishes his superiority over the people of the future by means of technology (simple matches in his case), just the way Rider Haggard's explorers triumph over the African natives.

With elements of both a time travel story and an imperialist romance, *Connecticut Yankee* provides a middle term between *King Solomon's Mines* and *The Time Machine* and may in fact have helped inspire Wells's book. In any event, the time travel motif enabled Twain to bring out what was implicit all along in imperialist romance. If a journey to the imperial frontier is a journey into the past, then the encounter with the so-called primitive non-European turns out to be a glimpse into Europe's own savage prehistory. In *Connecticut Yankee*, Twain exploits this blow to Britain's sense of its superiority for all it is worth. In the nineteenth century, the British gloried in their position as the most advanced nation on earth and trumpeted their superiority over their backward colonial subjects. But Twain's narrative pointedly reminds us that the British were once backward themselves and no better than the Africans and other natives they now look down upon. Moreover, if the British were going to make technology the standard of civilization, they were leaving themselves open to being surpassed by a more technologically advanced nation, which the United States was clearly threatening to become at the time Twain was writing.

Twain has great fun undercutting the pretensions of the British Empire in *Connecticut Yankee*. For one thing, he cuts it down to size. Here is how the great imperial capital, the nerve center of empire, appeared in the sixth century: "London . . . was a sufficiently uninteresting place. It was merely a great big village, and mainly mud and thatch. The streets were muddy, crowded, unpaved" (289).[21] As for the far-flung empire on which the sun never set in the nineteenth century, Twain shows that British power began on a much smaller scale in the sixth. King Uriens, for example, is "monarch of a realm about as big as the District of Columbia—you could stand in the middle of it and throw bricks into the next kingdom" (110). But more telling than the diminution of British dominion is the diminution of the stature of the British themselves. Twain presents them as savages:

> There were people, too; brawny men, with long, coarse, uncombed hair that hung down over their faces and made them look like animals. They and the women, as a rule, wore a coarse tow-linen robe that came down well below the knee, and a rude sort of sandals, and many wore an iron collar. The small boys and girls were always naked; but nobody seemed to know it. . . . In the town were some substantial windowless houses of stone scattered among a wilderness of thatched cabins; the streets were mere crooked alleys, and unpaved; troops of dogs and nude children played in the sun and made life and noise; hogs roamed and rooted contentedly about. (15)

Later, Twain makes the point explicit: "Measured by modern standards, they were merely modified savages, these people" (88).

The irony of such passages is clear when one views them against the background of British imperialist romance. Twain pictures the sixth-century British just the way British authors portrayed non-European natives in the nineteenth century. Rider Haggard himself recognizes the possibility of equating modern-day Africans with his British ancestors when he has his narrator refer to the "ancient Danes" as a "kind of white Zulus" (11). Perhaps echoing this striking formulation, Twain has his narrator call the sixth-century British "white Indians" (21). In the terms of the American frontier, this is Twain's most effective way of branding the British as savages, and, accordingly, he associates them with American Indians at several points (83, 89), even linking them to a specific tribe when he reduces the fabled Camelot to a "polished-up court of Comanches" (102; see also 30).[22] This is how Twain gives the British a dose of their own medicine. They have been looking down on the rest of the world as savages; in *Connecticut Yankee*, he reminds them of the primitive character of their own past. Twain brilliantly anticipated the opening of *Heart of Darkness*, where Conrad's narrator, Marlow, points out that what is now the center of the British Empire—London—was once a remote outpost on the periphery of the Roman Empire. Although the British now regard Africa as the Dark Continent, Marlow pointedly reminds his listeners of London: "And this also has been one of the dark places of the earth."[23]

In working out his portrait of the British as savages, Twain gives them exactly the moral and intellectual deficiencies they used to attribute to Africans and other subject people in their empire. The "natives" Twain's Yankee encounters in sixth-century Britain are superstitious and willing to accept the most improbable tales on pure hearsay as gospel truth. Because they have no critical spirit, their rulers manipulate them easily; the cheapest magic trick strikes these people as miraculous. As if he were following the script of *King Solomon's Mines*, Twain makes the Yankee's authority rest on his ability to predict an eclipse in front of the awestruck natives of Britain.[24] In a reversal of Rider Haggard's narrative, Twain's portrays the British as the scientifically backward people, incapable of grasping the order of nature. Twain correctly sensed that by the end of the nineteenth century, the United States was poised (along with Germany) to surpass Britain as the world's leader in theoretical and applied science. The eclipse incident also allows Twain to play with his own position in literary history. His narrator acknowledges that the eclipse trick is already a well-established topos in the literature of colonialism: "It came to my mind, in the nick of time, how Columbus, or Cortez, or one of those people, played an eclipse as a saving trump once, on some savages, and I saw my chance. I could play it myself, now; and it wouldn't be any plagiarism, either, because I should get it in nearly a thousand years ahead of those parties" (35–36). This is a textbook illustration of the paradox of turning belatedness into earliness. The Yankee openly admits that he is following in the footsteps of Columbus or Cortez—he must have read about their exploits and will be guided by their example. And yet, because he has traveled back in time to an era that predates them, he claims that they will be imitating him and not vice versa. The fact that Twain brings up the issue of plagiarism at just this point suggests that he might have been sensitive to the charge that he had stolen the eclipse incident from Rider Haggard's recent best-seller.[25]

But, more generally, the Yankee's comment on the eclipse tale captures Twain's anxiety as an American author—his concern that he is condemned to repeat stories that have already been told by his European predecessors. The threat of repetition is particularly troubling for a humorist. There is nothing worse than retelling old jokes. As early as chapter 4, Twain has his narrator complain about the staleness of the humor in Camelot: "I think I never heard so many old played-out jokes strung together in my life. . . . It seemed peculiarly sad to sit here, thirteen hundred years before I was born and listen again to poor, flat, worm-eaten jokes that had given me the dry gripes when I was a boy thirteen hundred years afterwards. It about convinced me that there isn't any such thing as a new joke possible" (29). Here the paradox of time travel creates a myth that is very useful to Americans anxious about their cultural indebtedness to Europe. If new jokes are never possible, then Twain as a humorist need not worry that an Englishman like Dickens got there first when it comes to comedy. If all humorists are doomed to recycle old material, then Americans are not at any particular disadvantage by virtue of coming at a later point in history. Twain's suggestion that every joke is, as it were, always already told levels out any temporal distinction between Europeans and Americans. The business of old jokes in *Connecticut Yankee* may stand for Twain's larger historical strategy in the work. The British claim cultural priority over the United States, but when Twain takes us back to the very source of the British literary tradition, he shows that it is not at all original, but rather already a site of repetition. With the people of Camelot themselves following old formulas and routines, Twain as an American need not feel bad if he lifts a scene or two from English literature.

Thus, in the eclipse incident, Twain's specific anxieties as an American author and, hence, a latecomer to the literary scene converge with his more general anxieties as an American living in the shadow of European culture and feeling potentially overwhelmed by it. He alleviates these anxieties by showing that the British were once subject to all the criticisms they now level against other peoples around the world. *Connecticut Yankee* reveals that there is nothing in the nature of the British that makes them inherently superior to other nations.[26] Their preeminence is merely the result of the luck of the historical draw and the head start it gave them in economic and cultural development. And whether or not Twain plagiarized the eclipse incident directly from *King Solomon's Mines*, he makes it serve the same function as a measure of political capacity. The chief problem with the superstitiousness of any people is that it unfits them to rule themselves. This is as true of Twain's Britons as it is of Rider Haggard's Africans. Any people that believes in magic will end up in thrall to charlatans and priests, who claim to exercise supernatural control over events in the natural world. In perhaps his most wicked blow to British self-esteem, Twain has the audacity to raise the question of whether the people who pride themselves on Magna Carta and the Glorious Revolution are even "capable of self-government" (193). To be sure, the Yankee concludes that they are, but only because he argues that *any* nation is capable of self-government—thereby undermining all pretensions to British exceptionalism. The British Empire rested on the claim that people in Africa and India were by virtue of their inferior natures incapable of ruling themselves; hence, the superior British had to step in and show them how to govern. Twain's fable, by contrast, shows that the British have no peculiar talent or knack for government; in fact, "Arthur's people were of course poor material for a republic" (192). Far from being able to set an example of good government for all the world to follow, the British in *Connecticut Yankee* have to be instructed by an American in how to manage their political affairs.

Here we come to the crux of Twain's critique of Britain in *Connecticut Yankee*—the British fail to measure up to the political standards by which they have been judging the rest of the world. Above all, the British claim to stand for the rule of law, and imperialist romances such as *King Solomon's Mines* fault native peoples for allowing their rulers to treat them arbitrarily and capriciously. But the Britain Twain presents in *Connecticut Yankee* is governed by despots, with no regard for the elementary rules of justice or the fundamental rights of the people. And Twain suggests that the legal and political abuses of medieval Britain did not disappear with the Middle Ages but have instead survived well into the modern period and in some respects still infect the country in the nineteenth century.[27] Twain dwells on the evils of an aristocratic regime and any sort of class privilege, and he views the Britain of his day as still characterized by an unjust class system. Thus, if the British are to learn about social equality and democratic government, it must be from the Yankee, who knows what the rights of the people are. Indeed, based on his American experience, he can cite chapter and verse from the democratic gospel: "I was from Connecticut, whose Constitution declares 'that all political power is inherent in the people, and all free governments are founded on their authority and instituted for their benefit; and that they have *at all times* an undeniable and indefeasible right to *alter this form of government* in such a manner as they may think expedient'" (93–94; italics in the original).

One of the chief lessons the Yankee seeks to teach the British is the value of religious freedom. He directs his criticism against the established church in medieval Britain—this means that in good Protestant fashion, he is attacking the Catholic Church, but his strictures would apply almost as well to the Anglican Church in the nineteenth century, which was, after all, an English *national* church, supported by public tax money.[28] The Yankee's argument against church establishment is positively Madisonian in character:

> We *must* have a religion—it goes without saying—but my idea is, to have it cut up into forty free sects, so that they will police each other, as had been the case in the United States in my time. Concentration of power in a political machine is bad; and an Established Church is only a political machine; it was invented for that; it is nursed, coddled, preserved for that; it is an enemy to human liberty, and does no good which it could not better do in a split-up and scattered condition. (125)

Echoing the argument for small, as opposed to great, factions in *Federalist* 10, Twain shows that he understands what is distinctive about the American political system envisaged by the Founding Fathers. And by choosing to focus on the issue of church establishment, Twain highlights one of the fundamental differences between the British and the American regimes—an issue on which the Americans stand on the progressive side for Twain and the British on the reactionary. Moreover, for Twain, the existence of an established church is a crime against freedom of thought in general. His fervent desire to see the power of the church broken is rooted in his conviction that it is the principal opponent of all progress, both moral and intellectual. As such, the church eventually identifies the Yankee as its great enemy and proves ultimately to be his undoing with the interdict it issues against him and all who support him. In the end, Twain's novel turns on the conflict between the Yankee, who stands for freedom, innovation, and progress, and the church, which stands for oppression, reaction, and the political, social, and economic status quo.

III

Thus, the political argument of *Connecticut Yankee* circles back to the cultural. The political differences between Britain and the United States are linked up with a whole series of differences in their ways of life. Brimming over with Yankee ingenuity, Twain's hero is the quintessential American. With his contempt for custom and the traditional way of doing things, he is free to experiment and strike off in new directions—even in several directions at once (he is the classic jack-of-all-trades). The Yankee is thus remarkably adaptable to changing conditions and ready to seize any opportunity that comes his way in the true entrepreneurial spirit of America. In all these respects, Twain contrasts his American hero with the British characters in the novel. Given their rigid, hierarchical society, they are set in their ways and incapable of changing with the times or making any progress. Twain comes up with a marvelous image for the rigidity of the British way of life—a medieval suit of armor. In recognizing the irrationality of wearing armor, the Yankee establishes his credentials as a progressive and reveals how different he is from the British in the way he thinks about the world:

> I wanted to try and think out how it was that rational or even half-rational men could ever have learned to wear armor, considering its inconveniences; and how they had managed to keep up such a fashion for generations when it was plain that what I had suffered to-day they had to suffer all the days of their lives. I wanted to think that out; and moreover I wanted to think out some way to reform this evil and persuade the people to let the foolish fashion die out. (85)

It is precisely because the Yankee has no faith in armor that he is able to defeat Arthur's knights so easily in battle. Locked into their armor, they lack maneuverability, while the Yankee, in true American cowboy fashion, is able to run rings around them and lasso them at will. Twain sums up the contrast he wishes to draw between the United States and Britain in the image of a mobile cowboy picking off clumsy armored opponents one by one.

For Twain, a democratic society will always have the edge over an aristocratic one because it will inevitably be more *inventive*. As an experiment in democracy, the United States embodies the very spirit of invention. By contrast, an aristocratic society like Britain, in which authority is grounded in ancestral rights, will necessarily resist innovation. In bitterly complaining about his lack of status in Arthur's court, the Yankee points to this contrast between Britain and America:

> I had the smith's reverence, now, because I was apparently immensely prosperous and rich; I could have had his adoration if I had had some little gimcrack title of nobility. And not only his, but any commoner's in the land, though he were the mightiest production of all the ages, in intellect, worth, and character, and I bankrupt in all three. This was to remain so, as long as England should exist on the earth. With the spirit of prophecy upon me, I could look into the future and see her erect statues and monuments to her unspeakable Georges and other royal and noble clothes-horses, and leave unhonored the creators of this world—after God—Gutenberg, Watt, Arkwright, Whitney, Morse, Stephenson, Bell. (257)

Although a number of the great inventors the Yankee mentions are in fact British (James Watt, Richard Arkwright, and George Stephenson), his point is that they were not sufficiently honored in their homeland. Britain would rather honor its aristocratic rulers than its inventors, even though the former oppress the common people, while the latter benefit them. And Twain views this problem as persisting into his own day. To the extent Britain remained an aristocratic society in the nineteenth century and put a premium on birth rather than merit, it continued to be oriented toward the past and unable fully to embrace the future.

All of Twain's criticisms of Britain essentially flow from his conception of the deficiencies of aristocratic, as opposed to democratic, society. As a democracy, the United States places its faith in the individual and the result is to set free the creative energies of its citizens and allow them to become productive to an unprecedented extent. Twain thus links democracy to capitalism and, specifically, the spirit of free markets and free enterprise. He has his Yankee defend the principle of free trade and attack the principle of protectionism, which he associates with the backward-looking imperialist ethos of Britain and its efforts to monopolize the commerce of its colonies. Twain implies that if the United States remains true to the principle of free enterprise, it will soon surpass Britain as the greatest economic power in the world. He was not alone in accurately predicting this development. As early as the late 1860s, John Stuart Mill was already speaking of the United States as "the great country beyond the Atlantic, which is now well-nigh the most powerful country in the world, and will soon be indisputably so."[29] Writing at the end of the nineteenth century (in 1898), Winston Churchill expressed concern about the way Britain was losing its lead in technology to the United States. In his account of the British reconquest of the Sudan, Churchill discusses a problem that arose when a strike at home prevented the British army from obtaining the railroad locomotives it needed to transport its troops to the front. The order had to be given to American industry, which quickly produced the railroad equipment Britain needed, leading Churchill "to institute a comparison between the products of the great commercial rivals":

> The American engines were sooner delivered and £1,000 cheaper. They broke down rarely. All their similar parts were interchangeable. If two engines had been disabled, the third might have supplied the material for the repairs. The fact that they were considerably faster soon won them a good reputation on the railway, and the soldier who travelled to the front was as anxious to avoid his country's locomotives as to preserve its honour. "They were," said one of the subalterns, "the products of a higher class of labour than that employed in England. They represented greater talent, though less toil. While appearance was not neglected, no 'finish' was wasted on unnoticeable parts. Thus economy was increased and efficiency preserved." There is no pleasure recording these facts.[30]

Except for the fact that Churchill the Englishman laments what Twain the American celebrates, this passage is in the spirit of *Connecticut Yankee* and its account of Yankee ingenuity. No doubt Churchill found this development all the more galling because in competing successfully with the British at manufacturing locomotives, the United States was beating Britain at its own game. The British had invented the railroad, only to find themselves surpassed by their former colony in railroad technology by the end of the nineteenth century. Thus, in suggesting that Britain was about to lose its position as the dominant economic power in the world to the United States, Twain found echoes within the British community itself.

In retrospect, we can say that Twain was right about the future of Britain, but was he right about its past? It is one thing to claim that at the end of the nineteenth century, the United States was on the verge of overtaking Britain economically. It is another thing to claim that the United States taught the British everything they knew. And that, of course, is the fantastic claim *Connecticut Yankee* makes. By the time the Yankee is through, he has taken credit for introducing every positive economic and political innovation into Arthur's Britain. In effect, he turns the railroad into an American rather than a British invention. In one of those paradoxes that time travel makes possible, the Yankee even suggests that America could only have been discovered by someone with an American's enterprising spirit. Toward the end of the story, we learn that the Yankee "was getting ready to send out an expedition to discover America" (315). At this point, it is easy to imagine protests from a justifiably indignant British audience, outraged by American ingratitude: "Did we give you colonials nothing? Do you think you could have discovered yourselves?"

Connecticut Yankee is a humorous book, and it would, of course, be ridiculous to demand historical accuracy of it. Twain makes no bones about the fact that he is having fun at the expense of Britain, and a large part of the fun is to rob the British of any of their claims to preeminence in the world.

Furthermore, Twain could offer his historical revisionism as just another example of doing to the British what they had been doing to the rest of the world. As we have seen, *King Solomon's Mines* tries to deny the Africans their own history. Rider Haggard suggests that the future of Africa will be European—only European science and technology are capable of developing the resources of the continent. But he also suggests that the past of Africa was European (in the broadest sense of the term). The presence of the mines of King Solomon suggests that non-Africans were exploiting the local resources long before the present inhabitants occupied the land. Rider Haggard thus presents African rule in Africa as a kind of interregnum—non-Africans once ruled the land, and they are about to do so again. The way Rider Haggard inserts Judaeo-Christian civilization into the ancient history of Africa provides a model for the way Twain inserts American civilization into the ancient history of Britain. Having established the principle that the nation that rules the world gets to write the history books, the British cannot complain when they end up on the losing end of historical revisionism.

In short, like many British authors, Twain has a polemical point to make by rewriting history, and once again, his efforts are rooted in his anxieties as an American former colonial. As a colony of Britain, America was overwhelmingly indebted to the mother country for its political tradition. *Connecticut Yankee*'s assertion to the contrary notwithstanding, the United States inherited the principle of the rule of law from Britain. Indeed, the legal tradition in the United States is in large part an extension of the British common law tradition. Although the United States created its own democratic institutions, they were in many cases modeled on British precedents. The United States did not opt for a parliamentary system of democracy, but no one would deny that the traditions of the British Parliament have influenced democratic procedures on this side of the Atlantic. Much of the theory behind democracy in America is derived from British sources; consider the importance of John Locke to the Founding Fathers.

It was, in fact, the overwhelming nature of America's political debt to Britain that forced Twain into the historical contortions and distortions of *Connecticut Yankee*. The book expresses the fascinating combination of cultural self-confidence and cultural insecurity that characterized late nineteenth-century America (and that is typical of the postcolonial condition in general). Even as Americans were beginning to feel their oats and were poised to dominate the world, they could not help looking back to their past and remembering how much of their culture was derived from Europe in general and Britain in particular. In psychological terms, *Connecticut Yankee* thus provides an overcompensating cultural fantasy. If American culture threatens to seem hopelessly derivative from British, Twain creates a history in which every positive aspect of British culture—rule of law, democratic institutions, free press, free trade, economic progress—turns out to be derivative from an American, and a perfectly average American at that. Obviously, Twain overstates his case, but that is the prerogative of a humorist. And one cannot fully appreciate *Connecticut Yankee* unless one entertains the possibility that Twain may have genuinely been onto something in claiming that the British political tradition was derived from the American. Up until, say, 1800, this claim would have been absurd, but in the course of the nineteenth century, the balance of political influence between the two countries began to shift. Britain certainly became more democratic during the nineteenth century. The series of reform bills broadened the electorate and opened up the political process in many other ways. The reformed parliaments in turn passed legislation that furthered the democratization of Britain, extending the reforms to other levels of government, including municipalities, and in general liberalizing political institutions in Britain. Undoubtedly, the driving forces behind these developments were indigenous to Britain. And yet, in trying to understand why Britain democratized as rapidly and extensively as it did in the nineteenth century, it is worth considering the potential impact of having a functioning and flourishing democracy on view just across the Atlantic.

I cannot explore in detail the complicated issue of the influence of the American democratic experiment on British political theory and practice in the nineteenth century; I will have to confine myself to the barest sketch of the subject. To read the most familiar nineteenth-century British authors—Thomas Carlyle or Matthew Arnold, for example—one would think that the United States served principally as a negative example in Victorian Britain.[31] Often these writers can barely conceal their contempt for the fledgling democracy of the United States, and they explicitly warn the British not to follow its example and especially its descent into vulgarity in every sense of the term. But if one turns to another group of writers in Victorian Britain, broadly speaking the genuine liberals, the classical liberals, one gets a different picture. In the writings and speeches of liberals such as Harriet Martineau, Richard Cobden, John Bright, and Herbert Spencer, one finds the United States constantly held up as a shining example of all that is best in modern political theory and practice, and these writers repeatedly urge Britain to follow the lead of America.

For example, these liberals were generally in favor of the disestablishment of the Anglican Church, and it significantly helped their cause to be able to point to the United States as a county without an established church that had not experienced the disasters predicted for disestablishment in Britain. The issue of church establishment in Victorian Britain was closely bound up with the issue of public education. Many liberals would not support public funding for education if, as was happening, part of that money went to support the teaching of Anglican doctrine in schools. In a speech on the subject in the House of Commons on April 20, 1847, John Bright revealed how important America was to his argument and, moreover, how significantly it figured in British political debate—so much so that it could be appealed to as an example by both sides in a controversy:

> The right hon. Gentleman tells us . . . what republican statesmen and leaders in the United States have said, what has been done or held by Washington, Jefferson, and the commonwealth of Massachusetts. But is there any comparison between the United States and the United Kingdom? Is there any Established Church in the United States? . . . Give us, if you please, the state of things which exists in the United States, and particularly in that State of Massachusetts. Free us from the trammels of your Church—set religion apart from the interference of the State—if you will make public provision for education, let it not depend upon the doctrines of a particular creed—and then you will find the various sects in this country will be as harmonious on the question of education as are the people in the United States of America.[32]

"Give us, if you please, the state of things which exists in the United States"—coming from an Englishman, Bright's words would have warmed the heart of the Connecticut Yankee, for they validate his claim that America has something to teach Britain. Indeed, given the way the example of the United States figured in British parliamentary debates, one might say that what Twain imaginatively portrays in *Connecticut Yankee* really did take place—America taught Britain a lesson in the value of church disestablishment.

On another issue dear to Twain—free trade—references to America abound in British debates, although, with its own protectionist tendencies, the United States did not always provide a positive model for Britain. Nevertheless, the great champion of free trade in Britain, Richard Cobden, told British audiences that they should look to the United States to learn something about the causes of economic prosperity:

> The men who write for Protectionist newspapers sometimes heap their scorn upon the inhabitants of the American republic. New York is that State of the Union in which there is the most pauperism, for to that State the stream of emigration from this country and from Ireland flows; and yet in that State, the most pauperised in the whole republic, there is only one pauper to every 184 of the population. It is true that they have not an hereditary peerage to trust to. They know nothing there of a House of Lords, seventy or eighty Members of which despoil their legislative power in the hands of one old man. It is not a wise thing for the hereditary peerage and the Protectionist party to direct the attention of the people of this country to the condition of the American republic.[33]

In speaking about the British aristocracy, Cobden here almost matches Twain's sarcasm, and, indeed, his comments on the corruption of the House of Lords anticipate *Connecticut Yankee*. Like Cobden, Herbert Spencer urged his British readers to contemplate "the unparalleled progress of the United States, which is peopled by self-made men."[34] In an analysis of the problems with British colonial policy, Spencer does something remarkable—he starts quoting the American Declaration of Independence at length in order to detail the abuses of British imperialism.[35] One would think that having the Declaration of Independence recited to them would be even more galling to the British than the moment when Twain's Yankee starts quoting the Connecticut Constitution. And yet, Harriet Martineau does something similar when, reporting from her travels to America, she cites the Declaration favorably to show why property in the United States will always be secure.[36]

Martineau provides a particularly interesting illustration of Twain's idea that the British had something to learn from America. In her autobiography, when explaining her decision to travel to the United States, she states that she originally wished to go to Switzerland and Italy, but she was persuaded to change her plans by Lord Henley. When she challenged him to give her a good reason to go to America, he cited the educational value: "Whatever else may or may not be true about the Americans, it is certain that they have got at principles of justice and mercy in their treatment of their least happy classes of society which we should do well to understand. Will you not go, and tell us what they are?"[37] I could go on citing cases of British writers wishing to be instructed by Americans, but I will limit myself to one final, extended example.[38] This passage from the *Leeds Times* reveals both sides of the British debate on the United States; it addresses those who condemn the example of American democracy, but it cautions them not to dismiss the lessons to be learned from it:

> The appearance of Dickens's work on America, has been the signal for an attack, by the Tory press, upon Democratic institutions and forms of government. It is discovered that there is a great deal of vice in America, that there is a "universal distrust" of public men, that its press is immoral and licentious, that its people are vulgar and spit horribly, and that they maintain slavery and a great many of the other abominations bequeathed to them by the Old World. All this is set down to the account of Democracy! It is Republicanism which has done it all! It is the Free Institutions of America which are to blame for all this. And accordingly, the inference attempted to be drawn is,—hold fast by the old world system,—stick to monarchy, aristocracy, and class legislation—and away with all dogmas of a full, fair, and free representation of the people. . . .
>
> The object of Democratic government is equal liberty, equal laws, and equal justice to all. If the Americans have not yet arrived at this consummation, it is no fault of Democracy; no more than the present misery of England is the fault of its Christianity. The wonder is, not that America is so bad as it is, but that [it] is not a great deal worse. . . . Has not the Democracy of America accomplished sufficient during the last fifty years, to enable us to infer still greater achievements from it in the approaching future? Surely the grumblers ought to be satisfied with America. Monarchy has no instance of national greatness or achievement, to be compared with America, since the beginning of the world.[39]

Judging by passages such as this, we may conclude that Twain had allies in England who shared his belief that if the British were to learn a lesson in democracy and good government, they would have to swallow their pride and do so from their former colonies in America. Twain's genius was to see that the best way of getting his anti-British message across was paradoxically to appropriate a British literary form. By parodying Arthurian romance and turning the form on its head, he sought to deconstruct the myth on which the British Empire had been fictionally founded. As a nineteenth-century American, he felt remote in time and space from the imaginative center of British literature. But by sending his Yankee back to sixth-century Camelot, Twain managed to reposition himself at the very fountainhead of British literature as he understood it. This movement from the periphery of the imperial frontier to the metropolitan center became a standard gesture in twentieth-century postcolonial literature, but Twain had pioneered it already in the nineteenth.

If it seems anachronistic to view Twain on the model of contemporary authors such as Rushdie and Coetzee, we are fortunate to possess a letter he wrote to his English publisher, Andrew Chattus, in which he outlines his intentions in *Connecticut Yankee*. He states clearly that he set out to criticize autocracy in England: "Now mind you, I have taken all this pains [*sic*] because I wanted to say a Yankee mechanic's say against monarchy and its several natural props."[40] Twain also makes it clear that his aim is to give the British a dose of their own medicine: "*We* are spoken of (by *Englishmen*!) as a thin-skinned people. It is you that are thin-skinned. An Englishman may write with the most brutal frankness about any man or any institution among us, and we re-publish him without dreaming of altering a line or a word. But England cannot stand that kind of a book, written about herself. It is England that is thin-skinned." Authors are notoriously not the most reliable interpreters of the meaning of their own work, and Twain may have had reasons for overemphasizing the relevance of his book to England in a letter to his English publisher. Nevertheless, we cannot simply dismiss Twain's own account of *Connecticut Yankee* and the fact that he insisted "that the book was not written for America, it was written for England." He could not have been more explicit in stating that he was out to turn the tables on the English and teach them a lesson: "So many Englishmen have done their sincerest best to teach us something for our betterment, that it seems to me high time that some of us should substantially recognize the good intent by trying to pry up the English nation to a little higher level of manhood in turn."

Even statements directed at the American audience for *Connecticut Yankee* point toward what we would call the postcolonial twist in the novel. The publisher's prospectus for the book virtually proclaims a postcolonial agenda:

> The work was written with an object—to show that true nobility is inherent, not inherited; that birth confers no rights not sustained by nature. . . . The book answers the Godly slurs that have been cast at us for generations by the titled gentry of English. It is a gird at Nobility and Royalty, and makes most irreverent fun of these sacred things. . . . The Yankee becomes the most noted personage in the Kingdom; he sets himself the task of turning the monarchy into a republic on the American plan. . . . Without knowing it the Yankee is constantly answering modern English criticism of America. . . . At the same time the Yankee illustrates in a practical way the advantages of a Republican government like that of America. It is a book that every man, woman, and child in this country should read and be proud of.[41]

The actual advertisement for the book was even blunter in its anti-British and pro-American sentiments:

> A KEEN AND POWERFUL SATIRE ON ENGLISH NOBILITY AND ROYALTY
> A BOOK THAT APPEALS TO ALL TRUE AMERICANS
> It will be to English Nobility and Royalty what Don Quixote was to Ancient Chivalry[42]

But perhaps we should leave the last word to an Englishman. In a February 1890 review of *Connecticut Yankee*, L. F. Austin showed that he understood Twain's comic strategy, and, indeed, he anticipated the whole flood of postcolonial literature in the twentieth century and the attempt at cultural protectionism that accompanied it:

> Did you notice the other day that this humorist gravely deplored the effect of European literature on the American mind? His countrymen are much too fond of reading about kings and queens and aristocrats. They cannot shake themselves of a bad old hemisphere from which they have nothing to learn. Is it possible, then, that Mark Twain's book is the first of a patriotic series, designed to emancipate Americans from their bondage? . . . Will Congress pass an Act to protect Republican principles from the insidious influence of books like *Little Lord Fauntleroy*?[43]

In the end, whatever else Twain may be doing in *Connecticut Yankee*,[44] his own account of the book, together with statements made by others, leave us with the image of the former colonial subject standing up to his erstwhile colonial masters. Perhaps Mark Twain was the Salman Rushdie of nineteenth-century America after all.

Notes

1. For a famous statement of this position, see Ngugi Wa Thiong'o, *Decolonising the Mind: The Politics of Language in African Literature* (London: James Currey, 1986).

2. The latter phrase, often attributed to Salman Rushdie, was popularized when Bill Ashcroft, Gareth Griffiths, and Helen Tiffin used it as the title for their book *The Empire Writes Back: Theory and Practice in Post-Colonial Literatures* (London: Routledge, 1989), which is still one of the best introductions to postcolonial studies. For a comprehensive collection of essays in the field, see Bill Ashcroft, Gareth Griffiths, and Helen Tiffin, eds., *The Post-Colonial Studies Reader* (London: Routledge, 1995).

3. In a 1979 interview in *Paris Review*, Rhys said, "When I read *Jane Eyre* as a child, I thought, why should she think Creole women are lunatics and all that? What a shame to make Rochester's first wife, Bertha, the awful madwoman, and I immediately thought I'd write the story as it might really have been." Quoted in Teresa F. O'Connor, *Jean Rhys: The West Indian Novels* (New York: New York University Press, 1986), 144.

4. For Bloom's analysis of this strategy in the case of John Milton, see Harold Bloom, *A Map of Misreading* (New York: Oxford University Press, 1975), 131.

5. See, e.g., George Lamming's *Pleasures of Exile* (London: Michael Joseph, 1960) or Aimé Césaire's *Une tempête* (Paris: Editions du Seuil, 1974).

6. This sense of cultural inferiority surfaces in contemporary reviews of *Connecticut Yankee*. The reviewer for the *Keokuk Gate City* (February 16, 1890) wrote, "America has produced as yet no writer of the first rank. Probably the future will say that our best work so far has been in humor." See Louis J. Budd, ed., *Mark Twain: The Contemporary Reviews* (Cambridge, U.K.: Cambridge University Press, 1999), 313. The reviewer dismisses Hawthorne and Emerson as writing for too "select" an audience and does not even mention Poe or Melville. He thus ends up pinning his hopes for the future of American literature on Twain.

7. See, e.g., chapter ix of the first book of volume II of Tocqueville's *Democracy in America*.

8. Jonathan Elliot, ed., *The Debates in the Several State Conventions on the Adoption of the Federal Constitution* (Philadelphia: J. B. Lippincott, 1896), 2:527.

9. See Mark Twain, *A Connecticut Yankee in King Arthur's Court*, ed. Bernard L. Stein (Berkeley: University of California Press, 1979), 2–3.

10. On Twain's relation to Scott and Tennyson, see Richard Slotkin, "Mark Twain's Frontier, Hank Morgan's Last Stand," in *Mark Twain: A Collection of Critical Essays*, ed. Eric J. Sundquist (Englewood Cliffs, NJ: Prentice Hall, 1994), 120, and Howard G. Baetzhold, *Mark Twain and John Bull: The British Connection* (Bloomington: Indiana University Press, 1970), 133, 348n27. Baetzhold points out that Twain's illustrator, Daniel Beard, drew Merlin's face on the model of Tennyson's. For Twain's particular hostility to Walter Scott, see his *Life on the Mississippi* (1883; repr., Mineola, NY: Dover, 2000), chapters 40 and 46. One passage is especially relevant to *Connecticut Yankee*: "Then comes Sir Walter Scott with his enchantments, and by his single might checks this wave of progress, and even turns it back; sets the world in love with dreams and phantoms; with decayed and degraded systems of government; with the silliness and emptiness, sham grandeurs, sham gauds, and sham chivalries of a brainless and worthless long-vanished society" (Twain, *Life on the Mississippi*, 208). Twain believed that the baleful impact of Scott's "maudlin Middle-Age romanticism" (185) was particularly strong in the American South, where it inspired an exaggerated sense of gallantry. Twain in fact held Scott "in great measure responsible for the [American Civil] war" (209).

Twain's attitude toward Scott helps explain the bitterness of his satire of the Arthurian legend in *Connecticut Yankee.*

11. The British reviewers of *Connecticut Yankee* reacted strongly to this aspect of the book, and thus, in effect, confirm Twain's intentions. William T. Stead endorsed the book, but worried that he would thereby offend the British public, who might find "a certain profanation in the subject." James Ashcroft Noble said that "the Arthurian legends . . . to us of the age of Tennyson, have become saturated with spiritual beauty and suggestiveness." The *London Daily Telegraph* wrote, "An attack on the ideals associated with King ARTHUR is a coarse pandering to that passion for irreverence which is at the basis of a great deal of Yankee wit. . . . [The] Yankee scribe chooses to fling pellets of mud upon the high altar." Reginald B. Brett said in the *Pall Mall Gazette*, "The quest of the Holy Grail was the symbol—in the old romance—of individual effort to arrive at perfection in personal life, to attain to high, unselfish, irreproachable conduct." All these quotations are taken from Stein, *Yankee*, 26–27. The marked tendency to treat *Connecticut Yankee* as blasphemous shows how the Arthurian legend had achieved a quasireligious status in Victorian Britain. See also Baetzhold, *John Bull*, 163, and Dennis Welland, *Mark Twain in England* (London: Chatto & Windus, 1978), 144–45. For the full text of the British reviews cited, see the section on *Connecticut Yankee* in Budd, *Contemporary Reviews*, 283–320. A reading of all these reviews, British and American, confirms that Stein's excerpts from them are perfectly representative. The reviewers again and again focus on the political dimension of *Connecticut Yankee*, they specifically view it as an American democratic attack on British aristocracy, and they constantly bring up Tennyson's *Idylls of the King* as a point of reference.

12. For a concise statement of Twain's intentions, see Slotkin, "Twain's Frontier," 121: "Twain apparently meant to contrast the progressive spirit of nineteenth-century American values with the regressive ideologies of traditional aristocracy, political monarchism, and established religion or superstition." A contemporary review of *Connecticut Yankee*, in the *Boston Literary World*, said that "the serious aim of Mark Twain's travesty is the glorification of American Protestant democracy" (Stein, *Yankee*, 22).

13. I cite *Connecticut Yankee* from Mark Twain, *A Connecticut Yankee in King Arthur's Court*, ed. M. Thomas Inge, Oxford World's Classics (Oxford, U.K.: Oxford University Press, 1997), 53. All subsequent page references will be parenthetically incorporated into the body of the essay.

14. Twain was not simply hostile to Malory; for his admiration for *Le Morte D'Arthur*, see Baetzhold, *John Bull*, 105–6, and Henry Nash Smith, *Mark Twain's Fable of Progress: Political and Economic Ideas in "A Connecticut Yankee"* (New Brunswick, NJ: Rutgers University Press, 1964), 49–50. For an excellent treatment of Twain's relation to Malory, see David R. Sewell, "Hank Morgan and the Colonization of Utopia," in Sundquist, *Critical Essays*, 147. Sewell views *Connecticut Yankee* as a critique of imperialism; see especially pp. 144–46. For a general discussion of Twain's view of imperialism, see Jim Zwick, "Mark Twain and Imperialism," in *A Historical Guide to Mark Twain*, ed. Shelley Fischer Fishkin (Oxford, U.K.: Oxford University Press, 2002), 227–55. For the view that *Connecticut Yankee* is a kind of proleptic critique of American imperialism, see John Carlos Rowe, "How the Boss Played the Game: Twain's Critique of Imperialism in *A Connecticut Yankee in King*

Arthur's Court," in *The Cambridge Companion to Mark Twain*, ed. Forrest G. Robinson (Cambridge, U.K.: Cambridge University Press, 1995), 175–92.

15. See Dennis Butts, introduction to *King Solomon's Mines*, by H. Rider Haggard (Oxford, U.K.: Oxford University Press, 1989), vii. All subsequent quotations from *King Solomon's Mines* will be taken from this text, with page references parenthetically incorporated into the body of the essay.

16. Louis J. Budd, *Mark Twain: Social Philosopher* (Columbia: University of Missouri Press, 2001), 134. For more on the parallels between *Connecticut Yankee* and *King Solomon's Mines*, see Justin Kaplan, *Mark Twain and His World* (New York: Simon & Schuster, 1974), 146. One can measure the popularity of *King Solomon's Mines* in the United States by seeing how frequently it is referred to in contemporary reviews of *Connecticut Yankee*.

17. Butts, "Introduction," *King Solomon's Mines*, vii.

18. See Anne McClintock, *Imperial Leather: Race, Gender and Sexuality in the Colonial Context* (London: Routledge, 1995), 244.

19. In *Connecticut Yankee* Twain speaks of "transpositions of epochs" (7).

20. For the relevance of *The Time Machine* to *Connecticut Yankee*, see Kaplan, *Twain*, 146–47.

21. Twain employs a similar strategy in an essay he wrote about Queen Victoria's jubilee in 1897, reminding his audience of the humble origins of the great imperial city of London: "No doubt there was a village here 5,000 years ago. . . . It was built of thatched mud huts. . . . The tribes wore skins—sometimes merely their own, sometimes those of other animals. The chief was monarch, and helped out his complexion with blue paint. . . . Some of the Englishmen who will view the procession to-day are carrying his ancient blood in their veins. . . . It was still not much of a town when Alfred burned the cakes. Even when the Conqueror first saw it, it did not amount to much." See Mark Twain, "Queen Victoria's Jubilee," in *The Complete Essays of Mark Twain*, ed. Charles Neider (Garden City, NY: Doubleday, 1963), 190. Twain also writes, "There will be complexions in the procession to-day which will suggest the vast distances to which the British dominion has extended itself around the fat rotundity of the globe since Britain was a remote unknown back settlement of savages with tin for sale, two or three thousand years ago" (196).

22. For background on Twain's attitude toward the Comanches, see Slotkin, "Twain's Frontier," 119.

23. Joseph Conrad, *Heart of Darkness* (1899; repr., New York: Norton, 1988), 9.

24. For an extensive discussion of the significance of the eclipse incident, see David Ketterer, *New Worlds for Old: The Apocalyptic Imagination, Science Fiction, and American Literature* (Garden City, NY: Doubleday, 1974), 213–18.

25. For more evidence that plagiarism was on Twain's mind when he wrote *Connecticut Yankee*, see Stein, *Yankee*, 23. The earliest mention of the eclipse appears in chapter 2 of *Connecticut Yankee*, and at that point, it seems that all Twain had in mind was to use the eclipse as a way for the Yankee to confirm that he had indeed been transported back to the sixth century. The fact that only later in the book (chapter 6) does Twain use the eclipse to establish the Yankee's hold over Arthur's Britain strongly suggests that he did in fact get this idea from reading *King Solomon's Mines*. On this point, see Stein, *Yankee*, 6n19, and Baetzhold, *John Bull*, 132n10. Some of the contemporary reviews of *Connecticut Yankee* already raised the issue of Twain's indebtedness to Rider Haggard. The reviewer for the *San Francisco*

Chronicle (December 22, 1889) observed, "So he [the Yankee] adopts the device which Rider Haggard has used with so much effect in his African romances, and threatens to destroy the sun unless he is released" (Budd, *Contemporary Reviews*, 288). The reviewer for the *Charleston Sunday News* (January 5, 1890) was so convinced of Rider Haggard's influence on Twain that he misremembered the plot of *Connecticut Yankee*: "Hank had been reading Rider Haggard's novels and determined to try the eclipse trick on King Arthur" (Budd, *Contemporary Reviews*, 298).

26. An American review of *Connecticut Yankee* noticed this aspect of the book: "Mark Twain has come up from the people. He is American to the backbone, and the assumption of natural superiority by titled English aristocrats and the terrible wrongs inflicted on the working people, evidently galled him beyond endurance." Quoted in Stein, *Yankee*, 26.

27. In a draft for a preface to *Connecticut Yankee*, Twain suggested that modern England was in fact his real source for the legal system portrayed in the book: "We do not know what the laws of the mythical Arthur's day were, and so, I have supplied the deficiency with the legal atrocities of a far later time; but I have invented none, for that was not necessary" (Stein, *Yankee*, 516). In a second draft for a preface (which also remained unpublished in his day), Twain pointedly contrasted American law with British: "There was never a time when America applied the death penalty to more than 14 crimes. But England, within the memory of men still living, had in her list of crimes 223 which were punishable by death! And yet from the beginning of our existence down to a time within the memory of babes stillborn England has distressed herself piteously over the ungentleness of our Connecticut Blue Laws. Those Blue Laws should have been spared English criticism. . . . They were so insipidly mild, by contrast with the bloody and atrocious laws of England of the same period" (Stein, *Yankee*, 517). Twain's friend William Dean Howells commented in a review of *Connecticut Yankee* for *Harper's Magazine* in January 1890, "The elastic scheme of the romance allows it to play freely back and forward between the sixth century and the nineteenth century; and often while it is working the reader up to a blasting contempt of monarchy and aristocracy in King Arthur's time, the dates are magically shifted under him, and he is confronted with exactly the same principles in Queen Victoria's time" (Stein, *Yankee*, 19).

28. For the critique of church establishment in *Connecticut Yankee*, see Budd, *Social Philosopher*, 127–30; he points out that the critique applies to Anglicanism as well as to Catholicism, with specific reference to the original book illustrations by Daniel Beard; Twain "had not stopped Beard from making the vestments of his prelates more Anglican than Roman or printing 'High Church' under a priest blown skyward by dynamite" (130). See also Baetzhold, *John Bull*, 117.

29. John Stuart Mill, "Chapters on Socialism," in *On Liberty and Other Writings* (1879; repr., Cambridge, U.K.: Cambridge University Press, 1989), 222.

30. Winston Spencer Churchill, *The River War: An Historical Account of the Reconquest of the Soudan* (London: Longman, Green, 1899), 1:298–99.

31. Carlyle, for example, classes the United States among the "lands that have no government." See Thomas Carlyle, *Past and Present* (1843; repr., New York: New York University Press, 1965), 264. Arnold was one of those who thought of American culture as hopelessly derivative from English: "America has up to the present time been hardly more than a province of England, and even now would not herself claim to be more than abreast of England." See Matthew Arnold, *Culture and*

Anarchy and Other Writings (1869; repr., Cambridge, U.K.: Cambridge University Press, 1993), 113. For Twain's feud with Arnold, see Budd, *Social Philosopher*, 118–20; Stein, *Yankee*, 12–13; Smith, *Fable of Progress*, 70–71; and Roger B. Salomon, *Twain and the Image of History* (New Haven, CT: Yale University Press, 1961), 96–97. See also Baetzhold, *John Bull*, 110–11, 119, and especially 120, where he reports a speech Twain gave at Yale University, in which, in the course of attacking Arnold, he said that the true purpose of the humorist is "the deriding of shames, the exposure of pretentious falsities, the laughing of stupid superstitions out of existence," thus making the humorist "the natural enemy of royalties, nobilities, privileges, and all kindred swindles, and the natural friend of human rights and human liberties."

32. Reprinted in Allan Bullock and Maurice Shock, eds., *The Liberal Tradition: From Fox to Keynes* (New York: New York University Press, 1957), 68–69.

33. Reprinted in Cheryl Schonhardt-Bailey, ed., *Free Trade: The Repeal of the Corn Laws* (Bristol, U.K.: Thoemmes, 1996), 157.

34. Herbert Spencer, "Over-Legislation" (1853), in *The Man versus the State with Six Essays on Government, Society, and Freedom* (Indianapolis: Liberty Fund, 1982), 324.

35. See Spencer, *Man versus the State*, 221–22.

36. Quoted in R. K. Webb, *Harriet Martineau: A Radical Victorian* (New York: Columbia University Press, 1960), 170.

37. Harriet Martineau, *Autobiography* (1877; repr., London: Virago, 1983), 1:270.

38. For more evidence of British authors and thinkers seeking to be instructed by American examples, see Budd, *Social Philosopher*, 131–32, 140–41. See also the review of *Connecticut Yankee* by William T. Stead that Budd includes in his *Contemporary Reviews*, 308: "Another circumstance which gives significance to the book is that it is the latest among the volumes whereby Americans are revolutionising the old country. The two books [by Henry George and Edward Bellamy] which have given the greatest impetus to the social-democratic movement in recent years have both come to us from America." Stead views Twain's popularity in England as evidence of the democratization and Americanization of the country. In defending Twain against his English critics, he writes, "Yet I make free to say that the vote of the mass of English people would be on the side of the American and against the English critic. For what our critical class has failed to appreciate is that the Education Act has turned out and is turning out millions of readers who are much more like the Americans in their tastes, their ideas, and their sympathies than they are to the English of the cultured, pampered, and privileged classes. The average English-speaking man is the product of the common school in America, of the public elementary school in Britain and Australia. His literary taste is not classical but popular. He prefers Longfellow to Browning, and as a humorist he enjoys Mark Twain more than all the dainty wits whose delicately flavoured quips and cranks delight the boudoir and the drawing-room." (Budd, *Contemporary Reviews*, 308). The way Stead draws connections among mass education, mass culture, and Americanization turned out to be prophetic.

39. Quoted in Webb, *Martineau*, 137–38.

40. This letter, dated July 16, 1889, is transcribed in Welland, *Twain in England*, 135. All the subsequent quotations from this letter in this paragraph are from the same page. Welland's analysis of this letter and of Twain's dealings with his English

publisher in general concerning *Connecticut Yankee* help illuminate the book; see especially 134–39. For further discussion of this letter and a collection of Twain's statements of his intentions in *Connecticut Yankee* that are in harmony with the letter, see Everett Carter, "The Meaning of *A Connecticut Yankee*," in *On Mark Twain: The Best from American Literature*, ed. Louis J. Budd and Edwin H. Cady (Durham, NC: Duke University Press, 1987), 194–96.

41. Stein, *Yankee*, 540. The advertising material for *Connecticut Yankee* was written by Twain's business manager, Fred Hall, but there is evidence that Twain approved it. See Stein, *Yankee*, 18.

42. Stein, *Yankee*, 541. The polemical thrust of *Connecticut Yankee* was evident in its Canadian reception as well. Welland, *Twain in England*, 142, reproduces a Canadian newspaper headline: "Mark Twain Coming to Canada: The American angry, however, with monarchists in general and the English people in particular."

43. Budd, *Contemporary Reviews*, 307.

44. I should make it clear that I am not offering a comprehensive interpretation of *Connecticut Yankee* in this essay. My "postcolonial" reading of the book is meant only to supplement other interpretations—not supplant them—and, indeed, to draw attention to aspects of Twain's achievement that have hitherto largely gone unnoted. As a result of concentrating on the Yankee as the champion of American democracy against British autocracy, I have presented Twain's protagonist in a basically positive light. I want to acknowledge the validity of the many negative readings of the Yankee that have appeared over the years. The Yankee is in fact a profoundly ambivalent figure, and Twain reveals a dark side to his character, especially toward the end of the novel. For a good summary of the divergent critical views of the Yankee, see Susan K. Harris, *Mark Twain's Escape from Time: A Study of Patterns and Images* (Columbia: University of Missouri Press, 1982), 44–46n1. On the ambivalence of *Connecticut Yankee*, see also Welland, *Twain in England*, 146, and Smith, *Fable of Progress*, 105. To put the matter simply: In contrasting America with Britain, Twain makes the Yankee symbolic of modernity, and in that sense a positive figure, but eventually Twain's doubts about modernity begin to surface in the novel, and he interrogates the Yankee and all that he stands for in a critical light. In short, Twain clearly regards the Yankee as marking an advance beyond what the British stand for, but it is by no means clear that Twain regards this advance as an unequivocal good. Twain's ambivalence about modernity is concisely stated in his "Queen Victoria's Jubilee" essay, where he points out that the monarch had presided over the greatest era of inventions in human history and had thus seen "every one of the myriad of strictly modern inventions which, by their united powers, have created the bulk of the modern civilization and made life under it easy and difficult, convenient and awkward, happy and horrible, soothing and irritating, grand and trivial, an indispensable blessing and an unimaginable curse" (195). Twain was particularly troubled by the development of modern military technology. In the horrific battle scenes at the end of *Connecticut Yankee*, he seems appalled at the way modern technology has introduced a whole new degree of brutality into warfare. To explore this question would require analyzing the way images of the American Civil War haunt the end of *Connecticut Yankee*, which would in turn require analyzing the important parallels Twain draws between medieval England and the antebellum American South (focusing on the issue of slavery). But these complicated questions lie beyond the scope of this essay, and, besides, they have already been investigated thoroughly in

Connecticut Yankee criticism. And although Twain's doubts about modernity certainly surface in the book, its main thrust remains a celebration of Yankee ingenuity and the modern spirit of America. Consider Twain's statement of his purpose in an autobiographical dictation on December 5, 1906: "I think I was purposing to contrast . . . the English life of the whole of the Middle Ages, with the life of modern Christendom and modern civilization—to the advantage of the latter, of course." Quoted in Stein, *Yankee*, 8n22. Or see Salomon, *Image of History*, 103, where he quotes Twain saying, "If any are inclined to rail at our present civilization, there is no hindering him, but he ought to sometimes contrast it with what went before and take comfort and hope, too."

3

Tom Sawyer

Potential President

Catherine H. Zuckert

The young protagonists of Mark Twain's two most famous novels—*The Adventures of Tom Sawyer* and its sequel, *The Adventures of Huckleberry Finn*—have often been taken to be quintessentially American. Like the new nation, Tom and Huck are young, boys rather than men, adventurous and fun loving, resourceful, inventive, and not particularly respectful or enamored of authority. They are, in a word, what Americans most want to be—free. Like the society in which they are raised—a small town on the Mississippi River in Missouri before the Civil War, a state on the border not only between civilization and the frontier but also between free men and slaves—the boys' future is undetermined. The fact that both Tom and Huck are orphans is probably not merely coincidental. Neither youth is defined by his family or background. Both represent, if from necessity, the possibility of becoming a self-made man. But is a self-made man necessarily a morally responsible individual? A good family man or fellow citizen? The stories Twain tells about Tom and Huck as they grow up give readers reason to wonder.

Although they share so much, there are also important differences between Twain's two most famous characters. Tom is and wants to remain "respectable." He does not willingly obey the orders of his elders, and he regularly seeks to evade the restraints involved in school, work, and church. But when he is caught, Tom good-naturedly takes his punishment. He is willing not merely to take risks but even to endure pain to get what he wants. He recognizes that there are rules. He himself cares a great deal about certain of those rules as he understands them—not the rules that tell people how to get to heaven but the rules for becoming a hero and acquiring fame or glory as he has gleaned them from novels. In other words, Tom cares very much what other people think of him. He wants to be recognized as better than others. In all his projects, Tom thus insists on taking the lead. He regularly organizes his young friends into "gangs" of pirates or robbers. They do not recognize the law of the land—at least in theory—but they have to play by the rules of his game, rules he takes from historical novels.[1] Whereas his friend Huck merely wants to escape from the constraints of what he calls "sivilization"—clean clothes, regular hours, school, church, and manners—Tom wants to be a leader, to give himself and others their rules.[2] In *The Adventures of Tom Sawyer* then, Twain depicts the character and practical education of a natural leader. As we will see, that character is definitely mixed.

In depicting the characteristic traits and development of Tom Sawyer as a natural leader, Twain speaks to a certain ongoing debate in American political thought. After the founding generation and the passing of the "Virginia presidents," nineteenth-century critics of American democracy began asking why great men never became president. As those of us who follow presidential elections know, people have been asking that question ever since. In his classic analysis *Democracy in America*, Alexis de Tocqueville gives the classic answer: no self-respecting man, certainly no gentleman, would do what is necessary to win a popular election.[3] A gentleman would not put himself forward as a candidate; that would involve a vulgar kind of bragging. He would wait for others to call upon him to serve. A gentleman would not lower himself to seek the favor and, hence, the votes of those he regarded as his inferiors. As James Fenimore Cooper shows so dramatically in his novels, the gentleman's fellow citizens would, therefore, accuse him (with reason) of thinking he was better than they were. They certainly would never elect him.[4] What sort of person does seek to become a leader in a democracy? Twain shows us in his depiction of Tom Sawyer.[5] In his *Autobiography*, Twain quipped, "Teddy Roosevelt is Tom Sawyer grown up."[6] In *The Adventures of Tom Sawyer*, Twain shows how such a potential president is born and raised.[7]

In *The Adventures of Tom Sawyer*, Twain tells the story of an obscure orphan of questionable moral character who becomes a town celebrity. At the end of the novel, one of the leading citizens suggests that Tom may have an even more glorious future:

> Judge Thatcher hoped to see Tom a great lawyer or a great soldier someday. He said he meant to look to it that Tom should be admitted to the National Military Academy and afterward trained in the best law school in the country, in order that he might be ready for either career or both. (181)[8]

The judge has an immediate interest in Tom's fate. The young man acquired his current celebrity, in part, by saving the life of the judge's daughter, Becky. She, too, feels gratitude—and more. Since Tom acquired a fortune at the same time he saved Becky, the judge cannot offer the young man merely a monetary reward. The judge can promise to help Tom in the future—not merely to get the wife of his choosing (and far superior social status to his own) but to attain a position of great public prominence. American presidents have been drawn preeminently from the military—successful generals—and the law. Judge Thatcher proposes to provide Tom training for either or both.

Should Twain's novel, then, be regarded as an extended explication of the classic American political promise—in this country, any young man can hope to be president? Or, is there something special about Tom Sawyer, in particular, that qualifies him to become chief of the world's first modern democracy? In *The Adventures of Tom Sawyer*, Twain shows that Tom possesses certain character traits—traits not to be found in his friend Huck, for example—that make Tom particularly suited or apt to become a popular leader.[9] Tom is courageous; he is willing not merely to endure pain, but even to risk his own life in order to obtain status and recognition. He is ambitious and imaginative. And he is not too terribly bothered or restrained by moral scruples.

Nevertheless, Twain also shows, potential popular leaders like Tom are not simply born. They have to be practically trained and educated. Attached to his own freedom and ease, Tom recognizes how important personal liberty and comfort are to his fellows. Ambitious himself, Tom also understands how important status—not merely "keeping up with the Joneses" but looking better than their neighbors—is to his purportedly egalitarian compatriots. And, Twain shows, Tom initially uses his insight into the passions and prejudices of his peers to get the better of them, to get ahead both economically and socially. At the beginning of the novel in the famous whitewashing scene, Tom thus shows himself to be a first-rate young entrepreneur. However, Twain indicates, to become a true leader of men and, thus, to achieve the recognition he most desires, Tom has to learn that it will not suffice merely to outsmart and outmaneuver others. It is necessary truly to serve their needs and interests. Simply cheating and lying to get or do what one wants eventually results—or so we hope—in public shame. To become the man he wants to be, to exercise the freedom Americans possess by nature as their birthright, to enjoy or realize the opportunities offered by an open, democratic society, Tom has to learn to be responsible. In order to be recognized as an outstanding young man, he really and effectively has to do things that benefit others. That is the only way one really "gets ahead" oneself. American presidents may not, indeed will not, be gentlemen, Twain suggests. They will, like most of their compatriots, be hypocritical and self-seeking or morally corrupt. But, they will not simply be vulgar and self-seeking. They will have to learn, actually and in reality, to be public servants.

Let me then trace the education of a potential president as Twain presents it in *The Adventures of Tom Sawyer.* That education proceeds in three stages. In the first third of the novel, Twain shows how Tom tries to attain the glory he seeks not merely by physically whupping, but primarily by outsmarting—or perhaps we should say duping—his peers. What we and Tom discover from his initial "adventures" is that people may grudgingly admire or even envy people who trick them, but they do not feel gratitude; they do not love or adulate those who openly exploit them. In order to achieve the status and fame he so passionately desires, Tom has to learn to take more account of the feelings, especially the vulnerabilities and fears, of his associates. In the second and central third of the novel, we thus see Tom display a "conscience." His "conscience" does not prevent Tom from doing what he wants or causing others pain, but it does cause him to suffer. Tom wants to get ahead himself, but he does not really want to hurt others. The most important lesson he learns in the entire novel thus appears to be that he can attain his ambitions, that he can become a hero and publicly adulated most effectively by risking his own life to save that of another.[10] Primarily by drawing a contrast between Tom and Huck, in the last third of the novel, Twain then shows how morally ambiguous and questionable Tom's "public service" is.[11]

Let me turn now to the novel itself and some of its more famous incidents to show how Twain portrays the education of a potential president. We begin with one of the most famous scenes in all of American fiction: the whitewashing of Aunt Polly's fence. A bit of background may be useful. In chapter 1, Tom's Aunt Polly suspects him of having played hookey from school to go swimming when he arrives home with damp hair. Tom parries her suspicions by pointing to his immaculate collar. He is caught only when his cousin Sid points out that the thread joining the collar to Tom's shirt is black rather than white. When Aunt Polly reaches for the switch, Tom diverts her attention for a moment and uses the opportunity to run away.

Twain reports that

> Aunt Polly stood surprised a moment, and then broke into a gentle laugh.
>
> "Hang the boy, can't I never learn anything? Ain't he played me tricks enough like that for me to be looking out for him by this time? . . . But . . . he never plays them alike, two days, and how is a body to know what's coming? . . . I ain't doing my duty by that boy, and that's the Lord's truth. . . Spare the rod and spile the child, as the Good Book says. . . . Every time I let him off, my conscience does hurt me so, and every time I hit him my old heart most breaks." (2)

She resolves to let him off that evening, but to force him to stay home and work on Saturday when all the other boys are off. There's nothing the boy dislikes more, she thinks, than good, hard work.

Aunt Polly does not really understand her young charge, we see. It is not effort nearly so much as public humiliation that Tom dreads. Next day, he is despondent, not so much at the prospect of having to work or at his lack of leisure and freedom as at the thought of how much fun the other boys will make of him for having to work. From the very beginning of his "adventures," we see that Tom cares more about his image in the eyes of others than he does about physical pain or comfort. That fateful Saturday morning, Tom has an "inspiration." Seeing a pal of his coming down the street, ready to rag him about having to work on Saturday, Tom pretends that whitewashing is a rare privilege, something a boy cannot do every day. Ben Rogers and a series of boys after him have to bargain with Tom, trading snacks or other prized possessions for the privilege of giving Aunt Polly's fence not merely one but three coats of whitewash. Twain concludes, "if [Tom] had been a great and wise philosopher, like the writer of this book, he would have comprehended that Work consists of whatever a body is *obliged* to do, and that Play consists of whatever a body is not obliged to do" (12). We readers learn even more. In the first place, we see that Aunt Polly's loosely Christian morals and conscience are not sufficient to enable her to discipline or control Tom; she has too much affectionate sympathy for his love of fun and freedom and too much admiration for his "high jinks" and clever stratagems to disapprove of him thoroughly or to keep him in check. Tom's education does not, in other words, take place in his family or in church. He has to learn to take responsibility for his actions and to acquire a certain amount of self-control someplace else, in another way—if at all.

We also see that it is not effort so much as perceived inequality or lesser privilege that grates on the citizens of the new republic. Aunt Polly thinks she is punishing Tom by making him work. It is not the work per se that daunts him or his fellows, however; it is the appearance of being less free or, as it turns out, more privileged that is of most concern to them. The most successful entrepreneurs do not sell useful products or services, Twain suggests, so much as they sell status or self-esteem.

As Twain shows in the next, almost equally famous incident, however, entrepreneurship is not enough to get Tom the recognition he seeks. To encourage his young pupils to learn scripture, the Sunday school superintendent had devised a system of rewards or incentives. For every two verses of scripture memorized and recited without too much coaching, each pupil received a small blue ticket with a passage of scripture on it. "Ten blue tickets . . . could be exchanged for a red one, ten red tickets for a yellow, and for ten yellow tickets the superintendent gave the student a very plainly bound Bible (worth forty cents in those easy times)" (21). The narrator explains,

> Only the older pupils managed to keep their tickets and stick to their tedious work long enough to get a Bible, and so the delivery of one of these prizes was a rare and noteworthy circumstance; the successful pupil was so great and conspicuous on that day that on the spot every scholar's heart was fired with a fresh ambition that often lasted a couple of weeks. It is possible that Tom's mental stomach had never really hungered for one of those

> prizes, but unquestionably his entire being had for many a day longed for the glory and the eclat that came with it. (21)

Hating the drudgery and boredom of mere memorization, Tom characteristically uses his wits to pursue his ambitions. He trades the various articles he acquired in exchange for the privilege of whitewashing for the biblical verse tickets. The day the county judge and his wife come to hear the recitations, Tom is thus in a position to gratify the desire not merely of the superintendent to "show off" his pupils, but the similar desires of the librarian, the young lady teachers, the young gentleman teachers, the little girls, and the little boys to "show off" before their distinguished guest, by marching up to the stage with nine yellow tickets, nine red tickets, and ten blue ones in his hand to exchange for a Bible. "It was the most stunning surprise of the decade," the narrator comments. "The boys were all eaten up with envy . . . [especially] those who had contributed to this hated splendor by trading tickets to Tom for the wealth he had amassed in selling whitewashing privileges. These despised themselves, as being the dupes of a wily fraud" (24). The fraud is exposed, however, when first the judge and then his wife ask Tom (who supposedly learned two thousand verses) to say who the first two disciples were. Hesitating, hemming and hawing in embarrassment, Tom finally blurts out "David and Goliath!" The pain of Tom's shame is compounded by the fact that the judge is the father of the new girl in town, whom he most wants to impress!

To make sure that his readers are not too critical of Tom for his commercial approach to biblical learning, Twain shows in the chapter following Tom's humiliation that the congregation as a whole is as bored by church services and sermons as the young boy. All laugh when a stray dog that has wandered into the service yelps, bitten by the pinchbug with which Tom has been covertly playing. "The neighboring spectators shook with a gentle inward joy, several faces went behind fans and handkerchiefs, and Tom was entirely happy" (29).[12]

It is impossible for an ambitious young man to lead a people if he does not share many of their feelings and tastes. Merely sharing in popular frustrations and relieving them will not suffice to bring that youth the adulation and affection he desires, however. He remains simply one of the crowd.

Tom cannot attain the distinction he wants through sheer effrontery or sharp trading. Such practices may arouse the envy of others, but they also produce resentment and anger. Nor, Twain shows, can a youth attain social preeminence simply with physical strength and moral fortitude.

Tom faces down each new fellow who comes to town—first in word and then with his fists. Nevertheless, as the young inmates of the town school know all too well, discipline imposed by force by their larger and stronger elders feels just like that—compulsion. The children may fear the switch of the schoolmaster, but they do not love or respect him. On the contrary, they seek any and every form of distraction they can find—to escape in mind, if not body, from the confinement.

Their desire for freedom—or perhaps we should say their dislike of confinement and constriction—makes the youths of St. Petersburg look with longing at the life of the son of the worst town drunkard, Huckleberry Finn.

> Huckleberry came and went, at his own free will. He slept on doorsteps in fine weather and in empty hogsheads in wet; he did not have to go to school or to church, or call any being master or obey anybody; he could go fishing or swimming when and where he chose . . . nobody forbade him to fight; he could sit up as late as he pleased . . . he never had to wash, nor put on clean clothes; he could swear wonderfully. (34)

For the same reason—because he acts out their children's desire to be free from convention—the adults citizens of St. Petersburg heartily disapprove of Huck. He

> was cordially hated and dreaded by all the mothers of the town, because he was idle and lawless and vulgar and bad—and because all their children admired him so, and delighted in his forbidden society. . . . Tom was like the rest of the respectable boys . . . under strict order not to play with him. So he played with him every time he got a chance. (33–34)

It was a relatively mild and therefore safe form of rebellion. As Twain comments late in the novel, Tom "did not care to have Huck's company in public places" (140).

Unable and ultimately unwilling to give up the affectionate care of their families, boys like Tom and his friend Joe Harper try to attain some of Huck's freedom, at least temporarily, by pretending to be outlaws. Escaping the supervision of their elders by going into the woods, they take turns playing roles—Friar Tuck, the Sheriff of Nottingham, even Robin Hood himself—and design their costumes literally by the book. Youthful romantics, Tom and Joe regret "that there were no outlaws any more, and wonder what modern civilization could claim to have done to compensate for their loss" (49). Looking for a more colorful, exciting, adventurous life, free from customary constraints and boring obligations like school and church, the boys say "they would rather be outlaws a year in Sherwood Forest than President of the United States forever" (49). Tom has not learned yet how to satisfy his desire for recognition as an adult in a democracy.[13]

As Twain shows when Tom and Huck unexpectedly witness the murder of Dr. Robinson by Injun Joe at midnight in the graveyard, Tom does not really understand what it is to be an outlaw or how dangerous it actually is. He is, after all, just a boy trying to have fun.

Tom and Huck had gone to the cemetery to see whether the dead cat Huck has acquired will actually cure warts the way people say. As Huck explains:

> Why, you take your cat and go and get in the graveyard 'long about midnight when somebody that was wicked has been buried; and when it's midnight a devil will come, or maybe two or three, but you can't see 'em, you can only hear something like the wind, or maybe hear 'em talk; and when they're taking that feller away, you heave your cat after 'em and say, "Devil follow corpse, cat follow devil, warts follow cat, I'm done with ye!" (36)

Standing by a fresh grave in the dark, the boys are thus startled, indeed frightened, when they hear voices. They are reassured when they recognize one as the voice of Muff Potter, town drunk. The other voice turns out to belong to a man worse than a devil, "that murderin' half-breed . . . Injun Joe." Joe takes the opportunity in the dark night to knife the young doctor who has hired the two derelicts to dig up a corpse for him to examine and blames the murder on Muff, who falls unconscious in the fight that leads up to the knifing. Frightened of what Joe will do to them if they reveal what they have seen and heard, Tom and Huck take an oath not to tell and initial it with their own blood.

Unfortunately, the narrator informs us, the fear that keeps the boys from cooperating with the law in the apprehension of the true criminal is not limited to the young.

> The villagers had a strong desire to tar and feather Injun Joe and ride him on a rail, for body-snatching, but so formidable was his character that nobody could be found who was willing to take the lead in the matter, so it was dropped. [Joe] had been careful to begin both of his inquest statements with the fight, without confessing the grave-robbery that preceded it; therefore it was deemed wisest not to try the case in the courts at present. (65)[14]

Law and justice are weak in America precisely because there are few individuals like Tom Sawyer willing to take the lead in an enterprise that promises to bring them pain, if not death—and Tom himself is not willing or prepared to take the lead in such a truly dangerous undertaking as yet. He has to develop his conscience—or to speak more precisely, he has to bring his conscience and his desire for recognition together. The story of that "reconciliation" occupies the central section of the novel.

Tom's conscience bothers him after the inquest; he does not rest easy with the knowledge that his remaining silent has led to the incarceration of an innocent man on the basis of false testimony by the murderer himself. As a result, Tom cannot sleep nights. Trying to mollify his conscience, Tom takes every opportunity to smuggle little treats to Muff Potter through the jailhouse window.[15]

However, Tom's conscience is, for a time at least, overcome not merely or even perhaps primarily by his fear of Injun Joe. Tom is depressed by a more general sense of gloom and doom. He has failed to acquire the renown or recognition he so passionately desires. His great enterprise in whitewashing was revealed as a fraud at the Sunday school exhibition, and his courtship of Becky fell apart after he inadvertently let slip that he was recently engaged to Amy Lawrence. "[N]obody loved him," he concludes. He decides, therefore, to run away. "[W]hen they found out what they had driven him to, perhaps they would be sorry." Meeting his "soul's sworn comrade, Joe Harper" whose "mother had whipped him for drinking some cream which he had never tasted," the aggrieved youths determine to leave home and move to an uninhabited island in the middle of the river, where they can live as pirates (70). Persuading Huck Finn to join them, they first "hook" some provisions and then take a raft. Arriving on the island, they are blissfully happy at first.

> They built a fire against the side of a great log twenty or thirty steps within the somber depths of the forest . . . cooked some bacon . . . and used up half of the core "pone" stock they had brought. It seemed glorious sport to be feasting in that wild free way in the virgin forest of an unexplored and uninhabited island, far from the haunts of men, and they said they never would return to civilization. (73)

But, Twain shows, the boys do not take pleasure so much in the beauties of a more natural existence as in the contrast between their current condition and that from which they previously suffered. "What would the boys say if they could see us?" Tom asks his companions. "It's just the life for me. . . . You don't have to get up, mornings, and you don't have to go to school, and wash, and all that blame foolishness" (73–74). Huck lives free of such restraints all the time, but the joy of escaping from the discipline of their regular schedule begins to wane for Tom and Joe as night falls. Saying their prayers inwardly, Tom and Joe both have a hard time getting to sleep. "It was conscience," the narrator explains.

> They began to feel a vague fear that they had been doing wrong to run away; and next they thought of the stolen meat, and the real torture came. They tried to argue it away by reminding conscience that they had purloined sweetmeats and apples scores of times; but . . . it seemed to them, in the end, that . . . taking sweetmeats was only "hooking," while taking bacon and hams and such valuables was plain simple *stealing*—and there was a command against that in the Bible. So they inwardly resolved that so long as they remained in the business, their piracies should not again be sullied with the crime of stealing. (75)

Tom and Joe think they want to be free to do what they please—more than anything else. What they discover—or what Twain shows his readers—is that they want, above all, to be seen by others to be doing what they please. These boys are by no means indifferent to the approval or disapproval of their parents and peers. On the contrary, what they most want is admiration and envy. To be admired they think they need to do something unusual, colorful, "gaudy." They believe that they will be envied not so much for their achievements, however, as for getting out of the unpleasant constraints from which others suffer. That is why they pretend to be "robbers" and "pirates." They certainly do not want to be, or to be perceived as, common "thieves."

Because they care so much about the opinions of others, whose moral teachings they have internalized in part in the form of conscience, the boys do not find the genuine beauties of nature and the pleasures of an easy existence satisfying for long. On the island, the narrator reports,

> They found plenty of things to be delighted with, but nothing to be astonished at. . . . They took a swim about every hour . . . they fared sumptuously upon cold ham, and then threw themselves down in the shade to talk. But the talk soon began to drag. . . . The stillness, the solemnity that brooded in the woods, and the sense of loneliness began to tell upon the spirits of the boys. . . . A sort of undefined longing crept upon them. . . . It was budding homesickness. (78)

The boys get temporary relief when a ferryboat comes looking for them; people in town think they may have drowned. "They felt like heroes in an instant. Here was a gorgeous triumph; they were missed" (79). But the relief does not last long. Human beings want to be surrounded by people who care about them. All three of the youths become homesick—even Huck. After his pals fall asleep, Tom thus sneaks back to town to see his family. Overhearing Aunt Polly mourning for him makes Tom feel so bad that he begins to write her a note to say that they are all fine, but then he has another, grander idea. He rushes back to the island where he convinces Joe and Huck to stay until Sunday—when they will sneak in, resurrected, as it were, to their own funeral. They march down the aisle as the minister begins to discourse on the text: "I am the Resurrection and the Life" (94). Relieved to see that the young men are actually all right, the members of the congregation join in to "Praise God from whom all blessings flow" with unusual fervor (95). The narrator reports, "As the 'sold' congregation trooped out they said they would almost be willing to be made ridiculous again to hear 'Old Hundred' sung like that once more" (95). Boys will be boys, and the people are happy to see them alive and sound—at least for the moment.

Nevertheless, the next day Aunt Polly complains to Tom about his lack of consideration for the feelings of those who love him most. Couldn't he have left some hint that they were just on the island? Tom wants people to love and admire him; for all his playing pirates and Indians, he does not really want to hurt others, especially the innocent who love and admire him already. He thus tells Aunt Polly about the note he wrote and then did not leave—which, as evidence of his affection and concern, greatly relieves her when she finds it in his coat pocket. Then, by taking the whipping that by right should have gone to Becky for tearing the pages in the schoolmaster's book, Tom learns that the best way to earn the admiration and affection of another is to take on one's own shoulders the pain they fear. He puts that lesson into practice in public in a most dramatic fashion when, overcoming his own fear of retaliation by Injun Joe, Tom testifies in court to what he actually saw in the graveyard that night and thus saves the life of Muff Potter. "Tom was a glittering hero once more," the narrator concludes. He was "the pet of the old, the envy of the young. His name even went into immortal print, for the village paper magnified him. There were some that believed he would be President, yet, if he escaped hanging" (124).

Tom has learned that a young man does not acquire glory so much by showing off or beating his fellows in contests—whether of fists or of wits—so much as by relieving the weak and the innocent from apprehension and suffering. Like Becky and Muff, the people so benefited greatly admire one's nobility and generosity. A young man can simultaneously satisfy the demands of both ambition and conscience, however, only if he can overcome his own fear of pain and death. It takes courage. Tom's desire for preeminence can be satisfied, in other words, only to the extent to which he shares in a real and old aristocratic virtue. There is a moral core or prerequisite for his success. As Twain suggests in two chapters depicting student recitations born out of fear of the whip and a temporary religious revival, the combination of courage and compassion represented by Tom results in more real and lasting benefits to others than moral teachings based on fear—of punishment—here on earth or in the hereafter.

It is also the courage born of ambition, of the desire, above all, to look good in the eyes of others, that distinguishes Tom from his friend Huck. Huck also has compassion for Muff Potter, but out of fear for his own hide, he would never have broken the oath he and Tom solemnly swore not just once, but twice, never to reveal what they had seen. Twain brings out the moral ambiguity of the desire for distinction that leads a person like Tom Sawyer to take the lead in performing real acts of public service by emphasizing the differences between Tom and Huck in the last third of the novel.

Like all red-blooded American youths, Tom and Huck want to strike it rich. They decide, therefore, to go in search of buried treasure. As with the cure for warts, so with buried gold, Tom informs Huck, there is a formula for success. One has to look "in a ha'nted house or on an island, or under a dead tree that's got one limb sticking out" (127). Confident that they will eventually succeed, although he admits it may take some time, Tom asks Huck what he will do with the money if they find it. And the differences in the young men's dominant desires come out in the resulting exchange. Huck says, "I'll have pie and a glass of soda every day, and I'll go to every circus that comes along" (128). As he admitted on Jackson's Island, the homeless boy often does not get enough to eat. His first desire is thus for food—especially for sweets. Huck is willing to sacrifice such physical comforts in order to maintain his freedom, however. As he indicates in his desire to see the circus, Huck joins or rejoins society, for example, as a "pirate" with Tom and Joe, for the sake of entertainment. Tom, on the other hand, displays his love of show and his more conventional, social desires for affection when he says that he is "going to buy a new drum, and a sure-'nough sword, and a red necktie and a bull pup, and get married" (128). Huck objects: he will be "more lonesomer than ever" if Tom hooks up for life with a woman. "No you won't," Tom unrealistically responds. "You'll come and live with me." He urges Huck to "get down to business" now and dig (129).

After they dig under several trees without success, the boys decide to try a haunted house—but during the day to avoid ghosts. When Huck remembers it is Friday, they fear it might not be an auspicious time to disturb spirits, so they decide to play Robin Hood outside and wait to go inside to explore until Saturday. Tom tells Huck that Robin Hood "was one of the greatest men that was ever in England—and the best. He was a robber" (132). When Huck asks who he robbed, Tom explains that Robin Hood only robbed "sheriffs and bishops and rich people and kings. . . . But he never bothered the poor. He loved 'em. He always divided up with 'em perfectly square" (132–33). Robin Hood is apparently the model for a democratic robber baron—or a noble redistributive politician. Law-abidingness is not nearly so important as whom you hurt and whom you benefit. Laws are made, after all, by people in power. Democratic heroes help the weak, the poor, and the powerless.

Next morning, when the boys return to the haunted house and postpone their digging in order to explore upstairs, they are once again surprised and frightened to hear voices—especially when they recognize one of the voices as belonging, once again, to Injun Joe. Disguised as a deaf and dumb Spaniard with a long white beard and serape, Joe has returned with a ragged companion to pick up a hoard of silver they left buried in the isolated shack. When they go to dig it up, they find another chest of gold coins left, they think, by another gang. The boys have found their buried treasure—only to see it carted away!

Having heard Joe say that they will bury the chest again under the cross at Number Two, Tom figures that Number Two must refer to a tavern that rents rooms. After Tom finds Injun Joe there lying drunk on the floor one night with no treasure in sight, the boys decide that Huck should keep a look out at night. When the robbers come back to pick up their treasure, he will notify Tom, and they will trail them.

Tom gets distracted from the treasure hunt by the picnic Becky Thatcher organizes by McDougal's cave. He and Becky have gotten lost in the lower corridors of the cave the very night that Huck sees Joe and his ragged companion return to the tavern, pick up a bag of things, and take off to do the "job" Joe insists they finish before he will let his "friend" leave—alive. It was a matter of "revenge," Joe had told his companion at the haunted house. As Huck follows them up Cardiff Hill past the Welshman's house onto the grounds of the Widow Douglas, the boy realizes with a "deadly chill in his heart,"

> this, then, was the "revenge" job! His [first] thought was, to fly. Then he remembered that the Widow Douglas had been kind to him more than once, and maybe these men were going to murder her. He wished he dared venture to warn her; but he knew he didn't dare—they might come and catch him. (149)

When they pause outside her house, waiting for her company to leave, he thus furtively backs down the hill till he can run to the Welshman to plead with him to help her. Knocking on the door, Huck entreats, "Please don't ever tell *I* told you. . . . I'd be killed, sure—but the widow's been good friends to me sometimes, and I want to tell—I *will* tell if you'll promise you won't ever say it was me" (150). Three minutes later, the old man and his sons, well armed, march up the hill.

Like Tom in the case of Muff Potter, Huck's compassion for the suffering of an innocent person who had been kind to him in the past overcomes enough of his fear to make him tell the authorities—or at least someone who can help. But, in contrast to Tom, Huck does not want to take credit or receive public recognition for his service or bravery. He'd rather remain in obscurity. He does not want to risk his life for mere fame. Is he simply a coward? Or, does his sense of his own vulnerability make him more truly egalitarian and humane?

The contrast between the responses of the two boys becomes even clearer after Tom saves Becky from starvation in the cave and at the same time discovers where Joe actually buried the treasure. He and Huck go back to the cave, and they dig up the chest. When the boys are brought to the widow's house, where the Welshman announces that it was Huck who saved her life, Tom informs the assembled crowd that Huck does not need the widow's support. He's rich! To the astonishment of the townspeople, the boys bring in and display the $12,000 in gold they have found.

Nevertheless, the widow takes Huck in.

> And the fact that he was now under the Widow Douglas's protection introduced him into society—no, dragged him into it . . . and his sufferings were

> almost more than he could bear. The widow's servants kept him clean and neat, combed and brushed, and they bedded him nightly in unsympathetic sheets that had not one little spot or stain. . . . He had to eat with knife and fork . . . he had to learn his book, he had to go to church; he had to talk so properly that speech was become insipid in his mouth; whithersoever he turned, the bars and shackles of civilization shut him in and bound him hand and foot. (181)

Huck bears with it for three weeks and then goes missing. After three days, Tom Sawyer finds him sleeping in an old empty hogshead. Huck is "unkempt, uncombed, and clad in the same old ruin of rags that had made him picturesque in the days when he was free and happy" (181). He tells Tom that despite the widow's good intentions and affection, he just cannot go back.

> The widder's good to me, and friendly; but . . . [s]he makes me git up just the same time every morning; she makes me wash . . . I got to go to church. . . . I got to wear shoes all Sunday. . . . [S]he wouldn't let me smoke . . . [or] yell . . . [or] gape, or stretch, or scratch, before folks. (181–82)

Huck has concluded that "being rich ain't what it's cracked up to be." He proposes, therefore, to give his share of the money back to Tom and to ask his friend merely to spare him a dime from time to time.

When Tom objects that everyone lives "regular" like the widow, Huck tells him that "don't make no difference. I ain't everybody, and I can't *stand* it. It's awful to be tied up so" (182). Huck does not want to give up the freedom he has to do what he wants, when he wants, in order to live the way other people think he should. He does not want anyone to know who he is or what he does, because he does not want to live by rules or under anyone else's command and control. He does not care what other people think. He simply does not want to be blamed—or held responsible.

Huck does want to be "one of the boys," however. He gets lonely. When Huck states his regret that just as he and Tom had found guns and a hideout in the cave and were all ready to rob, they had been dragged back into society, Tom sees his opportunity. "Looky here," he tells Huck, "being rich ain't going to keep me back from turning robber. . . . But, Huck, we can't let you into the gang if you ain't respectable." "Didn't you let me go for a pirate?" Huck reminds him. "Yes," Tom admits, "but that's different. A robber is more high-toned than what a pirate is—as a general thing. In most countries they're awful high up in the nobility." Huck pleads with Tom not to shut him out. "I wouldn't want to, and I *don't* want to," Tom assures him, "but what would people say? Why, they'd say, 'Mph! Tom Sawyer's Gang! Pretty low characters in it!' They'd mean you, Huck. You wouldn't like that, and I wouldn't." Huck agrees to go back to the widder's and stay there till he rots, if Tom will let him join the pirates. If he "git[s] to be a reg'lar ripper of a robber, and everybody talking 'bout it, [he] reckon[s] she'll be proud she snaked [him] out of the wet" (183).

The ending of the novel is, I believe, intentionally ambiguous. In his explicit "conclusion," Twain states that "[it] being strictly a history of a *boy*, it must stop here; the story could not go much further without becoming the history of a *man*. When one writes a novel about grown people, he knows exactly where to stop—that is, with a marriage; but when he writes of juveniles, he must stop where he best can" (184).

The narrator's report of the high opinion Judge Thatcher had formed of Tom leads us to believe in the end that Tom will marry Becky, that he will attend a military academy and go to law school, and that he will, one way or another, become a community leader. That would be the story of Tom Sawyer, grown up: Tom Sawyer as Theodore Roosevelt—or Bill Clinton, or George W. Bush, the youthful cutup who has compassion and a conscience, who asks forgiveness for his youthful indiscretions, who has given up his noble pretensions, finds religion, and runs for office to serve his fellow Americans. Taking the lead in all his endeavors, he is or has become the potential president.

By leaving the story a tale of a boy, Twain leaves the future open—or the result undetermined. Has Tom shown in his final manipulation of Huck's desires that he has become a responsible citizen and leader, that he sees the need to lead his fellows into society, to get them to accept customary regulations and order—for their own good? As we saw initially in the case of Tom and his Aunt Polly, sermonizing and moral discipline, even when affectionately imposed, do not succeed in civilizing or taming a spirited youth. Tom gets Huck to accept the order imposed on his life by the widow, where she and her good intentions could not, by appealing to Huck's love of adventure and fun. The appeal is, however, to Huck's desire to be a member of a gang of robbers, that is, to be one of a gang of young men who live outside the law, getting what they want through the use of force and violence. We are led to ask whether the means Tom uses to socialize Huck do not promise to undermine the obedience to civil and domestic order he would impose. In the murderous career of Injun Joe, Twain reminds his readers how ugly and dangerous the life of a "robber," a combination of a natural attachment to one's own freedom and equality with a willingness to steal and kill to get what one wants, looks in a grown-up.

In *The Adventures of Tom Sawyer*, I have thus argued, Twain dramatizes the problem of leadership in a democracy, if not in general. Like Tom and Huck, Twain shows, human beings are attached by nature to liberty. We do not want to be restrained by others, by customs, or by laws. We want to do what we please. Moral suasion, whether in the form of religious teaching or affectionate parenting, is not sufficient to institute order—or to protect the weak from the strong and ruthless.[16] People tend to obey out of fear—of violent death or of public opprobrium. Only a few, like Tom Sawyer, are willing not only to risk their lives but also to endure pain and shame—at least temporarily—in order to achieve the admiration, indeed adoration, of their fellows. Because they are willing to take the lead in all enterprises, such individuals perform an essential public service. Without such daring leaders, ordinary folks are too timid to take action against the violent and rapacious. Nevertheless, Twain suggests, we should recognize the true character of the beast. People like Tom Sawyer serve others not for the sake of the others; they serve because they glory in receiving glory. And they are perfectly willing, indeed happy, to use immoral and illegal means. We should reward such people with the fame they so desire—if and when they perform real public services. But we should not trust them. We should recognize that they are always scheming to "take" us. We should regularly remind them that we do not enjoy being "sold." We should hold them—and force them to hold others—responsible.

Notes

1. In *Mark Twain: The Fate of Humor* (Princeton, NJ: Princeton University Press, 1966), 140–41, James M. Cox observes that Tom "feels the pinch of school and the discipline of Aunt Polly, but he has no sustained desire to escape and no program of rebellion. What he does have is a perennial dream of himself as the hero."

2. Twain also contrasts Tom with Huck in *The Adventures of Huckleberry Finn.* In that novel, Tom is also presented as the leader, but the picture of Tom is much more negative than it is in *The Adventures of Tom Sawyer*, perhaps because Huck is the narrator. For the contrast from Huck's point of view, see Catherine H. Zuckert, "Twain's Comic Critique," in *Natural Right and the American Imagination: Political Philosophy in Novel Form* (Savage, MD: Rowman & Littlefield, 1990), 131–60.

3. Compare with Alexis de Tocqueville, "The People's Choice and the Instincts of American Democracy in Such Choices," in *Democracy in America*, trans. Harvey C. Mansfield and Delba Winthrop (Chicago: University of Chicago Press, 2000), I.ii.5, 187–90. In his novel *Democracy*, the scion of an American political family himself, Henry Adams says basically the same thing about his presidential hopeful, Senator Ratliff. In his famous explanation of why great men never become president, in *The American Commonwealth* (New York: Macmillan, 1898), 57–63, James Bryce connects the low character of American leaders to the requirements of party politics; but party politics are, after all, merely expressions of the requirements of democratic electioneering.

4. Compare this especially with James Fenimore Cooper, *Home as Found* (New York: Capricorn Books, 1961), and *The American Democrat* (New York: Knopf, 1959).

5. Twain gave a devastatingly funny critique in "Fenimore Cooper's Literary Offenses," in *The Writings of Mark Twain* (New York: Harper & Brothers, 1899), 22:78–96. He seems to have disagreed with Cooper about the character and potential of American political leadership as well.

6. Bernard De Voto, ed., *Mark Twain in Eruption* (New York: Harper Brothers, 1940), 49.

7. In the course of the novel, Tom Sawyer displays character traits associated with three, if not all four, types of presidential characters identified in "Presidents since Theodore Roosevelt" by James David Barber, *The Presidential Character*, 3rd ed. (Englewood Cliffs, NJ: Prentice Hall, 1985), 8. Like the "active-positive," Tom seeks and enjoys exercising power; like the "active-negative," he at times tries to compensate for a negative self-image; like the "positive-passive," he seeks affection. Unlike a "negative-passive," Tom does not seek positions of leadership from a sense of duty, although he does have recourse to the "rules" and proper "procedures." Because he is a boy, Tom's character has not yet been set by his experiences. He could become any of the likely political types.

8. Citations are to Mark Twain, *The Adventures of Tom Sawyer* (Mineola, NY: Dover Thrift Editions, 1998).

9. In a response to Barber, Erwin Hargrove, "Presidential Personality and Revisionist Views of the Presidency," *American Journal of Political Science* 17, no. 11 (November 1973): 822–27, pointed out that Barber's first two types were "close to Lasswell's 'democratic character' and 'political man.' . . . The 'political man' seeks attention and power in order to overcome low estimates of the self. The 'democratic character' has passed through his developmental stages successfully, and has outgrown the political drives. He does not need to dominate men"; Harold Lasswell, "Democratic Character," in *The Political Writings of Harold Lasswell* (Glencoe, IL: Free Press, 1951), 465–525. Lasswell's distinction could be applied to Huck and Tom. The admiration Huck displays for Tom, especially in his own book, *The Adventures of Huckleberry Finn*, raises questions about the extent to which the "democratic character" is superior to, or more mature than, the "political man."

10. In a provocative essay titled "Tom Sawyer: Hero of Middle America," *Interpretation* 2/3, no. 3 (spring 1972): 194–225, Harry V. Jaffa pointed out Tom's Machiavellian glory seeking. Jaffa did not see any development in Tom's character, however. Rather than trace the stages of Tom's education, Jaffa emphasized Tom's lying and his Protestant roots: "Tom is a hero of the new Calvinism, in which a new wine of worldly glory is poured into the old churchly vessel, and such success will henceforth be regarded as the hallmark of election and salvation" (197).

11. Most critics have denied that there is any real plot or organization to the novel. Compare with DeLancey Ferguson, *Mark Twain: Man and Legend* (Indianapolis: Hackett, 1943), 176, and James M. Cox, "Remarks on the Sad Initiation of Huckleberry Finn," *Sewanee Review* 62 (July–September 1954): 389–405. Most critics agree that *The Adventures of Tom Sawyer* depicts a boy's growth, but they see the structure in terms merely of themes rather than in stages. Compare with Walter Blair, *Mark Twain and Huck Finn* (Berkeley: University of California Press, 1962), 103, 151. I see each third, or stage, in the story of Tom's education as marked by one of the confrontations with Injun Joe: first in the graveyard and in court, second when Tom testifies against him, and third when they foil his attempt to take revenge on the widow and find the treasure buried in the cave.

12. On the service Tom performs by relieving the boredom of his fellow citizens, see Judith Fetterley, "The Sanctioned Rebel," *Studies in the Novel* 3 (fall 1971): 293–304.

13. Compare with L. Moffitt Cecil, "Tom Sawyer: Missouri Robin Hood," *Western American Literature* 4 (summer 1969): 125–31, reprinted in Gary Scharnhorst, ed., *Critical Essays on The Adventures of Tom Sawyer* (New York: G. K. Hall,

1993), 117: "Long ago Mark Twain recognized the generation gap. His distrust of the establishment . . . include[d] most adults. He saw that what the world calls 'experience' tends to make people bitter or bigoted or afraid. On the other hand, he admired the vitality and honesty of the young. Uncontaminated by the world, they are quick to recognize hypocrisy and bold to dream, to dare, and do. Mark Twain saw that there is a constant state of undeclared war in progress between adults and the young. . . . As innocent and mirth-provoking as the book may first appear, *Tom Sawyer* could well serve as a primer for those young activists and hippies who are protesting (sometimes too strenuously, it is true) against outmoded forms and attitudes."

14. There is a similar incident in *The Adventures of Huckleberry Finn* when Colonel Sherburn shoots the town drunk down in cold blood in the middle of the day and then taunts the mob that gathers at his doorstep. There is no real "man" among them, willing to risk his life in order to maintain the rule of law by punishing a criminal. Afraid of retaliation, these people take vengeance only at night, hooded, and in mobs.

15. Sid noticed that Tom never played coroner at one of the inquests his schoolmates held on dead cats, "though it had been his habit to take the lead in all new enterprises; [Sid] noticed, too, that Tom never acted as a witness" (65).

16. Twain indicates how skeptical he is about the effectiveness of compassion and forgiveness as the basis of public policy or law enforcement when he comments on the funeral of Injun Joe (who died of starvation after Judge Thatcher had the mouth of the cave boarded up): "This funeral stopped the further growth of one thing—the petition to the Governor for Injun Joe's pardon. The petition had been largely signed; many tearful and eloquent meetings had been held, and a committee of sappy women had been appointed to go in deep mourning and wail around the Governor, and implore him to be a merciful ass and trample his duty underfoot. Injun Joe was believed to have killed five citizens of the village, but what of that? If he had been Satan himself there would have been plenty of weaklings ready to scribble their names to a pardon petition, and drip a tear on it from their permanently impaired and leaky waterworks" (170).

4

Patriots and Philosophers

The Idea of Obligation and Race in William Faulkner's *Intruder in the Dust*

Joseph Romance

> No, I shall question him and examine and test him; and if it appears that in spite of his profession he has made no progress towards goodness, I shall reprove him for neglecting what is of supreme importance, and giving his attention to trivialities. I shall do this to everyone I meet, young or old, foreigner or fellow-citizen; but especially to you my fellow-citizens, inasmuch as you are closer to me in kinship.
>
> —Plato

> If the last generation of your country appeared without luster in your eyes, you might have passed them by and derived your claims from a more early race of ancestors. Under a pious predilection for those ancestors, your imaginations would have realized in them a standard of virtue and wisdom beyond the vulgar practice of the hour. . . . Respecting your forefathers, you would have been taught to respect yourselves.
>
> —Edmund Burke

William Faulkner occupies an important and controversial position in American letters. He stands foremost among our novelists of the twentieth century, and his importance to American cultural and intellectual life shows no signs of waning. However, this fame must be counterbalanced with some of the less savory aspects of his reputation. Faulkner's distinction rests not simply on the greatness of his literary craft but on the subject matter he chose to address, and one of the subjects he wrote about is central, not only to his beloved South, but to this nation as a whole—race. And, I should add, the things he said were not always so kind. In one interview concerning integration in the early fifties, Faulkner (probably drunk—but drunks and children tell no lies) said, "if it came to fighting I'd fight for Mississippi against the United States even if that meant . . . shooting Negroes."[1] The brutality of these types of statements often mask Faulkner's more central message—which was one of seeking reconciliation between the various groups that comprise America. His use of local speech coupled with a challenging syntax, reflecting his fidelity to place, if not certain prejudices, means that Faulkner is frequently misinterpreted and ignored concerning the political lessons he wants to teach. The result is that too often he is relegated to the cloistered abyss of English departments where real politics is banished (to be replaced by the postmodern variety of political discourse). It is my contention that Faulkner has many vital political lessons to teach. And his views, while apparently conservative, are, in reality, nuanced reflections upon the ways of transforming society. Furthermore, while I do not view Faulkner as a political radical—in fact he was quite conservative in many ways—his willingness to explore society's problems to their roots makes him a useful teacher. Even if we do not accept all of his teachings, he provides us with a depth of understanding that illuminates problems and aids us in solving continuing challenges. In brief, I believe that Faulkner wanted America to confront its racial problems that lie at the heart of American politics. Furthermore, he wanted us, all Americans, to realize our kinship with one another. Yet, to achieve this patriotic task would require us to accept our past and not reject it. This lesson resonates throughout his writings—but most forcefully in his novel *Intruder in the Dust*.

His main political lessons have to do with the relations of the races in America. In this way, Faulkner is particularly instructive to readers today. How Americans of European descent and African descent live together remains an issue without a final, comforting resolution. Faulkner is especially enlightening because he realized that both blacks and whites are bound together, and in being so bound, we have become one race—a race of Americans. And, while Faulkner obviously wrote at a time when questions of race were seen primarily through a black-white prism, I think what he writes applies with even greater force as America becomes more racially diverse. The particular stories he tells may have a striking resonance when it comes to blacks and whites; yet his more general concern about criticizing race relations, seeking a greater understanding of the common bonds between people, and the vitality of the past in shaping present realities carry far beyond Mississippi and Yoknapatawpha.

Faulkner educates precisely because he freely admits that he, too, is uncomfortable with what he says. He was too much a product of his own time and place ever to be completely free of the intolerance he learned from those around him. Yet, he was clear-sighted enough to recognize this fact and see prejudice as a problem to be confronted—if never fully resolved. In his writing, Faulkner explores the ties that unite the races and fully admits how difficult it is for whites to do this. In the process, he moves us to a different level of political thought, and it is my belief that Faulkner is political because he is a patriot in the truest sense of that word. By looking at our past—redeeming the lost parts and learning to accept but not whitewash the worst—we will become patriotic Americans. As John Schaar reminds us about patriots,

> He knows, for example—and the knowledge is almost instinctive—that only residents, not outsiders, can radically change a society's ways and customs without wrecking the society, for the changes are made from within, and that makes all the difference.[2]

This is an old teaching that recalls the ancient Greeks and the lessons most powerfully taught by Socrates of *The Crito*. To be loyal to a place or to a people requires that we love it. And true love can only be a worthy thing if we love something that is worthy. To make whites and blacks deserving of respect is the job of the political patriot in America, and it was Faulkner's task.

This charge is more difficult because it is fundamentally not about laws but about the character of human relationships. Long after Dr. Martin Luther King Jr. led the fight for legal equality, we discover today that legal issues are only part of the quest for a nation of equals.[3] Instead, it is increasingly clear that extending the vote and providing equal access to the public sphere is a necessary, but not sufficient, step in the long journey that America must travel. In realizing this—and many commentators have noted this for some time—it is also clear that we must fight for the hearts and minds of people.[4] Laws are only the first achievement (or sometimes the last official act) in what is the more central quest. As Faulkner said, the job of the writer is to chronicle "the human heart in conflict with itself."[5] This tells us what he saw as the most important role of the writer. In so doing, he realized that the transformation of American politics must come about when not only the laws have changed but the lived practices and beliefs of people are changed. This transformation must, by definition, be difficult, not merely because of whites' loss of privilege and power; rather, our difficulty exists because even the best and most liberal Southerners cannot easily adopt the right policy if it means rejecting the past. The sense of political identity we all maintain must allow for a reconciliation between past and present, and this reconciliation must find a way to allow people to view past sins and injustices with clear eyes; yet, such clear eyes must not result in a facile and blanket condemnation of the past, for this past helps define the present that is making contemporary judgments.

The easy answer of rejecting traditional racism is to reject the past in total. Faulkner is after something grander and much more difficult—how to reclaim the ancestors of Southern whites and still do the right thing. Faulkner was always interested in the past and in the problem of understanding how each generation owes all other generations a perpetual debt. In fact, the very idea of past, present, and future are intertwined in his writings. As he famously said, "That time is, and if there's no such thing as *was*, then there is no such thing as *will be*."[6] To redeem the past is to redeem the present and vice versa. Thus, the solution to any racial problems may not be what first appears obvious. Changing the laws and restructuring the economy may be quite painful. However, the real costs go deeper. The real challenges will only be met when Americans realize that we are all kinsmen, for the feeling of kinship is the most difficult and painful of all relationships.[7]

Faulkner's gift to us was to realize that America was a land of African Americans and European Americans. However, this banal observation reveals some more important truths. Too often today, as Americans of all races retreat into their own communities, we forget that the United States is an amalgam of many races. Race problems, this theory says, will then fade into history. In rejecting the idea of some synthesis about what it means to be American, we retreat into the separatism of identity politics, and this has implications that go far beyond simply the question of black-white relations in this country. At the opposite end of the spectrum of American politics, we have the stated or unstated belief of white Americans that the problem of race will be solved when black Americans start acting like "normal" Americans, which is just another way of saying "white." In a different, but related way, many black separatists want to free themselves from whites altogether. More moderate blacks and whites work together, yet they separate after work, and few have deep, abiding relations beyond making a living wage.[8]

Taken literally, the notion that we will have a race-blind society would mean that we will no longer see race. However, this suggestion is absurd—and not merely from a "practical" point of view. Race is too obvious, and the denial of this fact is ridiculous.[9]

At a deeper level Americans must accept the fact that we are a society of races, and blindness to this will blind us to our history. The problem with this theory—and it is often presented in a "benign" fashion—is that we Americans, all of us, are black. And white. We are, as the bigoted European observers of the eighteenth and nineteenth century called us, a mongrel nation. However, the importance of this point is most salient when we realize that it is not simply that African Americans must learn to be "white" but that Americans of European descent must learn that they are "black." This point is central to beginning to realize what it is we share together and how we can begin to glimpse the communality of American life.[10] As Ralph Ellison reminded his readers in the last sentence of *Invisible Man*, "Who knows but that, on the lower frequencies, I speak for you."[11] This should not be taken to mean that no distinctions exist between the various communities that make up American society. However, the entanglements of the different communities must be recognized and cherished as pivotal to the promise of American life.

One of the great strengths of our best novelists—writers like Ralph Ellison and William Faulkner—is that they see the entanglements while also cherishing the distinct strands of the particular communities. This is a lesson that resonates from the earliest political thought in America. As John

Winthrop observed, "That every man might have need of other, and from hence they might be all knitt more nearly together in the Bond of brotherly affecion."[12] Ellison eloquently summarizes this in his essay "What America Would Be Like without Blacks." In that essay, he recalls the ways various white Americans—Jefferson and Lincoln being the most famous—envisioned a new nation devoid of blacks. Not only would that be difficult (most likely impossible), but it would radically alter what it meant to be an American. To take one stellar example, there would be no Twain, at least as we understand him, and, thus, the entire history of American literature would be different and, most likely, diminished. The American language, the product of English speakers adapting to the land and to meeting non-English speakers, would have been altered in ways beyond comprehension. As Ellison writes, "Despite his racial difference and social status, something indisputably American about Negroes not only raises doubts about the white man's value system, but arouses the troubling suspicion that whatever else the true American is, he is also somehow black."[13] And, without blacks, as Ellison reminds us, there would be "no Faulkner."

Faulkner, as a Southerner, knew of the entanglements of communities better than most. This is obvious to many students and citizens of the South. Growing up so close to black Americans, white Southerners are keenly aware of how much the races are intertwined. Thus, the races have, together, forged one culture. This does not mean, of course, that equality exists. The fear of blacks and the need to maintain power and distinctions have made it all the more important for whites to maintain legal distinctions. Nonetheless, legal distinctions about race are artificial, and because of that, legal solutions are an imperfect way to solve the race problem. Faulkner, in his novels, reveals to his readers his awareness of the deeper need of white people to realize their fundamental community with blacks. This deep and abiding sense of obligation lies at the heart of his most overt race novel, *Intruder in the Dust*.

Intruder in the Dust is often criticized as one of Faulkner's less successful novels.[14] And there is a good case to be made against it. On purely literary grounds, the novel has problems. Faulkner's always opaque prose becomes even more difficult to understand. His insistence on using parentheses inside parentheses, his inventing of words, and his constantly shifting syntax test the patience of even his most loyal readers. While such writing works in the pages of *Absalom, Absalom* or *The Sound and the Fury*, it is less apparently successful here.[15] However, this should not distract us from the fact that this novel is also one of Faulkner's most powerful and undeviating political statements. His direct concern about race as a political problem, his increasingly rich and fully dimensional portrait of black people, and his abiding concern for the debts that white people owe to blacks combine to insure that the novel's strengths outweigh its weaknesses. Earlier novels deal creatively with the white man's problem with race; this novel deals more directly with everyone's problems with race. What makes it ultimately successful is that Faulkner moves beyond the "merely" tragic that characterizes the resolution of his previous novels. There is no sense of futility that is so powerfully expressed by Benjy's wail at the conclusion of *The Sound and the Fury*, for instance.

In many of his earlier, more famous novels, Faulkner was able to mark the depths of human existence and see how much failure lies at the heart of what we do. Furthermore, in his writing about a character like Dilsey ("they endured") in *The Sound and the Fury*, we find a genuinely sympathetic person. However, also striking is the inability of white people to connect and understand each other—either among themselves or with their black brethren.[16] *Intruder in the Dust* sounds a more positive note. People—white and black—can be redeemed. We can be restored by our willingness to see how much we are obligated to each other and how this obligation can only be repaid (or at least the interest on that debt can be maintained) by a willingness to see past society's prejudices and glimpse our common humanity. The apparent pessimism of Faulkner's early works is transformed into the more affirmative reconciliation of characters in this text.

The novel is about how Lucas Beauchamp, a man of mixed racial heritage, is caught after the murder of Vinson Gowrie. Such an action calls not for justice but the crude communal vengeance of a lynching. Why? It is not simply because a black man killed a white man; rather, it is because the black man in question is a particular thorn in the side of white society. Lucas Beauchamp is a man who refuses to "be a nigger first." His pride is legendary in the county, and Faulkner tell us that what makes Lucas even more frustrating to whites is that he "didn't even care" to follow the normal social requirements of treating whites with deference. He is the kind of man who refuses to come to town when the blacks and poor whites are expected to appear (Saturday); instead, he conducts his business on weekdays "like the white men who were not farmers, but planters, who wore neckties and vests like merchants and doctors and lawyers, as if he refused, declined to accept even that little pattern not only of the Negro but of the country Negro behavior."[17] Oddly enough, killing a white man is what many whites are "probably convinced all Negroes want to do," and now that Beauchamp has apparently conformed to expectations, a lynching can occur (48). The result will be a "nigger acting like a nigger and the white folks acting like white folks and no real hard feelings on either side . . . once the fury is over."[18] Beauchamp's alleged actions allow the community to return to its status quo. Yet, to understand how upsetting he is, we must explore Lucas in more detail.

Beauchamp is largely a solitary man with little interaction with his fellow blacks or whites. We also know that he is fiercely proud of his own ancestry. In the course of the novel, Faulkner recounts a telling encounter that occurred before the events of the novel. A group of drunk whites starts insulting Lucas, and he corrects their description of his lineage and insults the drunks in the process:

> I aint a Edmonds. I don't belong to these new folks. I belong to the old lot. I'm a McCaslin. . . . Yes, I heard that idea before [that he—Lucas—was "stiff-necked . . . sonofabitch"], and I notices that the folks that brings it up ain't even Edmondses.[19]

And when he is challenged by the drunks, he holds his ground and refuses to run from the scene; instead, he waits and finally leaves, "without haste, without haste," as Faulkner emphasizes.

This event precedes his arrest on murder charges and is merely Faulkner's attempt to provide the reader with background on the accused. Once in jail, Lucas appeals to young Charles "Chick" Mallison to help prove his innocence. Chick is a white boy and the nephew of one of the more distinguished lawyers in the town. In this sense, Faulkner is writing a traditional murder mystery. The actual working out of the mystery is, however, less important than the relationship between Chick and Lucas. In the course of the novel, Mallison will prove that the South can overcome its own problems and that he, himself, can redeem the failures of Southern society.[20]

After we are informed of Lucas's troubles, Faulkner moves the story back four years, and we hear how Chick, then 12 years old, first came to know Lucas. Chick has been invited out to the Edmonds' place to hunt. In the process he falls in the water, and in getting out, he meets Lucas Beauchamp. Lucas then invites him (insists really) to his house to dry his clothes and eat a meal. Chick realizes that what was offered was "not just the best Lucas had to offer but all he had to offer." At that moment, the central motivating event of the novel occurs—young Chick tries to pay Lucas for his kindness. However, to Lucas, monetary payment is impossible, even insulting. Lucas has extended to his guest a basic human consideration, and he refuses the money because such acts cannot be measured in monetary terms. Lucas acts as a dignified man extending a common courtesy, and he expects no payment:

> [Chick] . . . extended the coins: and in the same second in which he knew she [Lucas's wife] would have taken them he knew that only by that one irrevocable second was he forever now too late, forever beyond recall, standing with the slow hot blood as slow as the minutes themselves up his neck and face . . . "What is that for?" the man [Lucas] said, not even moving, not even tilting his face downward to look at what was on his palm: for another eternity and only the hot dead moveless blood until at last it ran to rage so that at least he could bear the shame.[21]

From that moment Chick feels indebted to Lucas, and over the ensuing years, he tries to repay him. However, each gift he sends to Lucas is repaid in kind. Lucas will not let Chick free, and this irony—a white "enslaved" by a black—gives the novel its moral force. This need for repayment is key to the story, because Chick, unlike virtually every other white person in the novel, recognizes and acts upon his obligation to a black man. This shame at his earlier action (or rather, his shame at a debt to a social inferior) allows Chick to question who he is and, more importantly, what values his society holds. From the point of view of the narrator, the story is less a murder mystery than a story about the relationship of Chick and Lucas.

Because he is indebted to Lucas, Chick is called upon to help prove his innocence. Lucas tells Chick that he must go out to the grave and dig up Gowrie and prove that it was not Lucas's gun that killed him. This is a powerful request—a sixteen-year-old boy is supposed to travel out from Jefferson and dig up a body in the middle of the night. He must violate the land (hence, the title of the novel) all for a black man. To add to Chick's challenges, the pressure of time is great because of the impending threat of a lynching—the county residents are not likely to wait long before they take matters into their own hands. The request—really a demand by Lucas—is extraordinary, and a lesser person than Chick would certainly refuse to act. What is striking about Chick is there is never any doubt that he will honor this call. All through the day of Lucas's arrest, Chick thinks about fleeing the town to get away from the eventual meeting with Lucas. However, as the day wears on, he is drawn to Jefferson and to seeing Lucas. He knows that his debt is now going to be called in: "'Me go out there and dig up that grave?' He wasn't even thinking anymore. *So this is what that plate of meat and greens is going to cost me*."[22]

However, before Chick can go, he returns home and finds that Miss Habersham is visiting Chick's uncle. Gavin Stevens, his uncle, is the lawyer whom Lucas has hired to defend him. Despite his being his lawyer, Lucas does not tell Stevens why he is innocent or how to prove it. Lucas is right, according to Faulkner, not to trust this information to Stevens as is soon revealed when Chick tells his uncle Lucas's version of events. Stevens simple does not believe Chick when he says that a different gun killed Gowrie. It is impossible for the old, more powerful members of the community—even a well-meaning one—to understand or even try to understand the words of a black man. Such accounts are immediately discarded or ignored. Chick faces the problem, at a less severe level of course, that faces the narrator of *Invisible Man*. Whereas people "refuse to see me," as the narrator of *Invisible Man* says, people refuse to hear Chick. (In this way, he is similar to Lucas himself.) Chick decides simply to disregard his uncle and proceed on to the grave himself. Yet, he soon realizes that he is not alone in either his pursuit of justice or his sense of obligation to Lucas. Miss Habersham, "whose name was now the oldest which remained in the county," grew up with Molly, Lucas's wife, and "had stood up in the Negro church as godmother to Molly's first child."[23] She feels a particular bond of friendship with Lucas (not only through his deceased wife). She has gone to see Gavin Stevens to see what can be done to help Lucas; however, Stevens is all ready to plead Lucas guilty of manslaughter and hope for the best. To Miss Habersham this will not do, and she joins Chick in his quest to prove Lucas's innocence. Miss Habersham and Chick are joined by the son of the Mallison's maid, Aleck Sander, who is bound to Chick as a close friend. This trio then embarks on the trip to Beat Four, where the body is buried.

What is utterly fascinating is the collection of people Faulkner chooses to assemble: an elderly spinster, a young black boy, and a young white boy. One would be hard-pressed to find a group of less politically powerful people in a Southern town, and Faulkner is telling us that such outsiders (in a political sense) must save Lucas—and by implication save the South. (I should note that Miss Habersham symbolizes both weakness [she's a woman] and strength [hers is the oldest name in the county]). Only these residents, who are powerless, yet, in the case Chick and Miss Habersham, respectable, are able to see beyond the prejudices of their community and act on their knowledge.

Just before the group gathers for its trek, Chick recounts a story about an old Negro, Ephraim, who was helpful in finding a ring that Chick's mother had lost. Ephraim explains why he helped Chick find the ring a week after it was lost and did not simply tell Chick's father the location right away:

> Young folks and womens, they ain't cluttered. They can listen. But a middle aged man like your paw and uncle, they can't listen. They ain't got the time. They are too busy with facks. . . . If you ever needs to get something done outside the common run, don't waste yo time on the menfolks; get the womens and children working at it.[24]

Later, Chick recalls more of Ephraim's wisdom that is revealing: *Get the womens and children at it, they works on the circumstances.*[25]

In the case of racism, the rules do not work justly, and yet, they are the rules. Laws made blacks second-class citizens, and yet, the law (such as the Thirteenth, Fourteenth, and Fifteenth amendments to the Constitution) cannot solve the problem. Men, like George Wallace, can claim that they are simply following the law and rightfully assert that legal principles are at stake.[26] Faulkner is using boys and women not because of some genetic argument that only the young and very old can see the truth, but rather because people not so rigidly bound by the conventional laws of society can see through to what is really happening. It is in this sense that Faulkner teaches us a philosophic lesson—a Socratic lesson about how people must develop a loyalty to truth that moves them beyond a slavish adherence to community beliefs. And yet, Socrates and Faulkner are in agreement that such loyalty to truth requires a commitment to make the community better. As the trio approach the grave, Miss Habersham observes that they are in search of "simple truth," and the narrator adds, "because truth was universal, it had to be universal to be truth and so there didn't need to be a great deal of it just to keep running something no bigger than one earth and so anybody could know truth."[27] (I cannot help believing that this is the most Socratic of statements, since Socrates claimed his ignorance was the foundation of his knowledge. I am not sure how, but it seems that Socratic ignorance and Faulkner's belief in the simplicity of truth are related at some level.) However, Miss Habersham immediately adds that, in this instance, the truth—of Lucas's innocence—must be brought to the town. The political world and truth must be brought together, and it is only people like Miss Habersham, Chick, and Aleck who have both the necessary distance and connection to achieve this.

It is in this context that I would like to address the central action of the novel and what sparked much of the critical controversy that accompanied the novel's reception. The trio returns to Jefferson, after digging up the body and proving something is wrong, and alerts Gavin Stevens, who joins them to find the sheriff. The sheriff, along with Stevens, returns to the grave and solves the mystery.

Along the way, Gavin Stevens delivers a long-winded speech defending the South.[28] His speech, attacking not integration per se, but Northern imposed integration, is seen as a thinly veiled presentation of Faulkner's moderate position on civil rights in the 1940s.[29] And, indeed, this might be the case. However, whatever Faulkner's stated position was in 1948, the novel tells us a slightly different story. It is my contention that Faulkner's central concern is with Chick, his ideas, and his relationship with Lucas. Thus, Chick's comments on his uncle's speeches are brief, but vital.

First, let us look at what Stevens says. He defends the South from what he perceives as Northern intrusion on the question of race:

> We are defending not actually our policies or beliefs or even our way of life, but simply our homogeneity from a federal government to which in simple desperation the rest of this country had to surrender voluntarily more and more of its personal and private liberty in order to continue to afford the United States.[30]

He goes on to say,

> That's what we are really defending: the privilege of setting him free ourselves: which we will have to do for the reason that nobody else can since going on a century now the North tried it and have been admitting for seventy-five years now that they failed.[31]

At first glance, these views seem to be Faulkner's views as expressed in public letters and speeches of the late 1940s and 1950s. However, as the author later said in reviewing his work, we should not take Stevens' thoughts as the final word on any subject. Faulkner later observed,

> That is, he knew a good deal less about people than he knew about the law and about the ways of evidence and drawing the right conclusions from what he saw with his legal mind. When he had to deal with people, he was an amateur, he was—at times he had a good deal less judgment than his nephew did.[32]

Yet, we do not need to go to Faulkner's later elaboration on his own work to illustrate this point. In the text itself, there is evidence that we should not take Stevens as the final word. First, we know that Stevens fails to believe his nephew when he first hears the possible explanation of Lucas's innocence. Furthermore, at various times late in the novel, Chick indicates that he, himself, does not always share his uncle's long-winded views of the world. After one rather long, tedious speech about cars and sex in American life, Chick insists, "That's not true." When his uncle persists, Chick replies simply, "I still don't believe it."[33] Chick sees things not through the eyes of his too-theoretical uncle but through those of a true philosopher—a seeker of wisdom free from the prejudices of society. His perspective is not the terrible fury of the lynch mob or the legal blindness of his uncle. The law is ignorant of the "circumstances" as Ephraim might say. We might add that the good-hearted uncle accepts that Chick does not believe everything that he, the uncle, might say. Despite these disagreements, the two—Chick and his uncle—do like each other and get along. Cushing Strout, in his essay "Twain's Huck and Faulkner's Chick," is right to see the connections between Chick and his uncle. Strout writes,

> Chick's sense of self is sponsored by his mentor. Ever since the boy can remember, he has felt "a blind and absolute attachment to his mother's only brother," for whom he does errands as "an intimation of his willingness to carry some of his own weight." It is his uncle who tells him about moral values: "Some things you must stop refusing to bear. Injustice and outrage and dishonor and shame."[34]

Strout is certainly right to remind us of the close bonds that unite the uncle and his nephew; nonetheless, Chick's sense of justice and his willingness to see beyond the community's sins prompt him to move past his uncle's innate caution. Thus, Chick must be willing to go beyond his uncle. The next generation must go beyond the generation in power.

Once they are finally forced to act, however, those who are sworn to uphold the law do just that. Stevens, once confronted with the evidence, swings into action. Furthermore, the sheriff, Mr. Hampton, guarantees that

Lucas is not lynched and implicitly believes the story Chick and Miss Habersham bring to him. The most legally minded characters in the novel do their duty, but their duty never encourages them to see below the surface and doubt the broader beliefs of the community. Duty and the law only encourage such people to act once they are prompted, but the law itself does not prompt.[35]

That said, we need to explore in greater depth Chick's perspective on what happens. For it is his perspective that defines the novel and provides a better glimpse of what I believe Faulkner wants to teach his readers. Chick sees not only his connection with Lucas (and despises this for some time) but the need to make his "own" white people better:

> when suddenly he realized that that was part of it too—that fierce desire that they [his only family] should be perfect because they were his and he was theirs, that furious intolerance of any one single jot or tittle less than absolute perfection—that furious almost instinctive leap and spring to defend them himself without mercy since they were his own and he wanted no more save to stand with them unalterable and impregnable.[36]

For Chick to redeem himself, he must redeem his fellow whites. However, that action requires him to act against many of values he has been taught all his life. Furthermore, his uncle's life of abstraction and "benign" withdrawal from life will not do.[37] The only way he can do this is to realize that what he owes his white kin is connected to his sense of obligation to Lucas. Chick must first see Lucas as human and, thus, like him, which occurs early in the novel. He recounts the time he saw Lucas shortly after his wife died and has a revelation: "He was grieving. You don't have to not be a nigger in order to grieve."[38]

Before we reach this point, however, Faulkner has been dropping hints all along that Chick notices something familiar—even familial—about Lucas. In the first few pages of the novel, there are at least three references to Lucas's reminding Chick of his own grandfather. When he first sees Lucas Beauchamp, he is wearing "a broad pale felt hat such as his grandfather used to wear"; then, after Lucas orders him back to the cabin, Chick thinks "that he could no more imagine himself contradicting the man [Lucas] striding on ahead of him than he could his grandfather."[39]

This confusion of Lucas with his own grandfather is enough to lead us to see Lucas not only as a man but as a man related to Chick. In a sense, Chick and Lucas are kin. Furthermore, the issue of race is more complicated than we might initially suspect in Lucas's case. Not only does Lucas have "white" blood, but "Edmonds's father deeded to his Negro first cousin and his heirs in perpetuity the house and the ten acres it sat in."[40]

What makes this even more racially complex is that the original owners of the plantation, the McCaslins, were Southern-born abolitionists. In their effort to overcome the sin of slavery, they did not legally set free their slaves; rather, they changed their actual, material conditions. The McCaslin brothers lived in that cabin and let their slaves live in the plantation house.[41] Thus, Lucas lives in the actual homestead of his white ancestors. His relative poverty is founded on the poverty imposed by his white predecessors. His pride may stem in part from being the only one with the right to live in that cabin. Who the true heir of the land is becomes staggeringly confusing in Faulkner's telling.

To return to Chick and his sense of obligation, we realize that he must act to redeem a man to whom he owes a debt, and this debt is forged in the image of his grandfather. So, when we come to the final confrontation between the would-be lynch mob and the defenders of truth, Chick is fighting for his ancestors, Lucas, and himself. His debt is real but still quite self-imposed, and it is self-imposed because Chick feels obligated to redeem the past. (I should note that when Lucas first helps Chick at the beginning of the novel, after Chick has fallen in the water, it takes the form of "negative" help. Lucas orders Aleck Sanders to withdraw a pole he was offering to Chick. In a physical, literal sense, Lucas forces Chick to save himself.) At this point, Chick explicitly recalls the past, and naturally for a Southerner, this past centers on the Civil War and Pickett's charge at Gettysburg:

> For every Southern boy fourteen years old, not once but whenever he wants it, there is the instant when it's not yet two o'clock on that July afternoon in 1863 . . . waiting for Longstreet to give the word and it's all in the balance, it hasn't happened yet, it hasn't even begun yet but there is still time for it not to begin against that position and those circumstances.[42]

This poetic imagining of the past is meant to show us what is possible, and in our recollecting of that past, the present can redeem time lost. The solution is not to turn back the clock in a literal sense but to purge the sin. However, to do this involves not rejecting the past but seeing one's connection with all the members of one's place, and doing so makes ancestors better, as impossible as that sounds. The society that enslaved the blacks and is about to lynch someone unjustly cannot be all bad if it created Charles Mallison, who will go to any lengths to save Lucas Beauchamp. It also produced Miss Habersham, "who is the oldest name in the county" and who fiercely looks the mob in the face (75). Toward the end of the novel, she sits in front of the jailhouse to make sure no one enters, while Gavin, Chick, and the sheriff travel to the grave site the next day to finally solve the mystery. This takes place after Faulkner has reminded us earlier in the novel that the past, and one's kinship with the past, can be a sign of good things. When Chick first sees Miss Habersham on the night the story takes place, she has "one of the round faintly dusty-looking black hats set squarely on the top of her head such as his [Chick's] grandmother used to wear."[43] Thus, as Lucas reminds him of his grandfather, and Chick must help a person who reminds him of his own family, the past, in the grandmotherly form of Miss Habersham, will be his ally. The past creates obligations that must be redeemed, but it also creates confederates to lighten the burden. In that way, Chick observes on his first trip to Beat Four that he is "the sum of your ancestry," who "had evoluted him into a secret resurrector."[44] And, thus, Chick has overcome Faulkner's earlier observation that normal attitudes about race in the South "[prove] again how no man can cause more grief than that one clinging blindly to the vices of his ancestors."[45]

All these ideas and ideals come together with a great deal of power and humor in the final scene of the novel. Lucas Beauchamp, now free, goes to Gavin Stevens' office to pay his debt. The two men negotiate for some time over whether he will pay anything and why. Finally, Stevens agrees to accept reimbursement for his expenses, which amounts to two dollars. Lucas pays Stevens in change, including fifty pennies. He tells Stevens, "I was aiming to take them to the bank but you can save the trip. You want to count um."[46] Steven insists that Lucas count the pennies himself. Finally, after this is done, Lucas remains seated, leading Stevens to ask, "Now what? What are you waiting for now." And Lucas replies, "My receipt."[47] These are, in fact, the final words of the novel. Thus, the story opens and closes with the notion of debt and repayment. In the final scene, with great and deserved dignity, Lucas pays his debts, and this serves as a reminder of his willingness to forgive the earlier debt that Chick incurred. However, as Cleanth Brooks perceptively writes, "It was Lucas, after all, who taught the boy that there are some things that one must not try to settle with a money payment. But token payment in this instance, meticulously counted out, not for services rendered, but 'for expanses,' is appropriate and even tactful."[48] The dignity of all those involved has been maintained, and Lucas has given Chick the ultimate gift of learning to accept the past and still act with justice.

The political lessons that Faulkner wants to teach are ones that are more important than ever. As America continues to progress on the legal front in its battle against racism, we realize that legality is only one part of the solution. We must learn that to be American says something—that we are not a collection of separate races and groups. We are, of course, that; yet, we are so much more. Race is often used to accuse minority groups of being exclusionary. However, as Faulkner makes clear, whites are usually more often at fault. In too many ways, whites expect blacks (and most other minority groups) either to be like whites or to be hopelessly different. In reality, the ties that bind are much stronger than we might admit. Furthermore, Faulkner asks us to realize our complicity in the corrupt actions of our ancestors. That said, the actions of our forefathers are not simply evil. The complexity of human relationships means we must recognize not only the failings but also the importance of all people involved in the community. Thus, as James Baldwin wrote,

> In short, we, the black and the white, deeply need each other here if we are really to become a nation—if we are really, that is, to achieve our identity, our maturity, as men and women.[49]

These lines of connection run not just between contemporaries but also back and forth through time. Faulkner's story is about a young man who finds his identity through an appreciation of the past and a sense of obligation to his fellow man—in this case a black man.

These teachings must not, however, blind us to Faulkner's failings. Laws are never the final solution to our societal problems. Nonetheless, I believe that Faulkner is a bit too dismissive of the role the law can play in the process of righting ethnic and racial conflicts. He was certainly right to point out the hypocrisy of Northerners, and the subsequent racial problems that arose in Northern cities confirm some of his observations. Still, we must recognize that laws can in reality prompt action. Faulkner's abiding effort to delve into the mysteries and failings of the human soul appears to have blinded him to the possibilities of "merely political" reform. He could only place his hopes in the actions of the individual and in the transformation of the human heart. As powerful as such reforms can be, the rules and procedures of political institutions can also work on the human soul and change, in the long run, the world and its inhabitants. The South was painfully slow in dealing with these issues, and I think without laws inspiring change, hearts may not change at all. Instead of seeing too sharp a distinction between rules and circumstances, we must see these phenomena as interconnected in the search for the dignity all Americans deserve. Yet, by reminding us of the complexity of circumstances, of the role of the past and the sense of social obligation that the law sometimes misses, Faulkner reminds us of the deeper connections that must exist among citizens. And this is a political lesson that is too often lost on political scientists and captured only by literature and our greatest writers.

Notes

1. Joseph Blotner and Noel Polk, eds., *William Faulkner: Novels 1942–1954* (New York: Library of America, 1994), 1099. Faulkner later said, "They are statements which no sober man would make, nor it seems to me, any sane man believe."

2. John Schaar, "The Case for Patriotism," *American Review* (May 1973): 90–91. It is also worth noting that Schaar singles out Faulkner (along with Robert Frost and Edmund Wilson) as one of the few to write "in the language of natural patriotism" (66).

3. This is something that Dr. King was well aware of and is implied in his "I Have a Dream" speech.

4. For a good discussion of many of these broader issues, see Clarence Page, *Showing My Color* (New York: HarperCollins, 1996). See also Tamar Jacoby's

thoughtful essay, "The Next Reconstruction," *The New Republic* (June 22, 1998): 19–21.

5. William Faulkner, "Address upon Receiving the Noble Prize for Literature," in *Essays, Speeches, and Public Letters by William Faulkner* (New York: Random House, 1965), 119.

6. Frederick Gwynn and Joseph Blotner, *Faulkner in the University* (New York: Random House, 1959), 139.

7. For a discussion of the theoretical issues of kinship, see Wilson Carey McWilliams, *The Idea of Fraternity in America* (Berkeley: University of California Press, 1974), ch. 1.

8. This issue is explored with care by Clarence Page in "Who Killed Integration? The New Apartness," in *Showing My Color*, 28–46.

9. A good example of this can be found in the way denials of seeing race are treated as starting points for comedy in many sitcoms.

10. I see this point as central to the novel discussed here and to virtually all of Faulkner's writings. The briefest statement of this belief can be found in Faulkner's "Funeral Sermon for Mammy Caroline Barr," in *Essays, Speeches, and Public Letters* (New York: Random House, 1965). He said, "She still remained one of my earliest recollections, not only as a person, but as the fount of authority over my conduct."

11. Ralph Ellison, *Invisible Man* (New York: Random House, 1952), 568.

12. John Winthrop, "A Model of Christian Charity," in *Puritan Political Ideas*, ed. Edmund Morgan (New York: Bobbs-Merrill, 1965), 77.

13. Ralph Ellison, *The Collected Essays of Ralph Ellison* (New York: Modern Library, 1995), 583.

14. There are two works that I draw on extensively to make some of my points: Cushing Strout's "'Working on the Circumstances': Twain's Huck, Faulkner's Chick, and the Negro," in *Making American Tradition* (New Brunswick, NJ: Rutgers University Press, 1990), and Cleanth Brooks, *William Faulkner: The Yoknapatawpha Country* (New Haven, CT: Yale University Press, 1963). Strout discusses the relationship between Stevens and Chick, and Brooks offers an excellent accounting of the idea of debt and redemption.

15. The best example of this criticism of the novel can be found in Edmund Wilson's pointed, if still positive, review, "William Faulkner's Reply to the Civil Rights Program," *The New Yorker* (October 23, 1948): 120–26.

16. *The Sound and the Fury* is probably the best example of this. All the white characters are lost and isolated from each other. Even the method of storytelling, the steam of consciousness used in the sections directly dealing with the white characters, reinforces the idea of their self-involvement. The final section is narrated in the third person and is largely centered on Dilsey. Notice, too, that in reference to Dilsey, Faulkner uses the plural "they." The black characters are seen in a more communal light.

17. William Faulkner, *Intruder in the Dust* (New York: Random House, 1948), 24.

18. Faulkner, *Intruder in the Dust*, 48–49.

19. Faulkner, *Intruder in the Dust*, 19.

20. And it is this idea of a murder mystery that disturbs so many critics. The idea of trying to prove himself innocent from behind bars is a good idea for a mystery; however, Faulkner certainly makes a mess of it. The complications of proving

Lucas innocent don't quite add up. The actions of the real murderer are often incomprehensible and illogical. However, in my opinion, that misses the point. One can broadly defend this novel as a mystery because, as one writer on the mystery has said of the genre, it is "an exploration of the relationship between Justice and Law, and—perhaps most important—a venture into forbidden things." See Wilson Carey McWilliams, "Democracy and Mystery: On Civic Education in America," *Halcyon* (1989): 43–56. In this sense Faulkner is a great writer because he deals explicitly with forbidden things—he dares to talk about race. For the more traditional criticism of the failings of the novel, see Brooks, *William Faulkner*, 279–94.

21. Faulkner, *Intruder in the Dust*, 15. The scene is central to the story, and many commentators have written about it. One of the better accounts is found in Joseph Gold, *William Faulkner: A Study in Humanism* (Norman: University of Oklahoma Press, 1966), 80–84.

22. Faulkner, *Intruder in the Dust*, 68.

23. Faulkner, *Intruder in the Dust*, 87.

24. Faulkner, *Intruder in the Dust*, 71–72.

25. Faulkner, *Intruder in the Dust*, 112. Cushing Strout makes much of Ephraim's comments in his essay "Working on the Circumstances: Twain's Huck, Faulkner's Chick, and the Negro," in *Making American Tradition* (New Brunswick, NJ: Rutgers University Press, 1990.)

26 As John Schaar observed, "The South surely had the better of the Constitutional argument, and only arms could clear the way for the definition of the American polity," in "The Case for Patriotism," 82.

27. Faulkner, *Intruder in the Dust*, 89.

28. Cushing Strout makes many of these observations about Stevens and his speeches in his essay on the novel. See "Working on the Circumstances," 161–62.

29. This was Edmund Wilson's interpretation in his *New Yorker* review.

30. Faulkner, *Intruder in the Dust*, 153. For parallels directly from Faulkner's nonfiction writings, see his "Letter to a Northern Editor," in *Essays, Speeches, and Public Letters by William Faulkner*, 86–91.

31. Faulkner, *Intruder in the Dust*, 154.

32. Gwynn and Blotner, *Faulkner in the University*, 140. These points about Stevens and this quote are discussed in Cushing Strout's perceptive essay "Working on the Circumstances."

33. Faulkner, *Intruder in the Dust*, 239–40. And his uncle, maybe realizing his own failure to convince Chick as important, says, "That's right. Don't. And even when you are fifty and plus, still refuse to believe it." It is not the sex and cars, which his uncle is discussing, that seem important to me. The more central point is that Chick is skeptical of his uncle's position, even if he respects him.

34. Strout, *Making American Tradition*, 159.

35. Like the warrior class in Plato's *Republic,* the men of duty in Faulkner's world act rightly, but they need to be told what to do. In this sense, Gavin Stevens and Mr. Hampton have souls of silver.

36. Faulkner, *Intruder in the Dust*, 209–11.

37. Gwynn and Blotner, *Faulkner in the University*, 141.

38. Faulkner, *Intruder in the Dust*, 25.

39. Faulkner, *Intruder in the Dust*, 6, 8. There is one final reference to Lucas's gold toothpick as being something his grandfather might have owned (12).

40. Faulkner, *Intruder in the Dust*, 8.

41. The account can be found in *Go Down, Moses* (New York: Random House, 1940).

42. Faulkner, *Intruder in the Dust*, 194–95.

43. Faulkner, *Intruder in the Dust*, 75.

44. Faulkner, *Intruder in the Dust*, 93.

45. Faulkner, *Intruder in the Dust*, 49.

46. Faulkner, *Intruder in the Dust*, 246.

47. Faulkner, *Intruder in the Dust*, 247.

48. Brooks, *William Faulkner*, 294. Brooks's interpretation of the novel, particularly the last scene, is insightful, and I draw upon it extensively to make my own concluding remarks.

49. James Baldwin, *The Fire Next Time* (New York: Dell, 1988), 97.

5

A Story about Nothing

Two Kinds of Nihilists and One Kind of Christian in Flannery O'Connor's "Good Country People"

Peter Augustine Lawler

"Good Country People" is, most obviously, a story about people who live in the country, none of whom is good or virtuous. The rough definition of a good country person, according to people in the country, is someone who is simple, trustworthy, Bible believing, and boring. Each of the characters, quite rightly, thinks of himself or herself as too sophisticated to fit that definition. So, for them, or at least two of them, the idea of a good country person is sentimental and condescending. From this modern view, country people are simple and good; city people are sophisticated and evil. But within all of us sophisticates, there is a longing to regress to simple, natural innocence. That longing is easily countered by our pride in our inability not to live in sophisticated awareness of the truth that nothing solid supports human morality or shame.

Our idea of natural innocence is an invention of modern intellectual pride. The idea is that some human beings (natural men) are below and others (the intellectually liberated) are above sin and that the innocent and the liberated are natural allies against the conventional or repressed—those whose lives are miserably distorted by the illusion of sin. The truth missing from the consciousness of all the characters is that sin is the natural condition of us all. They proudly believe in their unflinching realism, but none of them can see human beings as they really are.

All the characters in the story are modern human beings; they are like the people Flannery O'Connor thought would read her story—us. For them and for us, God is dead, and the idea of Him is repulsive and tyrannical. What we sophisticates think we know is that morality is nothing but seductive but empty words. What we know that good country people do not is that human love and human dialogue about what we have been given by nature and God are illusions. So, what we know that simple people do not is that the philosophy of the Greeks and Romans is impossible today and that Christianity is a trick played on the simple by the cunning. If love of each other is not really possible—if love itself is just an empty, seductive word—then love of God cannot be either.

"Good Country People" is also, quite obviously, a story about "nothing." Nothing, in one sense, means the absence of corrupt or virtuous human content. So, "nothing," or nihilism (a word O'Connor used in her letters), can mean that everything we believe to be distinctively human is an illusion or merely an arbitrary social construction. But "nothing is perfect," the favorite cliché of an easygoing nihilist, means that only the unconscious simplicity of natural innocence is perfect (264).[1] Those two modern definitions are perfectly compatible. Any self-conscious nihilist is too sophisticated to be perfect. Only nothing—the being without human content, a chimp or Rousseau's natural man—is perfect.

There are no chimp or dolphin nihilists, and so, the experience of nihilism is the one point of human distinction or pride that we cannot and, in fact, will not negate. We look down on the chimps because nihilism is not for them. Chimps know nothing of nothing and, so, cannot take pride in their liberation from something. They cannot incoherently take pride in knowing the groundlessness of pride. So, the nihilist takes pride in the fact that humbles Christians—only human beings are full of flaws or imperfections. It is natural for human beings without faith to take pride in sin, while still in some way longing for a world without it. So, when we think more clearly than the nihilist, we see what we want is a world in which we retain the pride and joy of self-consciousness but without its miseries and perversities.

The most intense reference to nothing in the story is a quote from the philosopher Martin Heidegger. He is quoted on nothing out of nowhere but not by name. Modern science is nihilistic because it denies the real existence of what cannot be captured by its method. The scientific view is that whatever exists can be accounted for technologically. So, what is beyond calculation and control does not, in truth, exist. Modern science says that what is nonmechanical or noncalculable about human existence is nothing.

The two characters in the story who read Heidegger have been seduced enough by the enlightened idea of sophistication to talk as if that nihilism were true, although they are too sentimental really to believe it. Neither follows Heidegger in viewing nihilism as a threat to our openness to Being and to all human excellence, but both really want nihilism not to be true. The two characters who do not read Heidegger are actually pretty perfect modern nihilists; their nihilistic insight is an uncanny natural capability, not a product of their education. Their nihilism is so methodical as to be almost mechanical. "Good Country People," in fact, presents characters who are amazingly, if not completely, mechanical in motivation; they are exaggerations of the beings produced by the doctrine of modern materialism or mechanism.

In this respect, O'Connor seems to follow Heidegger in chronicling the effects of scientific or technological nihilism. One danger, she thinks, is that the nihilistic or technological world might actually be able to breed the moral sense out of people, and nothing will be left but our instinct for self-preservation, cunning, curiosity, and cruel perversity. But as long as nonmechanical human longings persist in existing, the needs for love, morality, and God will be with us. Nihilism could become completely true only if mechanism or the technological account of nature were to become completely true. And we nonmechanical beings are too full of mystery to be able to reduce even nonhuman nature to a mechanism. For a genuine realist such as O'Connor, the stars, the woods, and the peacocks all point us toward the truth about the mystery of created being. Only the human being open to the truth about Being can see nature in all its glory; mechanism, in a sense, would become true if human beings disappeared because there would be no one (but God) able to see His creation for what it is.

We might say that the story has two natural and two conventional (products of enlightenment propaganda) nihilists. The story about nothing is also about the emptiness of modern, conventional claims to rule. Mrs. Hopewell rules because she is the mother (in a story with no fathers), the employer, and the property owner. But she lacks the self-knowledge and the astuteness really to rule; she is very easily tricked and manipulated. She is too sentimental and too scared—she is a utilitarian, or bourgeois, woman—really to be a nihilist.

Her daughter rules if wisdom should rule; she is a doctor of philosophy. But her degrees are no real evidence of insight; she is too blindly angry and self-pitying to have learned much at all from either books or her own natural experience. And we also learn that the truth is that she is miserable in her lonely liberation, and pride is an insufficient compensation for her lack of love. She is convinced that the miserable truth is that she is fundamentally unlovable, and so, she angrily refuses to have any of the experiences of a real woman, and, even with her books, without those experiences she cannot know much. She longs to learn that her philosophic opinion that there is no real foundation for love is untrue; as a real woman, despite her desperate efforts at self-invention or re-creation, she longs for friends, men, children, and God and to know that the truth about being human is good. She longs to be lovable and to be loved just as she is. Her self-deception and real human longings are those of the modern liberal or the secular, sentimental, Christian intellectual, and her failures open us to the genuinely postmodern world, to a return to the genuine primacy of both faith and reason.

The other two characters—the hired hand and the Bible salesman—are by convention merely service people. But Mrs. Freeman and Manley Pointer (note the names) have the natural cunning and mental liberation to rule effectively; they are tough, unsentimental nihilists who believe—not without some reason—that they are in touch with the truth about nature and human nature. It is tempting to say that they think of themselves as—and maybe they are—Machiavellian philosophers. They are generally happy enough in ruling or manipulating others in secret, although they cannot help but be indignant and resentful on occasion when their natural superiority goes unrecognized. But they know they could never rule openly or display clearly their natural excellence.

Their natural, or sociopathic, nihilism, their genuine insight into nothing, will always be hated—with good reason—by decent folks. And that hatred is more than a social prejudice or part of our instinct for self-preservation. The nihilistic insight not only produces a homeless and parasitical human life, but it is far from completely true. Sociopathic liberation caused by curiosity could not be *the* human good, although it is a distortion of *a* human good. It feeds off or empties the contents of the real goods that constitute human existence. And the inability of the uncannily liberated to experience those goods as real blinds them to part of the truth about the human soul, about what distinguishes human beings from machines and the other animals. The truth is that human beings must be somewhat—but not too much—at home to experience the truth about their homelessness.

We can say that the completely unconscious gratitude for what they've been given characteristic of "good country people" and the complete liberation of the characteristically curious and sociopathic philosopher are both human illusions. Extreme intellectual liberation from moral concern is actually quite ugly. It is also self-deceptive; such liberated beings deny the reality and goodness of the world that is the indispensable source of their physical and mental satisfaction. The nihilists win in this story only because it is missing a character who is both realistic or tough-minded and virtuous, who is loving without being self-indulgently sentimental. Such a character could see through Manley as easily as he could see through Hulga; the most penetrating human thinkers are not nihilists at all. The true antidote to nihilism is not unconscious nihilism but those who experience the truth about created being.

But that antidote cannot be the tradition-bred piety of country people who really are good. It turns out, after all, that their moral toughness—which we should not simplify or sentimentalize—is not usually strong enough to resist modern seduction. So, this story about the South today is full of godless and traditionless people. O'Connor is no Agrarian, although she agrees with much of the Agrarian criticism of the modern South, because she sees that the Christ-haunted South is, in the decisive sense, industrialized. There is a big difference between being Christ haunted and Christ centered! What the story lacks is a real Christian, especially a Christian with brains, maybe a proud and angry Cartesian who becomes a humble and wondrous Thomist. We are given some hope that the philosopher-daughter has learned enough from her humiliating seduction about her being and her longings as a woman with both a body and a mind to be open to that transformation. She has certainly learned enough from Manley's pointers to know that she is, most deeply, more a Christian than a nihilist: she is stuck with the human longings that point her in the direction of a personal God. If there is grace in the story, that is it. We can hope that this lonely, abused, and maimed Cartesian woman is ready for a friendly dialogue with a Thomist, but the appearance of such a Christian philosopher in her pathetic country life would certainly be miraculous.

All I have left to do is supply some of the details that support these conclusions about the teaching of the story.

Mrs. Hopewell

"Good Country People" is also, most obviously, the story of a strange but real relationship between a daughter and her mother and of the seduction of them both by a trickster-suitor Bible salesman. Each woman, despite her proud, utilitarian sophistication, is much less astute and penetrating than she thinks, and so, both are easy prey for a genuine nihilist, for someone who not only believes in, but has the genuine experience of, nothing. The two women pride themselves in their differences from one another. The mother thinks the daughter childishly lacks good sense and good manners, that she does not know how to present herself attractively to others. The daughter thinks her mother is exceedingly superficial and blind on many levels to the truth. Their criticisms of each other are both quite right, but the truth is that they are also quite similar in both their vanity and their blindness, and even in what they really think about human existence. For them both, as Friedrich Nietzsche or Heidegger would say, God is dead.

It is true that mother and daughter have quite different reactions to the words of Heidegger: "Science, on the other hand, has to assert its soberness and seriousness afresh and declare that it is concerned solely with what-is. Nothing—how can it be for science anything but a horror and a phantasm? If science is right, then one thing stands firm: science wishes to know nothing of nothing. Such is after all the strictly scientific approach to Nothing. We know it by wishing to know nothing of Nothing" (268). Mrs. Hopewell reads these words after opening her daughter's book to a random page and finding them underlined and "worked on." They "worked on Mrs. Hopewell like some evil incantation in gibberish. She shut the book quickly and went out of the room as if she were having a chill" (268–69).

Now we might want to say at first that any decent, sensible woman would be repulsed by Heidegger's preoccupation with Nothing and even feel the "chill" of the evil consequences of his thought. But that's saying far too much. Why would any ordinary woman be moved by those words at all? Certainly Mrs. Hopewell is not ordinarily moved by philosophy. Her daughter has a Ph.D. in philosophy and that fact leaves Mrs. Hopewell "at a complete loss." Being a philosopher, after all, is "something that had ended with the Greeks and Romans," and there is clearly no point in it any more (268). And when her daughter once angrily invoked the authority of the philosopher Nicolas de Malebranche against her, "Mrs. Hopewell had no idea to this day what brought that on" (268). Her sensible rejoinder had been "a smile never hurt anyone" (268). Ordinarily Mrs. Hopewell thinks gratuitous anger and thought make no sense, and she ignores them. Why should she care that Heidegger is worked up over nothing but Nothing in words that do seem like gibberish to any casual, and maybe any sensible, reader?

Mrs. Hopewell, in fact, thinks that real opinions about important issues make no sense. Her opinions are always to smile, be polite, and keep on the "bright side" of life (267). She talks, in worn out clichés, like a sophisticated moral relativist; "the most important was: well, other people have their opinions too" (264). Never impose your opinions on others or let them know what you really think—that can only lead to trouble. Understanding "deliberate rudeness" is beyond her; she thinks it "idiotic" (272, 268). Safe appearances are better than contentious truth; Mrs. Hopewell's obsession is with the utility of appearances. And she ranks other human beings, in fact, according to how well she thinks she can manipulate them with flattery. The only exception she makes to the "no rudeness" rule is badgering her daughter, and that's because she really does care for her. Her indifference to the opinions and actions of others is not so much deference to their moral freedom as it is a timid indifference to what is best for them.

Mrs. Hopewell is capable of getting sentimental and teary-eyed when thinking about her daughter's suffering and likely early death. But her sentimentality is childish and automatic because it is disconnected from genuine thought or moral goodness. Her sentimentality is, in fact, so platitude driven that it compromises her good sense; Manley manipulates it very easily to get invited to dinner. She is unable to come to terms with the real depth and corruption of other human beings or with the fact that pretty words cannot effectively hide or transform natural ugliness. So, Mrs. Hopewell refuses to acknowledge the first thing about the miserable predicament of her philosopher-cripple daughter, who has been maimed both in soul and body. She sentimentally tries to keep Joy a girl in her mind, someone she can readily understand without any problems, not a miserable adult deprived, seemingly for life, of "*normal* good times" (266).

Mrs. Hopewell is a rather extreme case of someone trying hard to immerse herself in what Heidegger calls "average everydayness," of someone trying to live a perfectly bourgeois existence. When she thinks of others, she thinks of herself, and when she thinks of herself, she thinks of others. That is, in part, because she is cut off from the moral depth that once characterized her tradition; she keeps her Bible in the attic. She, with some pride, knows that religion—like philosophy—has nothing to do with her life; she is too proud even to want to be called a Christian woman. Religion is for unsophisticated country people—like Bible salesmen and black farm hands. Religion is for simpleminded suckers (her real view of good country people), but such tricks will not work with her. The result is that her soul is almost flat, although, of course, not quite.

So, the "chill" Mrs. Hopewell gets from Heidegger is a glimpse of her moral emptiness, the nothingness of her own life. Her willful immunity to self-criticism breaks down for a moment, but the work Heidegger does on her soul does not last for long. It does not really disturb her usual liberation, not only from the depths of the Bible, but from much contact with human reality itself. Mrs. Hopewell divorced her husband early on and has only one child, we can assume, because her opinion is that love is too dangerous and more trouble than it is worth. Bourgeois sentimentality is a long distance from a tough acceptance of the world as it is. And so the platitude-driven Mrs. Hopewell is, on a purely human level, much less free than her Christian ancestors.

Joy-Hulga

Mrs. Hopewell has little to give her daughter but a name—Joy Hopewell. The name, of course, is cloyingly Christian. A good Christian experiences the joy that comes with hope in things unseen, the joy that is the grace that comes with believing in a loving God.

But the name Joy inherited has been emptied of its real content; for her mother, there is no real joy in life but only a sunny attitude projected onto others. We see why Joy could come so easily to believe in the philosophic doctrine that names are merely willful impositions that do not open us to the truth about natural reality at all, as well as in the power of naming to transform human reality.

Joy's real, angry objection to her name and sunny attitudes in general is that they do not correspond to her true condition. Her life, she thinks she knows, has been irreparably mutilated by an explosion that blew much of her leg off when she was ten. If that were not enough, she has a heart condition that condemns her to an early death. And her mother has not given her a clue about how her miserable condition might be transformed or redeemed.

So, Joy left home and sought refuge in philosophy, earning the Ph.D. But her physical condition forced her back home. Joy's education has freed her from "the last traces" of shame "as a good surgeon scrapes for cancer" (281). Joy takes pride in her liberation from the morality of her tradition, viewing what she had been given as a potentially fatal disease. She sometimes thinks of herself as having seen through morality to the truth, but the truth is, she was not given much to see through at all. She is full of the modern vice of ingratitude, but we are tempted to say she has not been given much for which to be grateful.

Joy's natural shame (which is, after all, quite weak without moral habituation) and her mother's vacuous platitudes are far too easy for her to overcome. She never takes moral or human questions very seriously. We want to say that education killed God for her, but He was never alive for her mother. Certainly, her escape is not from convention to nature in the manner of the philosophers of Greece and Rome. Joy is angry all the time, "with the look of someone who has achieved blindness by an act of will and means to keep it" (265). Her "constant outrage" (264) is most of all directed against natural reality itself, which she rationalizes with Heidegger's view that the study of Nothing is superior to the scientific study of something—nature: "Sometimes she went for walks but she didn't like dogs or cats or birds or flowers or nature" (268). More generally, "she seldom paid any close attention to her surroundings" (280), not even to "nice young men" (268).

Joy's escape from convention is emphatically not to discover the truth about being and human being. It suits her to be convinced from the beginning that there is nothing worth discovering anyway. Like her mother, she does not really care about the truth. She thinks, in fact, that the truth about her own nature is so terrible that she has no choice but both to deny and to overcome it.

Joy actually cares about the truth less than her mother, who thinks some about how to use words to exploit others for her own gain. Joy's angry rejection of the demands of practical life means that she pretty much sees nothing at all. She has no astuteness at all about how to live or use others for her own advantage. Yet, she still believes, as a liberated woman, that there is no reason for shame and morality not to give way to utility.

Her embrace of utility as a standard is inconsistent, unless she can say that something is useful for nothing. But she is not really nothing—she is a woman with a mind and a body. And if she had any sense—that might come either from attentively observing human nature or from practical experience—she might even know why shame is useful—even indispensable—for women.

Joy proudly believes that she has "[seen] *through*" to nothing; all human distinctions, all human hopes, and all appearances of beauty, ugliness, and excellence do not really exist (280). Her unflinching rationality, she imagines, allows her that rather singular insight. And that insight is, she says, her salvation; it allows her even to believe that those who do not share it—those who think that they are saved by God—are the ones who are damned (278). Her transvaluation of values saves her from the misery of any futile effort she might make to flourish in this natural world. The true world—the world of nothing—is the one in which she believes she excels, and in truth, without much effort. It is not hard to be good at nothing, but she still takes great pride in it.

Joy, as Nietzsche would explain, escapes into the world of nothing in resentment against her physiological inferiority in the visible world. In that respect, Nietzsche would add, she is a good Socratic. By denying the reality of love, flowers, and nice young men, she dismisses as insignificant her inability to be attractive to others. She has freed herself imaginatively from the misery she experiences as an embodied being. She imagines herself living "clear and detached and ironic" wholly in the world of the mind, where she can view the world of the damned bodies of others "from a great distance, with amusement but with pity" (278). From there, she wants to regard everything ordinary mortals do well—from having sex to raising children to dressing well—as a joke. But she fails to achieve any detachment or irony in her own case.

If life is a joke, Joy might think to laugh at herself. That contradiction, we can say, spoils the authenticity of most existentialist misery, as well as that of most modern pretensions to scientific detachment. What Joy really thinks is, mortal life is a joke, but through penetrating thought I have risen above *that*. But, of course, her thought really is full of the misery of her self-conscious weakness, dependence, and vulnerability. She is more determined by her bodily limitations that most of us; we rise above mere matter through the practice of virtue and the somewhat grateful, at least, assumption of the responsibilities given to human beings alone. And most of us have two good legs.

For Joy, philosophy is angry and easy, and it has nothing to do with curiosity or love. Believing—with the help of her mother—that her maimed body is unlovable, she takes refuge in the thought that love is an illusion. Her unusually maimed leg is both a cause and a sign of her unusually maimed soul. And her heart disease, of course, is both literal and metaphorical; her contracted heart, her moral and practical indifference are partly self-induced as ways of protecting her tender heart. We certainly see how reversible her heart disease is when she is seduced by a young man, who is not even nice.

Joy believes she follows Heidegger in seeing the natural world as a vast impersonal nothingness, and with the insight that seeing nothing but Nothing is wisdom. So, there is no wisdom to be found in the rational or scientific study of nature. But Joy is no real follower of Heidegger. For him, our anxious encounter with Nothing might be a prelude to our wonder about Being and the being who is open to Being. It might also culminate in our gratitude for the mystery of Being. Joy spends no time either anxious about or grateful for the mystery of her finitude and her openness to truth. And in that respect, she is fundamentally a modern thinker—a follower of Malebranche and Cartesians generally. She is in method a logical positivist who uses reason to devalue values. And she is a nihilist in the sense of being a technological thinker—a control freak at war with what she thinks is the truth about nature, especially her own nature. She believes she has taken off a blindfold, but really she has willed one into being.

Joy had rejected the name her mother gave her. She had named herself Hulga and had her name legally changed. From that point onward, she has responded to Joy in a "purely mechanical way" (266). She responds as a mere animal or mechanism and not as a free or willful human being. Her insight into nothing is, in part, that all naming is willful and arbitrary. She chooses the ugliest name that comes to mind to discard all the empty theological and metaphysical baggage associated with joy. Hulga knows there is not true joy. Because there is no foundation for joy and beauty, there is no reason to think that Hulga, by comparison, is ugly. She imagines the labor of her own self-creation as like the manly, "sweating" forging of Vulcan; it is an act of spirited male work and not womanly love (267).

Hulga imagines that she made herself out of nothing; her self-naming is the girl's "highest creative act." Because she made herself only for herself, it is hard to know why she had to name herself, much less get the law involved. Naming and law are ways of imposing one's will on others, as Vulcan could impose his will on "the goddess" (267). Hulga's self-creation was not really meant to be solitary. She childishly demands that others know of the anger and the suffering that brought Hulga into being, but not know Hulga. It angers her to have others call her Hulga, for them to communicate with her in more than a mechanical way. But it also angers her for others not to know that she made herself Hulga. As a singularly oppressed minority, Hulga engages in a most lonely form of identity politics.

Although she prides herself in being like other human beings only bodily or mechanically, over time even her body changes. Her mother notices that "every year she grew less like other people and more like herself" (268). Hulga has rejected her mother less than she imagines because they both believe that reality can be changed through redescription. And it is true that ugly names and sunny attitudes do have some effect as self-fulfilling prophecies. But deep down, neither Hulga nor Mrs. Hopewell really believes that naming is all that powerful in changing nature.

The Seduction

One dimension of the desperation of Hulga's self-creation is that she lacks other, living human beings with whom to share what she knows. She longs for intellectual friendship, to share Nothing with others. She does not find enough companionship in the authors—such as Malebranche and Heidegger—that she reads. Halfway, or inconsistently, she knows that consciousness is necessarily consciousness with others, and if there is any joy in discovery—even of nothing—it will be in sharing it. So, Hulga is depressed by the "dialogue" that is not really a conversation around her mother's breakfast table (265). And she makes it clear to her mother that if it were not for her disabilities, she would be at some "university lecturing to people who knew what she was talking about." Mrs. Hopewell pictures her as a "scarecrow" talking to other scarecrows, but scarecrows sharing the truth about nothing are still a community (268).

Hulga's longing for dialogue turns out to be the reason that she imagines seducing the traveling Bible salesman—Manley Pointer—who got himself invited to dinner. "She had lain in bed imagining dialogues for them that were insane on the surface but that reached below to depths that no Bible salesman would be aware of" (275). She imagines that "[t]rue genius" such as her own "can get an idea across even to an inferior mind" and, so, impart to another "a deeper understanding of life" (276). Inferior minds can be freed through conversation from shame and morality. Hulga imagines composing a dialogue that will somehow have the seductive power and "profound implications" of, say, a Platonic dialogue, but she does not connect her manner of seduction with anything erotic (275). And surely, there is no such thing as purely mental or dispassionate seduction! Hulga does not really consider why "nothing" would be attractive to anyone who found any joy at all in ordinary life or in being a Christian. Her rather groundless hope is that her seduction will free her from her intellectual loneliness; she imagines that her mind has freed her from physical desire and a more ordinary loneliness.

Hulga imagines herself as a sort of evangelist, being of use to another by sharing what she knows about salvation. Her imagined evangelical method has two parts. First, there is sexual seduction, which would produce shame and, so, "remorse" in the seduced good Christian. Second, there would be the instructive (for Manley) dialogue between unequal minds, which would turn remorse into "something useful" (276). Shame, it turns out, would not be replaced by nothing, but with utility as a point of orientation. What Hulga would do for Manley in particular, modern enlightenment aims to do for human beings in general.

Hulga's intention is far from evil; what would seem like corruption to others is redemption for her. Her intention is far from good; she does not consider Manley Pointer as a real human being, but only herself. One sign of the sentimental narcissism at the bottom of Hulga's allegedly rational nihilism is that she gives no real attention to the nature, the character, of Manley. In their first short meeting, there is a sign of his cunning that a real student of human nature—say, Plato's Socrates—would not have missed. But Hulga, just like her mother, identifies him too quickly with a platitude, or stereotype, reducing the story's most philosophic character to a rural Christian of simple virtue, to someone, in fact, without any of the greatness and misery or good and evil of a real human being. She very mistakenly and dangerously views him with intellectual contempt.

Hulga, in fact, is too blind and too inexperienced really to imagine what it would take to seduce another human being. So, at a crucial moment with Manley, she cannot tell the difference between seducing and being seduced (280). She has never really seen a flower, and at thirty-two she has never been kissed. The narrator of the story calls her a girl throughout; she is the closest thing we see in the country to an innocent. It makes considerable sense to view her, as all the other characters do, with contempt.

Hulga, in fact, views Manley at times as a child, and she presents herself to him, at first, as being only seventeen. The story has echoes of pedophilia. Hulga is afraid to be a woman and to be with a man. And she is, of course, in the decisive way not a woman; she does not do any of the things a grown woman does. So, her sexual imagination is, as O'Connor explains, both sentimental and pornographic. It is of seduction abstracted from the human risks and hard responsibilities that accompany real human sexual coupling. Acting on the pornographic imagination is irresponsible and illegal. The origin of pedophilia is surely the desire to dominate an innocent or to deprive someone of his or her humanity. And the desire to be the object of pedophilia is the unrealistic longing to be innocent, to surrender one's human freedom. Sexual sentimentality is a prelude to tyranny—that teaching is both personal and political, and it is one that Walker Percy learned from O'Connor and employed in *The Thanatos Syndrome.*

Manley awakens Hulga's longings as a woman; she learns quickly that she has repressed the ways in which her female body determines her being. Her encounter with Manley shows her just how much and in how many ways she needs men in her life. We cannot help but think that much of her misery would have been alleviated if she just had her father around. The sentimental narcissism of Mrs. Hopewell and Hulga is due in part to the fact that they do not really know and love men. That may be by choice in Mrs. Hopewell's case (we see her attracted to pretty young girls), but it is not true at all in Hulga's. We learn that the effectual truth of the theory and practice of women's liberation is the disappearance of men from women's lives. That usually means that they are deprived of what makes them whole human beings. Girls with cold mothers and no fathers have big-time self-esteem issues, even when they have two natural legs.

Manley teaches Hulga that she cannot really reinvent herself as a sort of sexless man. When they kiss at first, she experiences him as having the breath and stickiness of a child, and his mumbling is "like the sleepy fretting of a child being put to sleep by his mother" (279). Her rational detachment is immediately tempered, if not overwhelmed, by her maternal instinct. She then experiences loving surrender to another human being, which is "like losing her own life and finding it again, miraculously, in his" (281). At that point, of course, reason does give way. And finally, "Her brain seemed to have stopped thinking altogether and to be about some other function that it was not very good at" (282). Her willful resentment of her body is overcome by female sexual pleasure, which is an undeniable human good. But those experiences of surrender and pleasure are not strong enough to keep her from experiencing shame. As a real woman scared of a predatory man, she can now see what sexual degradation and obscenity really are. And she refuses to give in to them; she demands her leg—her independence—back once she sees how Manley intends to use her. Hulga quickly learns through experience that the effectual truth of shameless sexual liberation is to render women defenseless against naturally tyrannical men.

But it still takes Hulga too long to see Manley as a predator; she has surrendered her leg to him before knowing the first thing about him. At the moment of surrender, "She decided that for the first time in her life she was face to face with real innocence. This boy, with an instinct that came from beyond wisdom, had touched the truth about her" (281). Her conclusion is a matter of decision, not perception; it is willfully blind. The truth Hulga decides Manley has touched is that she is made different by her leg; she decides to imagine that he is full of instinctive compassion for her miserable plight. It turns out that she believes that she is most deeply not a liberated nihilist but simply a maimed girl cruelly deprived of normal good times. The depth of her maiming could not have been touched by reason but only by pure instinct. She decides that Manley "touched the truth" that is "beyond wisdom" without the need for dialogue at all (281).

Hulga gives in to the mindless sentimentality—the Rousseauean dream about the goodness of unconscious human nature—that lurks beneath the surface of modern or constructivist philosophy. From O'Connor's view, the heart of modern self-indulgence is the imagination that sin itself is a social construction to be overcome through compassionate social reform. But anyone with eyes to see—certainly any Christian—knows that sinless man is an oxymoron. It takes a very refined sentimentality to mistake a cunning sociopath for a natural innocent; it is not a mistake made by many women without lots of training in philosophy.

Manley Pointer

Manley, unlike the women he so easily tricks, really is detached from, and so knows how to manipulate very effectively, the conventions of human community. He is in no way genuinely attached to or at home with others, and he does not long to be at home. How he was raised is mysterious. He seems to be from no place in particular, "not even from a place, but near a place" (271). He moves as a traveling salesman from place to place, renaming or re-creating himself for others at each stop along the road. Once

Manley leaves town, he cannot be found because he has become someone else once again. He presents himself as a sincere, simple Bible salesman preparing himself for "Chrustian [*sic*] service," and he easily convinces the two not-so-simple women that he is stupidly earnest and boring (271). Having no identity of his own, he excels at becoming what people want him to be. His general policy in dealing with others is little different from Mrs. Hopewell's, but he is much better at implementing it because he is more genuinely self-conscious.

Manley has no sentimental or angry aversion to self-knowledge. He knows what he wants and that his desires are incompatible with social life. He must have had a mother, but we cannot imagine him having a wife or daughter. (To avoid the pregnancy trap, he uses protection.) Manley is a pure parasite, feeding off, for the moment, the identities of others. He wants a free dinner and a one-night stand. But that's not all. He has an "open curiosity, with fascination, like a child watching a new fantastic animal at the zoo" when looking at and thinking about Hulga (275). Like the zoologist, he regards her as one interesting specimen. And unlike Hulga, he is also interested in "what Mother Nature is wearing" (276) in the woods and in figuring out how to work artificial mechanisms for himself (281).

Most generally, his delightful curiosity is about figuring out how all things work; he seems to understand both nature and human nature rather mechanically. And he does not seem to be moved much by those human desires that are neither purely physical nor purely intellectual and, so, very specifically human. Because he lacks social instincts and moral breeding or habituation, we see in him clearly what a very intelligent human being would be like without morality. So, we see in him, not Hulga, what would be the perfect results of the nihilism of modern rationalism—a wise man taking pleasure in comprehending and controlling nature understood as pure materialism or mechanism. And before getting too moralistic, we must say that there is something charming and humanly excellent in Manley's childish delight in discovery. He is, in that way, a real philosopher and not some angry ideologue; he is an exaggeration of the moderation philosopher, as Hulga is an exaggeration of the modern intellectual. When it comes from natural discovery and invention, Manley—unlike Hulga—is no nihilist, which is not to say that he can see the true mystery of created being.

At first, Manley views Hulga with "complete admiration" and her wooden leg "reverently" (279). And he asks Hulga, "don't you think some people was meant to meet on account of what all they got in common and all? Like they both think serious thoughts and all?" (276). Manley certainly understands that she longs for moral or intellectual friendship, and he assumes she thinks he might be able to provide it. And he understands that without knowing about her "number of degrees," which do not impress him one way or the other (280). His standard is natural intelligence, not empty educational adornments. (When it comes to degrees, Hulga is no nihilist!) So Manley seems to assume that Hulga must have the natural insight to notice that he is not stupid; he underestimates the blindness of her anger and her vanity. He is genuinely surprised and "indignant" when she assumes he is simpleminded later (282–83).

When Manley hears Hulga say that she does not believe that "God takes care of [her]" or in God at all, he feigns astonishment (277). But he really is somewhat surprised because "[t]hat's very unusual for a girl" (278). It is certainly quite unusual and just plain stupid for a girl to announce her shamelessness to her new boyfriend. But in Hulga's case, it is a way of bragging about her wisdom—her liberation—as a prelude to both sex and dialogue. Manley wrongly assumes she means that she is "some girl"—a girl ready and willing to do it all (283). But he also assumes that she will have to say she loves him before he can have his way with her. Manley himself knows nothing of love, but experience has taught him that girls cannot help but connect it with sex. He has developed a "methodically" precise approach to conquest that works just about every time (279). He knows how to use kissing and talking to secure the consent that will make conquest easy and safe. And it turns out—despite her condescending words about the emptiness of the word love—that even Hulga's seduction depends upon love.

Once Manley hears her words of love ("Yes, yes"), he asks her for proof—to be shown where her wooden leg joins the real one. She is shocked by the "obscenity" of the suggestion, which seems to have nothing to do with sex (280). Shamelessly displaying her body might have seemed obscene to anyone else, but displaying the leg is so only to her. She imagines that to give up her real body is nothing, but surrendering her artificial leg would be surrendering her soul. And surely partly for that reason, Manley is more interested in possessing the leg than her body. But mostly he is interested in the working of the leg's ingenious mechanism.

We can say she reads a lot more soul into the wood than he does. So, we can also say, to her credit, that he does not understand Hulga as well as he thinks he does; his conquest of her is no complete proof of his comprehension of her. Because his methodical theory works so well, Manley cannot see—he has no reason to see—the mysterious dimension of human being. But Manley's uncanny inexperience with distinctively human social and political passions (with the exception of pride) still limits unrealistically his psychological or philosophical vision. In some ways, he teaches Hulga to know more than he himself does. The success of the modern conquest of nature is no proof of the complete truth of that understanding of nature.

Hulga is particularly moved by Manley's saying that her leg is "what makes you different" (281). But what she mistakes for an innocent's compassion is the most obvious form of materialistic reductionism. Human beings, Manley thinks, are pretty similar natural mechanisms, but Hulga also has an artificial one. Manley's methodical confidence suggests that his experience has been that women are pretty predictable beings. And his reductionism may not be all that wrong. Hulga's maimed soul is arguably the result of her maimed leg. If she were physically whole, she might not have taken psychological refuge in philosophy or nihilism. And normal good times with nice young men would have saved her more effectively from the emptiness of her mother's house. But we still have to say that her intellectual pride, angry self-pity, and womanly longings cannot be reduced to the mind or the body.

Manley never quite understands what a maimed female doctor of philosophy is like. He convinces Hulga for a moment that she can leave her leg off because "You got me instead" (282). So, he is confident enough in her physical and emotional dependence and intellectual liberation to reveal himself to her. He shows her what is really in his salesman's valise—only one real Bible and another hollow one containing whiskey, a pack of playing cards with obscene pictures, and a box of condoms. He presents these images of his liberation to her proudly and shamelessly, "like one presenting offerings at the shrine of a goddess" (282). He worships both her leg and her liberation now. But to Manley's surprise, Hulga will not even take a swig of whiskey. How could it be that someone who says she has seen through to nothing has no experience with and is too scared to try the most obvious human vices? Poor Hulga can have neither normal nor abnormal good times.

Hulga in frightened desperation calls Manley "good country people" and then a Christian to try to conjure up by naming the innocent she had imagined. Her inability really to know the first thing about him causes Manley to lose all admiration for her. Although he had been looking forward to sex, he is delighted enough with her wooden leg. It turns out that he collects such "interesting" mechanisms, and depriving her of her particular identity is plenty for him. He uses the name Hulga "as if he didn't think much of it" (283). The name has lost, or never really had, any meaning; Manley reveals the pretentious emptiness of her effort at independence through self-creation. So complete is his domination of her that she ends up thinking she sees him walking on water, although clearly Manley is only a man. Hulga is dead and gone; self-invention—not love—was the illusion. But we have no reason to believe that the woman can go back to being Joy because she was right to insist that she never really was joy at all. And joy cannot be one's own creation.

Real Nihilism

Manley leaves Hulga with nothing, with what she thought she would bring to him. Her intellectual pride turns out to be mere vanity; she is no match for one who combines experience and brains with genuine liberation. Her proud thought that she is essentially all mind and no body turns out to be pathetically false. The effects of her inexperience with men and with being a woman are more pathetic still. Manley arouses her longings as a woman without offering any real prospect of their satisfaction. Without her wooden leg, she is not even independent enough to leave the barn: she will be more humiliated by her childish dependence on her mother than ever.

Manley also leaves Hulga with knowledge of what it really means to believe in nothing. In a world of true nihilists, a girl without physical strength and experienced astuteness is easy prey. That world is far more cruel than the safe, if cold, bourgeois appearances that govern Mrs. Hopewell's home. There is something true about Mrs. Hopewell's thought that a cold world is better than a dangerous one. Manley tells Hulga, as if she should have known, that he does not believe "in that [Christian] crap" because "I know which end is up and I wasn't born yesterday and I know where I'm going" (283). That platitude shower reminds us of Mrs. Hopewell, and there's nothing on his list that a woman of sensible selfishness would not brag to herself about. But for Manley, the platitudes are really true; he cannot be tricked because he's fine with knowing that there's no real hope in life. He brags, as philosophers do, that he has come to terms with the utter contingency and finitude of his existence in every moment of his life. Nobody in the story believes that he or she believes in biblical crap, but Manley really does not believe.

Manley's last words to Hulga are "you ain't so smart. I been believing in nothing since I was born" (283). He has finally figured out that Hulga's nihilism is merely bookish and stupidly self-deceptive. Manley's insight is natural. But that means that his pride in his wisdom is groundless. It is a natural gift that required no cultivation on his part. The opinion of the Ph.D. is that nihilism is the result of an arduous educational effort that liberates one from the "cave" of belief or piety. Manley was never, to begin with, in the cave; he shows how easy or natural nihilism can be. O'Connor's view that nihilism is part of human nature and not just some sort of historical dispensation is, in a way, her most obvious criticism of Heidegger.

We have to wonder to what extent O'Connor means Manley to be a real human possibility. But he does correspond to a real dimension of human nature. For O'Connor, the combination of pure cunning with curiosity—unmoderated by social instinct, moral virtue, or religious faith—is one way evil appears in the world. Naive or modern intellectual efforts to show the repressiveness of all human conventions or to point to a return to natural innocence liberate Manley. The decay of moral and religious belief and tradition into mere utility make it easy for his sort of evil to prey on the world. The closest thing we experience to real innocents are not the Bible believers but those infected by the mixture of sentimentality and utility characteristic of modern enlightenment.

Mrs. Freeman

There are actually two natural nihilists—both called "good country people"—in this story. The other is Mrs. Freeman, the wife of "a good farmer" hired by Mrs. Hopewell to work on her place (264). Mrs. Freeman is a free woman because she is not, and does not pretend to be, moved by the appearances of good manners and because she, like Manley, has no social instinct or love at all. Literally, the first thing we learn in the story is that Mrs. Freeman wears "the neutral expression that she wore when she was alone" (263). And her point of pride is to make it clear that her opinions are not governed by others; she "could never be brought to admit herself wrong" (263).

Mrs. Freeman's previous employer told Mrs. Hopewell that she "was the nosiest woman ever to walk the earth" (264). So Mrs. Hopewell thinks she has no choice but to "give her responsibility of everything," to "put her in charge" (264), acknowledging, in effect, that her employee is actually a natural leader. Hulga has learned, to her disappointment, that it "was not possible to be rude" to Mrs. Freeman, that "a direct attack . . . never touched her" (266). Mrs. Freeman calls the girl Hulga in private, showing that she sees through her pretensions. And Mrs. Freeman, like Manley, is fascinated by Hulga's artificial leg.

But Mrs. Freeman's curiosity seems less childlike than Manley's; she perversely delights in human suffering. She loves hearing details of Hulga's horrible hunting accident, especially that "she had never lost consciousness" (267). Generally, she "had a special fondness for the details of secret infections, hidden deformities, assaults upon children. Of diseases, she preferred the lingering or incurable" (267). Mrs. Freeman seems less abstract, or more real, than Manley; her cunning and curiosity are mixed with other indecent human qualities. Perhaps that is because she is more embedded in social life—she has a home, a husband, and daughters. The combination of being sociopathic, sadistic, and socially ambitious makes her more dangerous than Manley; we might say she is a more political, or tyrannical, figure. But O'Connor still closes the story by calling attention to her and Manley's basic kinship—observing that her "gaze . . . touched him" (284).

Manley and Mrs. Freeman serve by convention but rule by nature. They rule in secret, and they almost deserve to do so. They both, in fact, are usually happy enough to do so, although she, too, sulks on occasion because her obvious superiority is ignored. What they lack, of course, is any true concern for those they rule. But Mrs. Hopewell and Hulga are short on that concern too, and they actually raise their indifference to the level of principle. So, the only political point of distinction the story leaves us with is competence, and the competence of the natural nihilists is rooted in their more genuine—if not complete—openness to and delight in the truth. The story lacks any character with any real contact with any tradition of thought or action that combines natural insight with moral goodness.

The Christian

If we look hard, we can find a Christian in the story—Hulga. Manley teaches Hulga that she is a Christian too proud or too unfortunate not to believe in Christ. Right after Manley says he cannot figure out why a believer in nothing will not join him for some whiskey and sex, Hulga hisses "You're a Christian. . . . You're a fine Christian! You're just like them all—say one thing and do another. You're a perfect Christian" (283). The Bible salesman as Bible salesman is exactly that kind of Christian. But Manley does not rely on fake faith to seduce Hulga in private.

According to her own definition, Hulga herself is a more perfect Christian. Even in private, she says one thing and does another. She uses the words of shameless liberation, but she acts prudishly, fearfully, and shamefully. It turns out that her only objection to the Christians is their hypocrisy. They speak of love, but they treat strange and ugly crippled girls with cruel indifference. She clearly longs for the true understanding and the true love that the Christian God promises her. At one point, she tells her mother, "If you want me, here I am—LIKE I AM" (266). But her mother refuses even to try to see her as she is, and no other human being—surely no innocent—will see her that transparently. When Hulga surrenders to her imagination of Manley's innocence, it is "like losing her own life and finding it again, miraculously, in his" (281). But he is not really the miracle for which she longs.

And finally, we must look closely at the words Manley uses to get Hulga to affirm his love for her: "I don't care a thing about what all you done. I just want to know if you love me or don'tcher?" (280). Manley, of course, does not really mean to give the redemptive message of Jesus in the Gospels. He is not referring to his indifference to Hulga's sins but to her "number of degrees," and his "look was irritated but dogged," not loving (280). But what Hulga hears, clearly, is that she can be redeemed for her sins through love, and for the moment, Manley looks like Jesus to her. She is ready to believe that what she is and what she has done can be transformed through love. It turns out that Manley's method works its charm on her only accidentally; only by being misunderstood does he win her loving submission.

Hulga self-indulgently longs for what the Christian God promises, but without Christian humility or the hard Christian view of sinful human reality. Manley points her toward all sorts of self-knowledge about her mind and body that should highlight in neon letters her ineradicable human dependence. But it is hard to see how she will be able to see why that revelation is good. Her humiliation must be accompanied by grace; it would be miraculous if her new knowledge were to point her in a Christian direction.

Hulga seems to have the misfortune of knowing no real Christians. But we can see how easy it would be for her to be seduced by a thoughtful and educated Christian—a Thomist who could point her in the direction of the goodness of created being. We are allowed to hope that she will be given the grace of meeting one. She may be ready for the dialogue that will transform her humiliation into humility. And there's no reason to believe that the dialogue will simply point her away from philosophy. She might surrender enough anger and self-pity to become genuinely curious about and delighted by nature and human nature for the first time. She might absorb something of what is good—even if in a distorted or reductionistic way—about Manley's life. We can see how the way back to Thomistic Christian realism might be through the eyes of a particularly wounded Cartesian.

O'Connor's story is Nietzschean insofar as it is a criticism of secularized or sentimentalized Christianity as a particularly self-deceptive form of thought. Its angry negation of real human excellence and responsibility is rooted in the resentment of the weak. Such Christianity nihilistically points to the destruction of the real world of human beings; it readies the world for cruel tyranny. A key teaching of this story is that, contrary to the thinking of Richard Rorty and other such soft, secular Christians, sentimentality is the most ineffective antidote to cruelty.

But unlike Nietzsche (much of the time), O'Connor can distinguish between secularized Christianity—modern liberalism—and true Christian realism—Thomism. In genuinely Christian ages, O'Connor wrote, people "felt less," but "they saw more, even though they saw with the blind, prophetical, unsentimental eye of acceptance, which is to say, of faith" (830). It is possible to be a Christian and to come to terms with the basic human experience of limitation, to be open to grace without being blind to nature.

Hulga, finally, is the most Christian character in the story because she is the most real, or least abstract, one. All real human beings have souls that are maimed to some extent or another; we all should be placed among the deprived or poor. And we all have longings that point in the direction of the Creator. Mrs. Hopewell is too cold and Manley and Mrs. Freeman, in a sense, too free to be real. And no one can say that their freedom by itself is humanly desirable.

Note

1. All page references are to *Flannery O'Connor: Collected Works* (New York: Library of America, 1988).

6

Ralph Ellison's Invisible Men

Pamela K. Jensen

> Today it makes little difference to Atlanta, to the South, what the Negro thinks or dreams or wills. In the soul-life of the land he is to-day, and naturally will long remain, unthought of, half forgotten. . . . To-day the ferment of his striving toward self-realization is to the strife of the white world like a wheel within a wheel: beyond the Veil are smaller but like problems of ideals, of leaders and the led, of serf-dom, of poverty, of order and subordination, and, through all, the Veil of Race. Few know of these problems, few who know notice them; and yet there they are, awaiting student, artist, and seer—a field for somebody sometime to discover.
>
> —W. E. B. DuBois, "Of the Wings of Atalanta"

Alexis de Tocqueville famously suggested that all Americans are Cartesians without ever having read René Descartes.[1] Although his remark points up the antiauthoritarian streak running through American society, it also has another implication. Leaving aside the *Discourse on Method*, which at least *sounds* useful, it is highly unlikely that Tocqueville's Americans would ever be caught dead reading a book called *Meditations*. And herein lies a quandary. The one thing, above all, that democratic peoples need—to which Tocqueville's own mammoth book attests—is the one thing our harried lives disincline us to undertake, namely, meditations, and, in particular, a meditation on democracy itself.[2] Our ears are bound to prick up, then, when we encounter an American writer who makes just such a meditation central to all his literary works, as Ralph Ellison does. Moreover, while we have to concede that *Democracy in America* is a project conceived by an aristocrat, Tocqueville himself suggests that democratic poets and men of letters will be drawn to make democracy their theme, in this sense anticipating Ellison's orientation. Or, to state the matter differently, Tocqueville's and Ellison's accounts of American democracy converge in the importance they each ascribe to the "abstract and futuristic" ideal that guides it.[3]

I would like to explore here one of Ellison's most important treatments of democracy in America, his essay "The Little Man at Chehaw Station: The American Artist and His Audience," originally published in *The American Scholar* in 1977 and republished in 1986 at the head of his second collection of essays, *Going to the Territory*.[4] I hope to show that "The Little Man" serves both to deepen our reflections on liberal democracy and to enhance our understanding of *Invisible Man*.[5]

Ellison believes that every American artist has the responsibility to reflect on our fundamental political principles and that every American artist has the responsibility to elevate the standards of art, accomplishing the latter by doing the former. Put in other words, in a democracy every artist must share in the deliberative functions of a citizen, and every citizen must take "personal moral responsibility" for improving his country.[6] The special civic role Ellison accords to artists (and novelists, above all) has to do with the power of *logos*, of the Word, in our democracy: we live on "a terrain of ideas," and our community is formed by the "sacred principles" enshrined in our founding documents (LM, 17). "In our national beginnings . . . was the word *democratic*, and since we vowed in a war rite of blood and sacrifice to keep its commandments, we act in the name of a word made sacred," always referring back, whether positively or negatively, to principles of justice enunciated by the founders (LM, 18). Since our politics and our self-understanding are shaped by our persistent tendency to recur to first principles—though, to be sure, competing, even contradictory, interpretations of those principles abound—Ellison expects a more dramatic and potentially explosive political landscape than is foreshadowed in *Federalist* 10: "a conscious awareness of values describes the condition of the American experiment, and often much of our energy goes into finding ways of losing that consciousness. In the beginning was not only the word, but its contradiction."[7]

That we are essentially a language, or symbolic, community also means, says Ellison, that a premium is placed on the writer's ability to foster communication among the members; to do that well, of course, the writer must know his audience, that is, the country, in its full complexity, being continually attentive to patterns and possibilities, heretofore unrecorded or unnoticed, in our history. In a variety of ways, Ellison calls attention in his writings to what is happening on "the lower frequencies," in the "underground" where people live who fall under the radar, below "the threshold of social hierarchy" or, as he also puts it, "outside of history,"[8] people who nevertheless have fully absorbed the "body of assumptions about human possibility" expressed in our "great documents of state."[9] Having repudiated a union conceived of in racial, ethnic, or religious terms, we need also to concede that the regime principles, including the right to self-government, touch us all. Ellison's signature metaphor for the "omnipresent American ideal" is the Territory, promised land for all those who seek "the democracy-sponsored opportunity to have a second chance" (LM, 27). Originally incarnate as the old Indian Territory that so powerfully attracted emigrating slaves and, later, freedmen, and that developed into Ellison's own (and Woody Guthrie's and Will Rogers') home state of Oklahoma, the Territory remains as the imagined venue of perfect freedom and equality, the ever-looming and never-vanishing frontier to which, like Huck Finn, we democrats regularly dream of cutting out to.[10] But Ellison also uses the Territory in another sense, as a metaphor for the unknown but not unknowable plane of American existence, the field the true American artist must explore. The task of the writer in democracy, in brief, is to make the invisible visible, and in the service of this enterprise, Ellison enlists the aid of the "little man."

The Little Man

The "little man" is Ellison's metaphor for a refined and highly cultivated sensibility that expresses itself in obscurity, a sensibility that, in democracy, can no longer be "the exclusive property of a highly visible elite" (LM, 6, 10). It is a "random," hence unexpected or incongruous, but inevitable effect of the dismantling of aristocratic privilege: "certain assertions of personality, formerly the prerogative of high social rank" spread to the "anonymous and lowly" (LM, 9).[11] The "mysterious enrichment of personality" that the little man represents results from the "random accessibility" to the finest products of the arts and intellect that arises from "America's social mobility, its universal education, and its relative freedom of cultural information" (LM, 8). Since the little man cannot be explained by reference to his socioeconomic background, we can only infer the specific circumstances of his provenance (LM, 8). Inverting the orientation of those who celebrate the democratizing potential of the Internet, Ellison, for his part, likens the wide, open democratic cultural scene to "the memory banks of some computer systems" (LM, 10).

Ellison became acquainted with the little man at Tuskegee in the mid-1930s, following a dressing down from one of his music professors for a sub-par trumpet recital. Since he was at the time hoping to become a classical composer, this was a rebuke that stung. In lieu of the sympathetic reassurance Ellison sought from another teacher, Hazel Harrison—a professional pianist with avant-garde leanings and, as will become clear, something of a little man herself—instead invoked "the little man" to explain why, "in this country," in particular, it is necessary that an artist always perform to the utmost of his capacities: "you must *always* play your best, even if it's only in the waiting room at Chehaw Station, because in this country there'll always be a little man hidden behind the stove" (LM, 4). As Ellison glosses, an artist must recognize that "any American audience will conceal at least *one* individual whose knowledge and taste will complement, or surpass, his own"

(LM, 9). While the little man is not necessarily African American, Ellison emphasizes those who are in order most pointedly to make his case, in the process merging literary criticism and symbolic political action.

Though "[s]omething of an autodidact," or self-made man, the little man is not a mere diamond in the rough, endowed with a "raw" talent and good natural instincts (LM, 11). Although he is not a part of the "visible cultural elite" and may lack other formal credentials, he stands quite securely on a high rung of the real cultural meritocracy, the realm of culture realizing at least some of Jefferson's hopes. He is a stealth critic, consumer, and even producer of art, reclusive and secretive in general, but surefooted and voluble in his element. Hazel Harrison attributed to him knowledge of "the *music*, and the *tradition*, and the standards of *musicianship*" required for whatever one sets out to perform, and she implied strongly that he will not give an A for effort (LM, 4).

And before we start to hum the "Fanfare for the Common Man," we ought not to confuse the little man with "the *little* guy," the lowest common denominator. If Ellison designates the little man as a "representative of the American audience writ small," it is specifically because he means to point to the "enigma of aesthetic communication" in America, to expose the fact that every American audience is a mystery, plumbing the depths of which requires a deeper "cultural introspection" on the part of artists and of all Americans than is customarily made, and without which an artist cannot be said to understand his subject matter or to perform his function in a democracy, which is to disclose the nation to itself (LM, 6, 25).

The typical American audience does not, then, respect the lines of race, religion, region, or class and evades the social and political barriers, including segregation, erected in their names. Cultivated taste is rather to be found "floating, as it were, free in the crowd," creating a kind of community within the community (LM, 10). The precise places where free-floating cultural information will penetrate can by no means be decided in advance, but the little man displays a sense of entitlement to appropriate it and self-government with respect to using it, making his or her own contribution to the gross cultural product (GCP) undeterred by the "authorities" or self-styled arbiters of taste; freely translating into one or another of our vernacular languages even "the chilliest of classics"—as Ellison says jazz also does, and as he says Mark Twain did—and otherwise morphing everything into new matter to suit new creative purposes. Thus, *Romeo and Juliet* becomes *West Side Story*, and *Emma* becomes *Clueless*. But if it is the case that democracy undermines a strict line of demarcation between high and popular art, it is also true that the little man has an unerring knack for fitting form to function.[12] He knows when the vernacular is appropriate, when to stick to classical modes, and when to show the nexus between them; he is, moreover, a stickler for the standards that inhere in vernacular forms themselves, preferring his art "without frills."[13] If he is predisposed toward experimentation and against "canonical" thinking and irreverent toward authority in general, he also vehemently repudiates high-minded efforts to dumb things down in order to make them more "accessible." So, if you're going to make a rock musical out of *Aida*, be prepared to see him standing in the wings.

Although he can be found anywhere, the little man has the Show Me State in his genes. To all outward appearances, and based on his customary cohorts and the fact that he does not travel first class, he could be confused with Joe Six Pack (though it is unlikely he would ever have deliberately chosen to be in Phil Donahue's audience). He might nod in partial agreement with people who say they don't know art but know what they like because he, too, knows what he likes, but he also knows art. First and foremost, then, he is meant to caution artists to live up to the highest possible standards of their craft: out of an "unaccountable knowingness," acquired through "familiar but uncharted channels of culture," he possesses refined and rigorous criteria of judgment (LM, 11). "Which is to say that, having been randomly exposed to diverse artistic conventions, the little man has learned to detect the true transcendent ambience created by successful art from chic shinola" (LM, 11). The little man at the Chehaw, Alabama, train station is, then, to put it briefly, a connoisseur lying in wait for con men and for elite (and probably effete) snobs. Although like a latter-day Socrates he's always ready to pull the pretentious down a peg or two, he is not essentially motivated—as Friedrich Nietzsche, for one, predicted—by ressentiment. While not a social climber himself, he is the declared enemy of "social climbing and of social exclusion," especially if he detects in an artist's oeuvre an effort deliberately to lord it over him or to keep the literary club exclusive (LM, 12). And woe betide the artist who treats the American audience "as though it were as easily manipulated as a jukebox" (LM, 12).

Like some other knobby-kneed long shots who are "misunderestimated," and also like Brer Rabbit, the little man exploits his perceived disadvantages to the hilt, savoring his eventual victory in advance. Ellison likens him to Hamlet because he, too, somewhat puckishly puts on masks to challenge all comers. Ellison's description of the American audience as "an instrument" on which the artist plays "as a pianist upon a piano" also distinctly echoes the terms in which Hamlet taunts Rosencrantz and Guildenstern (LM, 10–11). Mocking their ham-handed and rather desperate efforts to get him to confide in them, Hamlet dares Guildenstern to play a recorder, to get *it* to talk. When the feckless and unskilled Guildenstern cannot oblige, Hamlet touchily retorts that yet

> you would seem to know my stops, you would pluck out the heart of my mystery, you would sound me from my lowest note to the top of the compass. . . . 'Sblood, do you think I am easier to be played on than a pipe? Call me what instrument you will, though you can fret me, you cannot play upon me.[14]

Now the little man has his own "stops," his own range of perspectives, his "filial, sacred, racial" pieties, which constitute, in effect, the rhetorical stops through which he responds to art. And he, too, can be "fretted" if not deftly handled. And "what frets him utterly is any attitude that offends his quite human pieties by ignorance, disdain, or disregard for his existence" (LM, 13). He is thus "repelled by works of art that would strip human experience—especially American experience—of its wonder and stubborn complexity" (LM, 13).

Like the narrator of Ellison's masterpiece, the little man is also an invisible man, indeed, a close relative of his literary forbear, and, like him, the little man is also called "an underground-outsider." Of him it is also said that "[d]rawn to the brightness of bright lights, he cloaks himself in invisibility" (LM, 11). In his love of bright lights and ability to turn his invisibility to advantage, the little man really does resemble the narrator of *Invisible Man*, who has conned the equivalent of Con Edison (Monopolated Light and Power) out of both light and power so that he can fill—really fill—his underground cavern with light, making it brighter than any spot on Broadway: "Nothing, storm or flood, must get in the way of our need for light and ever more and brighter light. The truth is the light and the light is the truth. . . . Before I lived in the darkness [i.e., was blind] but now I see."[15]

Although the narrator remains invisible to others, he bathes his surroundings in light in order not to lose sight—so recently gained and so hard-won—of himself. But both he and the little man seek light and not the limelight, taking advantage of their anonymity to get a better view and to confound hierarchal expectations, which lead one to judge on appearances (LM, 11). With, so to speak, their dark glasses on, these masters of disguise have taken more than a page from the slippery Rinehart's book—the Protean con man of *Invisible Man*—without surrendering to Rinehartism.[16] They exhibit the same ingenuity in exploiting the "interstices" of American life, which present an "incalculable scale of possibilities for self-creation" to the adventurous soul but put their freedom to better use than Rine the runner cum righteous reverend.[17]

Like the liberated narrator, the little man may also feel impelled at some point to broadcast his invisibility to the world. Indeed, "the *obligation* to make oneself seen and heard [is] an imperative of American democratic individualism."[18] Ellison himself chose to obey this imperative by inventing a character who became "visible" only as a disembodied, but eloquently articulate and increasingly self-conscious, voice; we have to hear him to see him, and he's not taciturn. Ellison says he chose this tactic in order to be true to a social reality that was not frequently reflected in literature. He asked himself "why most protagonists of Afro-American fiction (not to mention the black characters in fiction written by whites) were without intellectual depth."[19] Notwithstanding their subjection to the "most extreme forms of the human predicament" or participation in the most wrenching social struggles, they were nevertheless "seldom able to articulate the issues which tortured them."[20] There are enough exceptions to the rule, however, "to provide the perceptive novelist with models."[21] Further, "if they did not exist it would be necessary, both in the interest of fictional expressiveness and as examples of human possibility, to invent them."[22] And this is especially true in American democracy, where traditional impediments to human development have no standing. Ellison speaks in the same terms of the little man, conveying the thought that he is not an anomaly of our culture, but somehow typical:

> But out of a stubborn individualism born of his democratic origins, he insists upon the cultural necessity of his role, and argues that if he didn't exist, he would have to be invented. If he were not already manifest in the flesh, he would still exist and function as an idea and an ideal because—like such character traits as individualism, restlessness, self-reliance, love of the new, and so on—he is a linguistic product of the American scene and language, and a manifestation of the idealistic action of the American Word, as it goads its users toward a perfection of our revolutionary ideals. (LM, 7–8)

Art and Democracy

As a reminder that the American audience is more "democratic" than it might seem, the little man poses a significant "rhetorical challenge" to the artist. If an artist cannot readily identify in advance who is *in* his audience, including not knowing on which side of the color line its members might originate, he must learn how to "fashion strategies of communication that will bridge the many divisions of background and taste it might contain" (LM, 9). To envision, or *see,* the little men out there, he has to penetrate a number of prevailing myths, look beyond stereotypes, and question comfortable assumptions (LM, 31). At least implicitly, Ellison's remarks in "The Little Man" emphasize the need for white writers to accommodate astute and varied black readers. Conversely, in the introduction to the thirtieth edition of *Invisible Man*, published in 1982, Ellison discusses the same "rhetorical challenge" from the point of view of a black writer who intended in his novel to reach out to heretofore unknown white readers.[23] In both cases, he insists that democratic artists must create lines of communication where there were none before and avail themselves of the underutilized ones that already exist. To meet this challenge, Ellison says, he sought to reveal "the human universals hidden within the plight of one who was both black and American" in order to communicate "across our barriers of race and religion, class, color and region."[24] In so doing, he hoped to foil "the many strategies of division that were designed, and still function, to prevent what would otherwise have been a more or less natural recognition of the reality of black and white fraternity."[25]

Reflecting on the unexpected ways in which his study of "comparative humanity" had touched readers, Ellison says that he was gratefully able to rediscover the truth of the narrator's closing lines: "Who knows but that on the lower frequencies, I speak for you?"[26] Gambling with "the reader's capacity for fictional truth," the ability to "identify" with well-drawn characters, a good novel makes possible an encounter with the heroic, but perhaps also with the all-too-human, in oneself, as with Mr. Norton's revelation of his share in the human condition, made possible by his run-in with the tragicomic predicament of the aptly named Trueblood.[27] Such encounters make for a novel's "permanent interest" or significance, even if, as Ellison thought regarding some of the episodes of *Invisible Man*, the immediate issues were rapidly resolving themselves in an ever more democratic America.[28]

Art contributes to the progress of democracy because it is, as a work of the imagination, inherently integrative: it forms a whole out of disparate parts not normally found together, and it also envisions new possibilities within the given social reality—at its most serious, art "is a thrust toward a human ideal."[29] Thus, "even if true political equality eludes us in reality—as it continues to do—there is still available that fictional vision of an ideal democracy in which the actual combines with the ideal and gives us representations of a state of things in which the highly placed and the lowly, the black and the white, the Northerner and the Southerner, the native-born and the immigrant combine to tell us of transcendent truths and possibilities."[30]

An artist who is fully aware of the little man's "incongruous existence" is bound to be somewhat discomfited, perhaps to the point of disavowing him "as a source of confusion, a threat to social order, and a reminder of the unfinished details of this powerful nation" (LM, 7). That is to say, the invisibility of the little man is a sign that we have not yet fully recognized equality and do not want to face the facts, but perhaps also of our unwillingness to confront the implications for ourselves of America's fluid and continually shifting social lines. Part of Ellison's intention in shining light on our invisible men is to compel us to look both at where we have fallen short as a nation and where certain issues of justice have already been resolved, making us better than we think we are.[31]

It is certainly the artist's right to ignore the little man or to disdain him "as one who aspires beyond his social station or cultural capacity," but he does so at his peril (LM, 12). He will not succeed in turning the little man against a cultural heritage he deeply feels as his own, but he will also miss out on the chance of perfecting his own art. Ellison characterizes it as a double breaking of faith: art is faith in the ability to communicate to all readers via language or symbolically, and democracy is faith in the ideal of a refined cultural sensibility available to all (LM, 15). Awareness of the little man pushes novelists to delve more deeply into their cultural materials, in the process enriching our knowledge of American democracy by showing more of its possibilities. The little man is both gatekeeper and tour guide of the Territory. In the first part of the essay, then, Ellison presents the little man as a "cautionary figure who challenges the artist to reach out for new heights of expressiveness" (LM, 15).

The fact that every reader reads from a distinctive perspective reflecting his life experience aids the author "in achieving the more complex vision of American experience that was implicit in his material," as when an African American reads the Civil War source of Nick Carroway's family fortune in *The Great Gatsby* or, as "an insider-outsider" himself, incorporates "Gatz-Gatsby's experience into his own and his own into Gatsby's," perhaps, from hard experience, seeing through the fatal illusions of "social mobility" that dominate that character (LM, 14).[32] The new dimension of meaning the novel acquires with its readers' help is essential to its completion. Every work of art, Ellison argues, is unfinished in itself; it requires audience participation in order to fulfill its potential. In the sometimes rocky "antagonistic cooperation" or dialectic—the tango—that occurs between artists and audience, readers accept or reject a novel based on whether it affirms or distorts their own sense of the American experience (LM, 7).[33] Reach out to the little man, then, and "even the most avant-garde art may become an agency for raising the general level of artistic taste" (LM, 15).

An artist who takes the little man into account as part of his audience necessarily opens himself up to changing the content of his work: pitching it not only *to* the little man but also writing *about* him and the cultural nooks and crannies in which he can be found. In this sense, the little man is a "lightning rod," attracting new insights and possibilities and stretching the artist's own imaginative potential.

The little man does not demand that the novelist exaggerate his centrality, but he wants images of American experience that "resonate symbolically with his own ubiquitous presence" (LM, 13). In our one nation indivisible, he is a part of the story. Ellison writes, "As a citizen, the little man endures with a certain grace the social restrictions that limit his own social mobility, but *as a reader* he demands that the relationship between his own condition and that of those more highly placed be recognized" (LM, 14). Since American experience is of a whole, he wants "the interconnections" revealed—not out of vanity but "because he sees his own condition as an inseparable part of a larger truth in which the high and the lowly, the known and the unrecognized, the comic and tragic are woven into the American skein" (LM, 14).

To forward this enterprise, as noted earlier, it is necessary for writers to endow their characters with the requisite moral and intellectual consciousness, to create characters "who could think as well as act."[34] Art and democracy can converge only when both are working toward the goal of creating a "conscious, articulate citizenry," prepared to govern because capable of self-government and of moral discrimination.[35] The "more chastened view of political possibility" dominating our post-Reconstruction history notwithstanding, Ellison avers he saw "no reason to impose undue restrictions upon my novelist's freedom to manipulate imaginatively those possibilities that existed both in the Afro-American personality and in the restricted structure of American society. My task was to transcend those restrictions," as Mark Twain had done.[36] Although African Americans "were usually defeated in their bouts with circumstance, there was no reason why they, like Brer Rabbit and his more literary cousins . . . shouldn't be allowed to snatch the victory of conscious perception from the forces that overwhelmed them."[37]

With reference again to *The Great Gatsby*, and in an implicit criticism of Fitzgerald, Ellison finds it ironic that the witness who could have identified Daisy as the driver of the car that eventually led to Gatsby's murder was a black man whose ability to communicate, and thus pass moral judgment, was "of no more consequence to the action than that of an ox that might have observed Icarus's sad plunge into the sea" (LM, 15). Ten years earlier, Ellison leveled a similar criticism at Richard Wright in *Native Son*: "[Bigger Thomas] was designed to shock whites out of their apathy and end the circumstances out of which Wright insisted Bigger emerged. Here environment is all—and interestingly enough, environment conceived solely in terms of the physical, the non-conscious. . . . Wright could imagine Bigger, but Bigger could not possibly imagine Richard Wright. Wright saw to that."[38]

As Ellison sees it, Wright's ideological stance got in the way of his art. And he objects to a political position that prevents Wright or any African American writer from being able to give an account of himself in his own work. Among other things, Wright and those who use his work as a standard for African American writing "leave no room for the individual writer's unique existence," which includes coming under the plural influences available in any context and, in turn, developing one's own response to them.[39] "Wright was able to free himself in Mississippi because he had the imagination and the will to do so. . . . The same is true of James Baldwin, who is not the product of a Negro store-front church but of the library, and the same is true of me."[40] Thus, for Ellison, "Wright as *writer* was less interesting than the enigma he personified: that he could so dissociate himself from the complexity of his background while trying so hard to improve the condition of black men everywhere; that he could be so wonderful an example of human possibility but could not for ideological reasons depict a Negro as intelligent, as creative or as dedicated as himself."[41]

If it is not already clear, Ellison might hasten to add at this point that all serious literature must deal with "the moral core" of society, and in America, "the Negro and his status have always stood for that moral concern."[42]

Ellison thought that, with the notable exception of William Faulkner, American novelists since Mark Twain have been evading "our great moral theme," the signature moral issue of our country. "The moral imperatives of American life that are implicit in the Declaration of Independence, the Constitution and the Bill of Rights were a part of both the individual consciousness and the conscience of those writers who created what we consider our classic novels . . . and [for all] the reluctance of contemporary writers to deal explicitly with politics, they still are."[43] In addressing these issues from the vantage point of "that fragment of the huge American experience" he knows best, Ellison saw himself contributing "not only to the growth of literature but to the shaping of the culture as I should like it to be. The American novel is in this sense a conquest of the frontier; as it describes our experience, it creates it."[44]

The Melting Pot

> "[At the widow's] everything was cooked by itself. In a barrel of odds and ends it is different; things get mixed up, and the juice kind of swaps around, and the things go better."
>
> —Huck Finn, from Mark Twain's *The Adventures of Huckleberry Finn*

The little man's surprising ability to pop up in any of America's characteristically mixed assemblies will, Ellison hopes, spark a new awareness of the fundamental importance of America's cultural pluralism, our "unity-in-diversity." And so we come to "the melting pot," of which the little man is a proud product.

According to Ellison, while acknowledging the terms of the melting pot in principle, Americans have freely defaulted on their responsibilities in practice (LM, 26). Nevertheless, he insists that the concept was never so "abstract" as to be more than a blinding myth, nor so literally descriptive as to mask the discrimination undertaken in its name. The melting pot is then neither a fiction nor a subterfuge designed, like so many of the promises offered to the narrator of *Invisible Man,* merely to anesthetize him and keep him running in place, appealing to his sense of logic in an Alice-in-Wonderland world, or, as he might put it, "Bledsoing" him six ways from Sunday.[45] Since the little man stands on the solid ground of a real cultural pluralism, he could admit the melting pot to be a "conceit" or hope, without rejecting it as merely "a con game contrived by the powerful" (LM, 27).

Ellison calls the "melting pot" our historical metaphor for "the goal of cultural integration" but notes as well that the idea has come under assault nearly as frequently as it has been invoked (LM, 25).[46] He directs his own staunch defense of the melting pot against the proponents of "ethnicity" in his day: "So today, before the glaring inequities, unfulfilled promises and rich possibilities of democracy, we hear heady evocations of European, African and Asian backgrounds . . . proclaiming the inviolability of ancestral blood" (LM, 21). In our own day, attacks on the melting pot have arisen under the banner of the politics of "difference" and the ideology of multiculturalism and in new debates over immigration.[47] Whether one considers the melting pot in terms of its feasibility or its desirability or both, Ellison can contribute to our current conversations.[48] At the outset, however, he would reject both sides of a debate in which, because a complex social reality is oversimplified, a repellent choice is offered: either the bland uniformity generated by market forces or a defensive insularity. The alternative he proposes for black Americans is a "personal affirmation of integration along with keeping the distinctive identity of our people alive."[49]

At the time Ellison was writing, his opponents tended to seek unity without diversity; today his opponents are more likely to celebrate diversity without unity. Wariness about the costs of inclusion arises today in order to spare cultural groups from being absorbed into an America that, it is claimed, is not, and to some extent cannot be, their own. By contrast, Ellison forwards an argument against exclusion, on the grounds that all of America's culture groups are cocreators of the whole. He does not so much call on America to affirm separate cultures, then, as to recognize and affirm separate contributions to a common culture developed under the auspices of our regime.[50] He means even the latest waves of immigrants to feel welcome on these grounds.[51]

As Ellison understands our cultural past, it is not that there was less diversity, but rather that there was more hope in the goal of integration. His writings are guided by an effort to revive and solidify that hope, both for the sake of African Americans and for the sake of democracy. He believes opposition to the melting pot lends support to continued racial discrimination, indeed strengthens a deleterious and dangerous categorization of Americans by race, and betrays America's fundamental ideals and historical practices. He is thus less worried about the effacement of cultural difference than he is about the imposition of a permanent outsider status on African Americans. If his argument about the formation of American culture and the relation between democratic politics and culture has merit, it might still be offered on behalf of the melting pot today.

On the question of the feasibility of an American melting pot, and with special regard to African Americans, Ellison strenuously disputes the central claim of the widely influential *Beyond the Melting Pot*, published in 1963 by Nathan Glazer and Daniel Patrick Moynihan: "the point about the melting pot is that it never really happened."[52] Ellison counters that "the realities of discrimination and racism notwithstanding," culturally "the melting pot melted" and that the "irrepressible" process is continuing at an accelerating pace (LM, 21, 27). The attempt to pretend otherwise only aggravates race relations, occasionally prompting brutal racial assaults where there had been none before (LM, 21).

With respect to the desirability of an American melting pot, Ellison argues that our future as a democracy stands or falls with our attachment to it; culture is *the* repository of the democratic faith, bearing over time the most consistent traces of self-government and equality. Even when the democratic process is thwarted in politics or social life, it operates freely in the realm of culture. And our culture is integrated, even if the rest of society is not. Above all, exploration of the melting pot reveals the innumerable and most consequential exercises of freedom that are, and always have been, even within the strictures of unfreedom, a crucial part of African American heritage; the record of these activities is a measure of African American participation in American society and of its inclusiveness.

The American "people" is not an undifferentiated mass, but rather a congeries of regional, religious, racial, and ethnic groups—the overlapping and constantly shifting "minority groups," to any number of which each of us, by heritage and elective affinity, belongs. We are "not only a political collectivity of individuals, but, culturally, a collectivity of styles, tastes, and traditions" (LM, 16). When Ellison speaks of our "cultural pluralism," he means something different, however, from Horace Kallen, who popularized the term early in the twentieth century to counter what he saw as an all-too-robust assimilation effort by a kind of racial and ethnic essentialism, insisting on the intrinsic separateness of the groups comprising America's "federation of ethnicities."[53] When Ellison, by contrast, speaks of our "nation of nations," he means to imply our complex wholeness: America is a totality produced by the reciprocal exchanges among its various subgroups (i.e., from many, one). Nor would he accept the implicit premise of Kallen's argument that cultural forms can somehow be hermetically sealed or static in America, where everything is subject to change. On the contrary, the evolution or metamorphosis of all cultural forms and practices as they come into contact with one another yields an ever more "American" synthesis or composite, in which the past is continually adjusted to the needs of the present.

Indeed, in its extravagant diversity, "the whirlpool of odds and ends" comprising "the general American culture"—the "eclectic mix of forms and modes," fusions, syntheses, and amalgams present here—suggest that our melting pot democracy is as motley and many-colored, as full of varied sights and sounds, as is the democratic city Socrates describes in Book VIII of *The Republic*. Socrates, to be sure, affects to disparage the Athens he depicts, dubbing it an ever-changing spectacle especially appealing to "women and boys" but presumably to be shunned by the serious person. Ellison might hasten to point out that as Socrates left Athens less than the halt, the blind, and the lame, there is perhaps more to his world than is contained in his philosophy. In any case, like Socrates, Ellison welcomes the philosophical and psychological investigations democratic life supports. The rich variety of human types in democracy educates the integrative imagination, enabling us to understand more by letting us project ourselves into multiple personalities, "and you don't have to take an ocean voyage to do it."[54]

Ellison's designation of American society as a "whole" might seem an ill-chosen term for a "whirlpool of odds and ends," the clashing ingredients of our culture (LM, 20). Despite the centrifugal forces that are at work in the very notion of self-assertion, Ellison argues that the elements in the American compound combine to produce a whole because each is integral to the end result, the sign of a level playing field that permits and has always permitted interpenetrations of one cultural "stream" or "idiom" by another, fostering cross-pollinations and, above all, interdependencies. Innumerable anonymous donors work independently but in tandem to "achieve" American identity. The "general American culture" is a creature of all and no one: we are all "inheritors, creators, and creations of a culture of cultures" (LM, 29).

Everything is interrelated, or as Hazel Harrison would say, "all-shook-up," in this country (LM, 32). We are no longer free, if we ever were, literally to dissociate from or to escape one another. There are plenty of reasons not to acknowledge these reciprocal exchanges and the debts they incur—most notably the fear that, literally as well as culturally, there may be fewer than six degrees of separation between any one American and another—but perhaps there are even more reasons to notice them for what they signify, namely, that the democratic process is operating (LM, 28). "All social barriers," Ellison contends, "are vulnerable to cultural styles."[55] It is precisely at the level of culture, rendered even more malleable because everything is translated into the vernacular, that "ethnic resistance is least effective."[56]

In general terms, Ellison traces opposition to the melting pot to an anxiety about democracy that comes into being with it. Echoing Tocqueville's account of the development of democratic "individualism," Ellison notes the isolation or alienation inevitably produced with the dismantling of hierarchal or aristocratic society, the concomitant of the creation of new potentialities for the individual, that is, of "an open society in which the individual could achieve his potential unhindered by his ties to his past" (LM, 20).[57] As Tocqueville explains, in democratic societies, the constant communication and intermingling of all classes of society lead them to "imitate and envy each other," which circumstance, in turn, "suggests a host of ideas, notions, and desires to people that they would not have had if ranks had been fixed and society immobile. In these nations the servant never considers himself entirely a stranger to the pleasures and works of the master, nor the poor man to those of the rich; the man in the fields strives to resemble someone in the towns, and the provinces, the metropolis."[58]

At the same time, the immobile social structures that served in their own way to integrate aristocratic society by creating stable relations among its constituent elements—relating both classes and generations to each other—evanesce; equality breaks the social chain, and "sets each link apart."[59] With the sundering of all steady connections to others, the pervasive sense arises that one owes nothing to anyone, cannot rely on anyone, and is compelled to sink or swim on one's own. Theoretically, at least, the liberation from social constraints knocks out both any preexisting ceiling and the floor. As Ellison puts it, "So despite any self-assurance [a person] might achieve in dealing with his familiars, he is nevertheless (and by the nature of his indefinite relationship to the fluid social hierarchy) a lonely individual who must find his own way within a crowd of other lonely individuals" (LM, 19–20).[60]

Thus, again following Tocqueville, Ellison conveys just how demanding democracy is on the individual, pointing out the burdens or responsibilities that come with our endowed rights. No one is exempt from the mandate of self-government. Each individual is encouraged, literally, to make something of himself—to become a self-made man in his identity and not just in his bank account—and is, indeed, obliged to do so, only to find that in the "universal tumult" of democracy, where he is equal to everyone else, the solid privileges of a few have only given way to the unrelenting competition of all.[61] Ambition is simultaneously unleashed and thwarted. The game, or rather, the rat race, is afoot.

Since equality detaches everyone from a secure mooring and makes it seem that each can rise and fall only by his own efforts, we are prone to a kind of perpetual disorientation: there are, Ellison says, "no easily recognizable points of rest, no facile certainties as to who, what or where (culturally or historically) we are" (LM, 20). Our ardor for equality notwithstanding, we intuit that there can never be enough of it to reassure us that no one is looking over our shoulders or dogging our heels; someone is always poised to offend us by making us feel the precariousness of our position—to which circumstance Tocqueville imputes our national "restiveness."[62] Since we can never be certain that everyone else will renounce their ambition and settle down quietly as "last men," we cannot, even if we want to, renounce our own.

To find at least some insulation from the crowd, some foothold in the flux of American society—even if only a rickety set of floorboards and a couple of slap-dash walls—Ellison says, again following Tocqueville, we are prompted to create exclusive groups founded on arbitrary distinctions, with the hope of achieving on a new, artificial footing what aristocracy had achieved on the basis of birth.[63] Race and ethnic classifications (with their attendant parochialisms) fit the bill, particularly insofar as they allege some permanent disability that would prevent potential rivals from displacing us, rivals on whom we can instead project our own fears or shortcomings.

In order to become the self-actualized person promised by democracy, it is necessary for one to choose "that psychic uncertainty which is a condition of achieving his potential, a state [one] yearns to avoid" (LM, 20). Hunkering down in cultural or racial enclaves is a way for the spiritually or characterologically timid to allay anxiety. The tendency to hug familiar shores and stay "within one's own" shows the looming Territory once more, not in its aspect as the alluring venue for freedom, but its flipside, the menacing or terrifying, boundaryless unknown. Thus, although we have been cooperating pragmatically across racial, ethnic, and religious barriers since before the nation as such existed, we have also regularly sought somehow to opt out of the democratic process by "symbolic acts of disaffiliation," acts of will equivalent to pulling a blanket over one's head. However much this willful blindness helps in the short run, Ellison might say, the historical facts are stubborn things.

Racial discrimination is, for Ellison, the most obvious *effect* of this circumstance arising in democracy, rather than its cause. Indeed, as he sees it, the desire for exclusion increases in tandem with the actual "melting" of hierarchal barriers and the opening of new opportunities, advancing as equality advances. Hence, he detects the greatest opposition to our "cultural wholeness" in those who have "made it," the "descendents of peasants, or slaves, and inhabitants of European ghettos" (LM, 19–20).

Ellison does not at all deny that our diverse pasts and traditions can provide important sources of comfort and "morale" (LM, 26). Purged of the hierarchal conditions that may have given rise to them, they may, in fact, be preserved as something even more precious than before. But he does mean to caution against an overreliance on them (LM, 19–20). It is also true, however, that in a society as fluid and swiftly changing as our own, tradition as such has no standing—especially when compared to the "next new thing"—and "identity" is therefore always going to rest at least as much on choice as on inheritance. As a consequence, Ellison thinks we will never be able to suppress a deep-seated intuition that we must meet the requirement for self-definition in a free society, nor altogether to resist its positive appeal. At home, within our elected or inherited cultural family, then, there is always "a brooding strangeness," and in the underlying sense of alienation we often feel when abroad, a frequently ephemeral, but nevertheless undeniable feeling of kinship or "sense of fraternity"(LM, 20–21). Thus, like W. E. B. DuBois, Ellison finds a sort of "double consciousness" in America—not, however, as the special burden of African Americans, but as the legacy of all Americans. Because we can neither fully embrace nor completely repudiate our principles, deep down the American condition is "a state of unease" (LM, 20–21).

While not denying that black opponents of the melting pot evince a justifiable impatience and frustration at America's slowness to live up to its own political ideals, he also holds it to be possible that their most defiant self-assertion may conceal the same lack of self-confidence exhibited by white opponents: "They are frightened by the existence of opportunities for competing with their white peers on a basis of equality that did not exist for us. . . . [T]hey are in the position of pioneers who must enter an unknown territory armed only with knowledge and skills which they have brought with them from the past, but instead of plunging in and testing themselves against the unknown, they choose rather to argue with the deficiencies of the past."[64]

To which Ellison's central response is, "no excuses." He combines the demand for inclusion of all the parties in order to meet the requirement of equality with the demand for responsibility in order to meet the requirement of freedom.[65] This is true whether one is a white segregationist or a black nationalist, whether one seeks to celebrate a quasimythic past in which there did not seem to be so many potential competitors or detractors, to scapegoat those who do exist, or, from the same anxiety and distrust of democracy, to repudiate the entire past or to abandon the goal of integration altogether. America's inability to prevent the democratic process from operating, despite all obstacles, and in those very people for whom it could not be assumed in advance to operate, is a fact of our unrecorded history that preserves hope and bolsters the overall struggle for freedom or civil rights. Proper recognition of the melting pot takes away the excuses from those who do not relish, or who wish altogether to avoid, individual responsibility—the price of freedom—and, by exposing the groundlessness of their claims, also from those who want to suppress recognition of our cultural diversity because they do not want to pay the price of equality. And he makes his case by pointing to the optimism about democracy that existed in earlier generations of African Americans amidst far greater social and political restrictions: they showed no signs of "trying to withdraw in a pique or of surrendering their investment in the experiment."[66]

Even when "clouded in slavery," the past displays virtues needed in the Territory. Although the members of earlier generations may have been unseen or invisible to others and, in a most poignant irony, may have made contributions to American society that frequently went unrecognized or unattributed, "they saw themselves in all the movements of American life no matter how confused the scene."[67] No one may have been watching, but history was happening all the same. Ellison, in fact, frequently refers to the incalculable effects of their efforts.[68]

The lessons Ellison draws from our unrecorded history give him the ammunition to refute the view that would pit "ethnicity" against "assimilation," with the latter option meaning a kind of sell-out by blacks to "white" culture or an adulteration of "white culture" by blacks. Although he prefers the word integration to assimilation,[69] integration cannot be understood as an effort to gloss over an inveterate antagonism, or even separation, between black and white culture, since neither exists. There is, says

Ellison, no such thing as "white" or "black" culture: American culture is itself the product of integration. "[T]he values of my own people are neither 'white' nor 'black'; they are American. Nor can I see how they could be anything else, since we are a people who are involved in the texture of the American experience. . . . The terms in which the question is couched [whether to adopt 'white' or 'black' values] serve to obscure the cultural fact that the dynamism of American life is as much a part of the Negro American's personality as it is of the white American's."[70] And again: "I recognize no American culture which is not the partial creation of black people. I recognize no American style in literature, in dance, in music, even in assembly-line processes, which does not bear the mark of the American Negro."[71]

African Americans are not then being asked to sign on to an American project that they had no hand in creating. And Ellison would reject the notion that the ground for a more inclusive "society" in the future is a kind of reparation for the sin of cultural exclusion in the past. Indeed, in the American melting pot, "one of the strongest forces shaping the general American culture has been what I call the Negro American idiom."[72] And again: "for all the harsh realities of the social and economic injustices visited upon them, these injustices have failed to keep Negroes clear of the cultural mainstream; Negro Americans are, in fact, one of its major tributaries."[73] Subject to general American values, "we in turn influence them—in speech, concept of liberty, justice, economic distribution, international outlook, our current attitude toward colonialism, our national image of ourselves as a nation."[74] And "most American whites are culturally part Negro American without even realizing it."[75]

Like the ever-so-talented ten drops of black pigment, folded into a colorless base to produce the paint called "Optic" White—pride of Liberty Paints, and the government's number one choice for our national monuments—America's blacks have always been essential in the American cultural mix.[76] To see them, it is necessary to penetrate the gleaming surface, trace effects back to their sources, and in general, to conduct an investigation like "Western pioneers confronting the unknown prairie."[77] If the sociologists and literary narrators of our history themselves show the grit to cut out for the Territory, refusing to be fooled by a trompe l'œil themselves, they will make the same discovery about our cultural composition as the narrator of *Invisible Man* made about that paint's chemical composition. If they eschew their opportunity, they will set back the struggle for freedom and further disenchant Americans with the democratic faith.

While Ellison by no means underestimates the many efforts to retreat from democratic pluralism then, he does insist that every such enterprise is doomed: there are no cultural Berlin Walls in America; at most one hides behind a semipermeable membrane, where all the radios are two-way, as illustrated, for instance, by a white boy shouting racial epithets at a public swimming pool while listening to Stevie Wonder on his transistor (LM, 21). In response to the concerns expressed by some today about the potential fragmentation or balkanization of our society along ethnic, religious, or racial lines, Ellison would remind us that pragmatic cooperation across all these lines, with all attendant cross-pollination, shows no signs of letting up; E pluribus unum—from many, one—still, he would say, describes us; it is our "fate."[78] Despite all efforts not to notice, the process of "Americanization" occurs apace. Responding to his own opponents, he insists, "Yet while this latest farcical phase in the drama of American social hierarchy unfolds, the irrepressible movement of American culture toward the integration of its diverse elements continues, confounding the circumlocutions of its staunchest opponents" (LM, 22).

Having been endowed by democratic equality with both the necessity and the encouragement, culturally speaking, to be both a borrower and a lender, we freely make "improvisations on the given" as we craft our identities. "It is here, on the level of culture . . . if we would but recognize it, that elements of the many available tastes, traditions, ways of life and values that make up the total culture have been ceaselessly appropriated and made their own—consciously, unconsciously, or imperialistically—by groups and individuals to whose backgrounds and traditions they are historically alien" (LM, 27). It is, in fact, through this "process of cultural appropriation (and misappropriation)" that we have *become* Americans. From the Pilgrims forward, and not excluding slaves, everyone has played "the appropriation game," counting even our most opportunistic cultural moves "among our many freedoms" (LM, 28). In this process, nothing is sacrosanct; everything is, so to speak, profaned, or turned into grist for someone else's mill, new matter to be endowed with new form by others. "In this country it is in the nature of cultural styles to become detached from their places of origin."[79] Thus, in a culture that is literally "poetic," we have from the outset "pressured the elements of the past and present into new amalgams," with jazz and the works of Mark Twain again serving Ellison as prime examples (LM, 29). Earlier, the Pilgrims famously borrowed from the American Indians. Slaves laid aside their tribal identities and became a single group, learned English and changed it, borrowed freely from the imagery and religious symbols of the Old and New Testaments, and, in turn, left their marks on language, music, imagery, and dance.[80] At Frederick Douglass High School, Ellison and his fellow students (ignoring those who said they were "expressing a desire to become white") enthusiastically applied themselves to learning European folk dances. Ellison also talks about middle-class white kids doing their best to sound like black Baptists, "appropriating the style—and profaning it, as it were—they are simply trying to attain some vague ideal of perfection."[81] That is to say, Ellison's examples strongly suggest that he thinks cultural integration is motivated not by self-hatred, but by self-love.[82]

Ellison actually endows culture with some of the same properties as Montesquieu gives commerce: it behaves like a free man, insouciantly picking up and moving wherever the climate is most congenial, leaving razed cities or newly planted ones in its wake.[83] Cultural artifacts, like books, are portable and cater to the individual tastes of the person. As Tocqueville found Shakespeare in a log cabin, and Francis Parkman French wine along a remote stretch of the Oregon Trail, and Ellison Hemingway in a barbershop,[84] so America at large shows innumerable possibilities for metamorphosis, not only in the culture at large but also, with a large nod to the little man, in the "self-creating personality" (LM, 30).[85]

In several essays, Ellison returns to the remarkable fact that Hazel Harrison, decamped at Tuskegee, was a friend of the composer Sergey Prokofiev and had a signed score from him on her classroom piano, a cultural object sitting there with as much incongruity, he says, as "a Gutenberg Bible on the altar of a black sharecropper's church"(LM, 30). But that's the point. This artifact of contemporary music, traveling with her from the inner musical circle of Berlin to Tuskegee, Alabama, representing the "unstructured possibilities of culture in this pluralistic democracy," defies the logic of "a society ordered along racial lines" and plays havoc with our conventional understanding of social order, morphing Tuskegee itself from a racially segregated rural college into an advanced outpost, albeit a largely undetected one, on the frontiers of music (LM, 30–31).

Once glimpsed, the Territory Ellison prepares us to explore is by no means entirely a cause for celebration, and Ellison points to it with the same ambivalence—the "divided" voice, the "yes and no"—with which he ends *Invisible Man*.[86] We may be inclined to avert our eyes, in other words, because it continually serves to check the celebratory tone of official recorded history. Hence, he tells Hazel Harrison's story from two competing perspectives. It simultaneously exposes race prejudice on the part of the ill meaning and defeats racialist thinking by the well meaning. If, on the one hand, she exemplifies the possibilities of self-creation here, on the other, she exemplifies the contradictions between American reality and its ideals: she left a nazifying Germany to return to an America "not yet ready" to receive her (LM, 3).[87] Properly contextualized, these contradictory elements extend our national self-knowledge and make a more fully human history possible. "Perhaps we are able to see only that which we are prepared to see," says Ellison, "and in our culture the cost of insight is an uncertainty that threatens our already unstable sense of order and requires a constant questioning of accepted assumptions" (LM, 31).

And in the culminating vignette of the essay, Ellison recounts how, a few years later, he crashed into that truth. His own sense of social order and logic was assaulted, not *literally* by a little man behind a stove, but by an equally effective quartet of big men in front of a fireplace: guardians of the furnace room of a Harlem tenement, where, at the end of an appropriately long descent, Ellison was collecting signatures for a socially progressive petition (LM, 32–33). Behind a closed door, he heard four black men vehemently arguing, and in the saltiest possible language, about which of two famous sopranos at the Met was better. He learned that custodial work was only their day job; at night and for years they had been working as extras at the opera, and in the process had become very well-informed aficionados.

According to Ellison, such stories dominate our unwritten history—our vernacular culture prepares us for "the emergence of the unexpected, whether it takes the form of the disastrous or the marvelous."[88]

With his analysis, Ellison intends to clear up the "insidious confusion" between race and culture that operates to the detriment of a full understanding of our past and of the complex processes of self-definition in America (LM, 28). Race is a sociological concept, or as we might say, a social construct, the imposition of a status based on color as if color were the sole determinant of heritage and as if heritage were itself a prison—viewed without regard to the individual human personality and the myriad responses free human beings make to their heritage, including availing themselves of opportunities to reshape it. Race is a willful surrender to a "given"; culture is created through self-assertion and, so, attests to human freedom.[89]

Ellison is himself not always wild about the results produced by, especially, the commercial appropriation and subsequent trivialization of cultural objects, and he acknowledges as well that there may be an outcry from the original owners, especially when there is no public attribution of their claim.[90] But, with a Millian optimism about the marketplace of ideas and cultural practices, he is always ready for "new possibilities" that might turn up.

In this context, Ellison recounts at length an encounter he had with a quintessentially self-made man, a jumbled but serenely self-confident "man of parts," who had transformed himself stylistically into a unified, traffic-stopping whole (LM, 22–24).[91] He was most definitely a democratic man, earning the designation not because he gave equal weight to every kind of activity, but rather because his central activity was self-expression (i.e., a variant of self-government). His blithe co-optation of America's multicultural heritage made him a sort of walking illustration of E pluribus unum. He was of motley lineage and even more motley styles. On a bright afternoon on Riverside Drive in New York City, Ellison observed him posing in a literally autofocused photo shoot in front of his car—a pied-combo of Volkswagen and Rolls-Royce—stunningly decked out in English boots and riding breeches, a dashiki and, atop his Afro, a Homburg.

Clearly, whatever identity he presumed to project, he was "a product of the melting pot and the conscious or unconscious comedy it brews," and Ellison commends him for exercising that "precious American freedom" to liberate at will anything he wanted from America's walk-in costume closet, especially objects that had solemnity associated with them in their original contexts (LM, 23). An antiestablishment attitude, made in America, let him play irreverently upon the symbolism of status, property, and authority, as it were, to suggest "new possibilities of perfection," or as we might say today, of reinventing himself, as if to say, no matter where it came from, I have made this all mine.

It could certainly be objected today that in this description of free-wheeling "aesthetic gesturing," Ellison anticipates our weakness, not our strength, that he witnessed the sort of playful posing and incongruous juxtaposition of styles—the irony—that bespeaks our postmodern inability any longer to take anything seriously. Yet, for Ellison, the young man's irony and irreverence toward tradition, his will to transgress, jerry-rig, improvise, and, in general, show off, seems specifically commendable as the antidote to the posture taken by those who can only calibrate aesthetic issues on a moral scale: "the opponents of the melting pot concept [who] utter their disavowals with an old-fashioned, camp-meeting fervor—solemnly, and with an air of divine revelation" (LM, 24). That is to say, moral indignation and hot zeal may need countermanding by the irrefutably cool.

The motley man also illustrates Ellison's insistence that in our vast cultural store, it would be wrong to declare certain things off-limits for any racial or cultural group, as not belonging to them, impeding a person's natural inclinations to appropriate as his own whatever happens to be available, with the important proviso that, as Hazel Harrison points out, making something truly your own is a matter of severe discipline and personal conquest (LM, 31).[92]

In lieu of a "usable cultural tradition," everything is improvised in the national as well as in the individual quest for identity. All are engaged in a competition to dominate our corporate experience, and all have an equal chance to affect the others. Nor is it possible to "express" or "affirm" or "celebrate" one's cultural tradition without it ceasing to be private property. In America, affirming culture means asserting it, via an act of will, against something else, and making claims on its behalf.[93] Thus, the poetic or form-giving activity in which we are engaged is also intrinsically political. The resulting "antagonistic cooperation" or dialectic is a sign that no one group "has managed to create the definitive American style."[94] Cultural interaction is not like one of those Cuban Chinese restaurants in which the two cuisines make separate but equal claims from opposite sides of the menu: here the twain always meet and fuse. Because it is achieved by "the clash of group against group," however, the cultural mix does not submerge all the sharp and spicy flavors into some bland and "tasteless soup," in which no flavor is any longer identifiable because all have been effaced.[95] The "melting" is a sort of alchemy in which distinct cultural elements are transmuted, as the sparks fly, into something new, something more than the sum of its parts. The resulting product is different from that of the past, but no less vibrant and richly multifarious for all that. If something is lost, a phoenix may also rise. "Our old familiar pasts become, in juxtaposition with elements appropriated from other backgrounds, incongruously transformed, exerting an energy (or synergy) of a different order than that generated by their separate parts—and this with incalculable results" (LM, 29).

On the significant effects of the democratic dialectic, the Protean little man makes his mark. That is to say, he is present in one or another variant of the archetype on which Ellison frequently calls in his exercises of cultural excavation. In addition to serving as the conscience of the artist, he can also show up as one of those creators of culture whose contributions have heretofore been appropriated without proper attribution or as one of those "agents of culture," without whom Ellison, for one, denies he himself could have existed as a writer: the "dedicated individuals," working beneath the scope of the recording historian's eye, who nevertheless exert a wide influence and "compel the democratic process to work."[96] For instance, "if you are surprised that there are now so many Afro-American opera and concert singers, I'd remind you that it didn't happen accidentally. God didn't reach down and say, 'All right, Leontyne Price, Shirley Verrett, Betty Allen, Jessye Norman, Simon Estes, you may now sing opera as well as your native Negro spirituals.' No, this came about because there were agents of culture among us who embraced the ideals of art and found ways of imparting them to their students, conveying that, as Americans, they too were heirs to the culture of all ages."[97]

Of his own teachers Ellison says, armed with faith in themselves and in the democratic ideal, "they were conditioning us to take advantage of such opportunities as the built-in logic of the democratic process would throw our way."[98] Further, "we were being taught to discover and exercise those elements of freedom which existed unobserved (at least by outsiders), within our state of social and political unfreedom."[99] Indeed, they did something "that those who were charged with making our ideals manifest on the political level were not doing."[100] But though occurring in private, their activities were suffused with public meaning. If the act of citizenship is essentially to assert what it means to be an American, this is not just practice for citizenship, but the thing itself. To call the broadening of one's "personal culture" by appropriating and absorbing the culture of others one of "our most precious of American freedoms" is to declare it a civic act. (LM, 28).[101] And, in this sense, "the culture of the United States has always been more 'democratic' and 'American' than the social and political institutions in which it was emerging."[102]

To the argument about the relationship between politics and culture in America that politics unites us while culture divides or differentiates us, Ellison might respond that while politics unites us in theory, our culture unites us in fact, but it does so by defying hardened social or racial categorization coming from the top down with a kind of grassroots politics. Competition and "random points of access" to cultural objects make culture resistant to the concentration of power; in turn, an ever-shifting cultural center supports diversity of opinion and ways of life.

Politics and Culture

For Ellison the "melting pot" is shorthand for principles of the Constitution in action: the "melting" occurs under a definite aegis, the principles of justice enshrined in our founding documents.

We are dedicated to principles that are conceived "linguistically," to concepts "committed to paper" or codified during the period of our revolutionary break with traditional forms of society (LM, 17).[103] These principles are "spiritual" and "abstract," that is, "ideals" or regulative norms, because rather than describing what is, they tell us what ought to be, viz., "all men are created equal." For Ellison, the essence of our founding documents is the transcendent vision, the ideal society, to which they commit us (LM, 17–19). Following his reading of Kenneth Burke, the power of ideas to set man in motion is specifically owing to their standing as moral imperatives. Morality itself is a construct of human freedom imposed on the data of nature. At the deepest level, human freedom is the ability to conquer nature (i.e., to negate a "given and amoral condition") by an "endless series of man-made or man-imagined positives" (LM, 18).[104] Self-creation is not simply prompted by democracy but is the human condition altogether, although democracy ostensibly removes the external impediments to the human activity.

Our freedom in this sense is implicated in the very way in which the nation exists—as "spirit," an entity of heart, mind, and imagination, rather than a set of boundaries or an extent of terrain. Despite the significance of American geography for Ellison, American democracy—that "abstract and futuristic concept"—does not exist so much in space as in time, or in the tension between time and timelessness. Because democracy is something "predescribed" rather than established, it is for us what Burke calls a "god-term," a sublime, quasidivine standard against which we are perforce compelled to measure ourselves (LM, 18). The regime is then constituted by a dialectic between spirit and flesh: the Word insists on being instantiated or made flesh, impelling us to close the gap between the ideal and the real.

Both culturally and politically, we are a country perpetually in the process of becoming itself. Tocqueville might attribute to the belief in the infinite malleability of men that prevails in democratic peoples Ellison's adherence to such "a fugitive ideal of perfection" as that adumbrated by the Territory.[105] Ellison might respond that it is not just that as democrats we are oriented toward the future rather than, as aristocratic societies are, the past, but also that this orientation derives specifically from our regime. We are not just driven forward by a vague faith in progress but are set on a definite trajectory by our founding documents, which give us, along with our entitlements, a sacred charge or duty. For Ellison, then, the original birth of freedom, like the "new birth of freedom" of which Lincoln spoke, fundamentally means the acceptance of responsibility for "unfinished work" (what Ellison similarly calls "unfinished details"), such as that left us by the dead on the battlefield at Gettysburg. Our principles set stumbling blocks in the way of the recalcitrant, inescapable imperatives in the way of the half-hearted and apathetic, and stirring, if fugitive, goals in the hearts of all.

Not only is there a tension between the ideal America and the real world but also between various interpretations of our principles by the individuals and culture groups comprising the society. "As a nation, we exist in the communication of our principles, and we argue over their application and interpretation as over the rights of property or the exercise and sharing of authority" (LM, 18). As a language community, bound together by conflicting opinions about justice, we give daily evidence of both the power and the misuse of *logos*. The Constitution's "sacred words" are promises, a contract for future performance, on which the nation may renege (and has frequently). We often find these words indigestible and have, in fact, cultivated a "national habit of word-eating." The melting pot, a culture of inclusion to which all belong, is mandated by our founding documents. Yet, for many, "our cultural diversity is as indigestible as the concept of democracy on which it is grounded" (LM, 19). But even at our worst, we rationalize or justify our actions by reference to the Word. And "these principles—democracy, equality, individual freedom and universal justice—now move us as articles of faith. Holding them sacred, we act (or *fail* to act) in their names" (LM, 18). As "articles of faith," our principles are as much matters of sentiment, especially hope and fear, as of calculated or self-conscious reason. "By arousing in the believer a sense of the disrelation between the ideal and the actual, between the perfect word and the errant flesh, they partake of mystery" (LM, 19).

The relation between politics and culture is in Ellison's view determined by the primacy of politics, but the primacy of politics lies in the demands and entitlements that our principles, because they are ever-present, unleash in our culture. Even our everyday actions are "enactments of ideals grounded in a vision of perfection that transcends the limitations of death and dying" (LM, 19). The ideals prod us to turn the symbols and signs we hold as our creed into policy and "social forms," and they seek to extend themselves into every aspect of our conduct and all areas of life, including aesthetics. They "interrogate us endlessly as to who and what we are; they demand that we keep the democratic faith" (LM, 18). Our founding fathers committed our principles, so to speak, to flypaper.

This circumstance gives a certain character to our politics. American citizens relate to one another through words, through the symbols and signs of our principles that demand something of us; our union is simultaneously ephemeral and Plymouth Rock–solid, determining how we act in all spheres of life, and how we praise and blame, as the narrator's grandfather in *Invisible Man* unmistakably attests.[106] Properly understood, our political conflicts are not about economic interests that adjust themselves in the halls of Congress, if not in the marketplace. The centrality Ellison assigns to the struggles of black Americans for freedom and equality in America is owing to the light those struggles shine on the true core of American politics, the "tragic knowledge" they impart, namely, that "the true subject of democracy is not material well-being, but the extension of the democratic process in the direction of perfecting itself. And that the most obvious test and clue to that perfection is the inclusion, *not* assimilation, of the black man."[107]

The factions formed as a consequence do make American politics a species of identity politics. For one thing, our conflicts threaten to take the combatants to the mat, most frequently in a "war of words" that replaces a real war, although our ideals also led us to the Civil War and to violent conflicts since then.[108] Above all, Ellison suggests, to be an American is to participate in a dialectic or contest over our identity—both proponents and opponents of the melting pot act from the same impulsions.[109] "But indeed it is in the name of these same principles that we ceaselessly contend, affirming our ideals even as we do them violence" (LM, 18). We stand united even when we are divided.

Conclusion

> "Ralph Ellison, *alone* of the world famous Afro-American novelists, never denied his American identity, his American birthright, his complex responsibilities as a participant in the analyzing of American meaning, which is the job of the intellectual, and the remaking of American life in the hopefully immortal rhythms and tunes of art, which is the job of our aesthetically creative."
>
> —Stanley Crouch, "How Long? So Long," in
> *The All-American Skin Game, or The Decoy of Race*

Ralph Ellison was a man who kept his balance in the maelstrom of racism and race-based politics, whether originating in the progressive or the retrograde parties. In his way of plumbing the depths of E pluribus unum, he also glides across the equality-difference continental divide that has confounded democratic theorists in recent years. If he promotes equality to cure invisibility, he also promotes individual responsibility to preserve freedom. He is a master at simultaneously holding two opposing thoughts in an energizing and illuminating tension—never losing sight of either and always poised to bring out the one, if his audience is only willing to entertain the other. He tells his stories from competing perspectives so that we will miss neither the "unstructured possibilities" in America nor the "unfinished details" of our work. And that contrapuntal mode repeats itself when we juxtapose his most important essays with *Invisible Man*. He also bristles when either an "individual" vision or the historical experience of one's cultural subgroup is underrated or depreciated, and he demands that both be seen in terms of their own complexities and of the unity of human experience altogether. If you forget the individuality of *his* vision by designating him as a spokesman for a group, he will remind you; if you emphasize *only* his personal independence—as if he were unique, an exception among African Americans—he will also remind you.[110]

Ellison is an unusual writer among contemporary American literary figures in his insistence on the close harmony between art and democracy; he does not deem it necessary for the artist, so to speak, on principle, to take a standpoint outside of democratic (i.e., bourgeois) society. Perhaps this is because he has a more elevated understanding than most of what democracy is. For him, as noted earlier, both art and politics at their best are "a thrust toward a human ideal." That is, in democracy, art serves politics by keeping the democratically conceived ideal of the Territory—"ever to be sought, ever to be missed, but always there"—keenly before us, making up for whatever "interruptions in our moral continuity" mar our history.[111] Ellison is also an unusual democrat among democrats. While he regards greater inclusiveness as the key to improving both American democracy and American literature, his understanding of the grounds of inclusion of other, especially African American, voices, and what he hears in them, depart from both current identity politics and current academic fashions.

As many commentators have pointed out, Ellison's overriding theme is the unity of all human experience and the stubborn intransigence of individuality; no human being—unless is he is, like the narrator of *Invisible Man* at the beginning of his journey, invisible to himself—is reducible to the conditions or the names imposed on him, whether by segregationists or by sociologists. Exhibiting a bit of the ire or "democratic touchiness" of the little man in his essay, Ellison volubly resents the imposition of, as we might say, "otherness" on African Americans. By contrast to our usual understanding of that freighted term, however, what annoys Ellison is a refusal to see African Americans as the free, self-governing selves they have always been, the agents, within the greater or lesser restrictions of their circumstances, of their own lives, rather than as passive recipients of their self-understanding at the hands of the powerful. This refusal may persist even among those who think "their hearts are in the right place" on this issue: sometimes they write "as though Negro life existed only in light of their belated regard, and they publish interpretations of the Negro experience which would not hold true for their own or for any other form of human life. . . . Prefabricated Negroes are sketched on sheets of paper and superimposed upon the Negro community; then when someone thrusts his head through the page and yells, 'Watch out there, Jack, there're people living under here,' they are shocked and indignant."[112] Hence, Ellison laments that white sociologists or black protest novelists might, from "good will and a passion for abstraction," end up inflicting a new kind of invisibility and dehumanization on African Americans generally, perpetuating the problem they would like to see resolved. By introducing us to the little man and all the implications that follow in his train, he means to work against that possibility.

Ellison once wrote that all the seven deadly sins have been imputed to black Americans except the sin of pride.[113] At times, racial pride has seemed to demand separation in order to permit the fullest possible differentiation of one group from another. Ellison's equally intense commitment to African American pride led him, however, in another direction: toward the insistence that we learn to see the sometimes invisible activities in which free men engage without seeking prior permission and the subsequent network of human interconnections that entails. By contrast to W. E. B. DuBois, Ellison argues that most African Americans have always "recognized themselves as themselves" and have, in addition, seen even their oppressors' humanity clearly.[114]

Unlike Tocqueville's account of democracy, Ellison's is written entirely from within. The very juxtaposition so fundamental to Tocqueville is no longer important. While pointing out the features of a new order erected on the debris of aristocracy, Ellison scarcely gives a second glance to what is no more and is not susceptible to the slightest nostalgia regarding it. He embraces democratic ideals fully, freely, and without reserve, and, in particular, he seeks to promote political and social equality without harboring any of the hesitations Tocqueville expresses. As a full-throated democratic partisan, Ellison sometimes expresses the sentiments and ideas that Tocqueville anticipated as likely features of democracy, yet in his own way, Ellison is not uncritical in the friendship he extends to it. Although not poised between two social orders, Ellison resists the outsider status imposed on him because of his race, denying him full participation in the civic rights that are his due as an American. It is not surprising then that when Ellison, by contrast to Tocqueville, identifies problems for American society, they come from antidemocratic, that is, antiegalitarian moves, moves that he considers to be betrayals of democratic procedures and ends.

Nor does he exhibit a Tocquevillian alarm at the possibilities of a tyranny of the majority exerted over opinion such that the free individual can, in effect, disappear; this is not to say that he does not himself worry that the individual, and especially the individual African American, may "reduce himself to a cipher," that is, do to himself what "the entire history of repression and brutalization"—slavery, reconstruction, and Jim Crow—has been unable to do.[115] In Ellison's view, modern sociological and ideological concepts have more to do with instructing African Americans in self-hatred or a feeling of inferiority than the facts themselves, so he criticizes those concepts mightily.[116] Should it ever happen that a greater political and social equality would be obtained under the auspices of such specious conceits, should the positive freedom African Americans have enjoyed be denied by the prevailing intellectual or political leadership, such that the strength to be drawn from the actual history of African Americans would be overlooked, then, Ellison worries, equality could, indeed, have the effect of effacing cultural diversity and particularity: there would be nothing deemed worth preserving from the past once outside pressure for living a certain way was removed. In the worst case, social equality could generate a desire to negate the African American past and offer up a series of excuses in one or another sort of victimization to sap individual aspiration.[117]

For the most part, however, Ellison exhibits an optimism about individuality—the presence of "original and energetic characters"—and the preservation of high aspirations in a free society that we are more likely to associate with J. S. Mill than with Tocqueville. To put it another way, for Ellison, in contrast to Tocqueville, associations are not the requisite democratic device, the artificial "aristocratic persons" needed to replace the actual individuals of importance in aristocracy. Ellison seems to locate the solution, both to the concentration of power and to the leveling or standardization of the personality, not in institutions of any kind but in the fruitful tension between the political and the cultural arenas and particularly in cultural decentralization. As he understands it, culture is both more egalitarian and inclusive and more meritocratic than politics. And unlike some of its proponents today, Ellison explicitly links cultural diversity to individual freedom: "Let man keep his many parts and you'll have no tyrant states."[118] If there are fewer little men in the shadows and more of them coming out of obscurity into the mainstream, we can still take Ellison's ideas as an exhortation to live up to both the political and literary ideal.[119]

Ellison insists that democratic equality and cultural excellence are inextricably and permanently linked. Nor does he see democracy on a course that causes it to drift gradually but inevitably downward toward the lowest common denominator. Ellison's *little* man throws down the gauntlet at the *last* man, the endpoint toward which some have seen democracy heading.[120] Leaving Nietzsche aside, in *The Road to Wigan Pier*, George Orwell's nightmarish vision of the future depicts as victorious the socialist (i.e., more perfectly democratic) ideal—a baneful, even poisonous, amalgam of equality and technology, an ideal that, in a variation on the little man theme, urges us to make the world safe for "little *fat* men."[121] Orwell also mocks an imaginary British progressive who cheerily wonders, "Why must we level *down*, why not level *up*?"[122] For his part, Ellison seems to take that position more seriously. Invoking his namesake Ralph Waldo Emerson and also Walt Whitman, Ellison speaks of the widely dispersed "cultivated democratic sensibility" of self-governing, responsible, educated men of conscience that was the original promise of democracy, an ideal important in understanding the "cultural necessity" of postulating the existence of the little man and of taking note of him where he actually exists (LM, 7).

Here Ellison touches on our own intense interest in the "undefined aspects of American experience": like the white teenagers' enthusiasm for "soul," we all seek "the homeness of home," embarking on enthusiastic quests for whatever looks authentic or lies at the "roots" of America, insulated from the corporate makeover. And, driven by democratic impulsions, we are already "suspicious of easy assumptions of superiority based on appearance," a fact perhaps accounting for our own fascination, maybe even obsession, with invisible men, hence with our own hunt for the little man, whether in the form of unsung heroes, quirky buffs, or just plain extravagantly talented people—in any case, some "true American original" who fits into his region and conveys something of both the vastness of the country and the prodigal individuality within it. We have gone on the road with Charles Kuralt, still sit happily in films like *Good Will Hunting* or *Finding Forester*, and stand in wonder at the fact that, behind the mild and bland exterior of a file clerk at the Veterans' Administration in Cleveland, Ohio, is a comic book artist extraordinaire, one Harvey Pekar, whose life and times are the subject of the film *American Splendor*. Ellison would see our fascination with unearthing the invisible man as an act of democratic faith and would only ask us to keep the little man's nose for excellence as we sleuth. As an artist and a critic he always did.

Throughout his life, Ellison evinces the ambition not simply to participate in but to lead American letters, raising artistic standards by exemplifying them. When he died without completing his long-awaited second novel posthumously published as *Juneteenth*, the novelist Charles Johnson offered a partial explanation of why that novel was taking so long: Ellison wanted "a book that would be an epic dialogue with the finest writers, going back to Homer and Virgil and Shakespeare and others. The books that are on the top shelf of our library, that's where Ellison wanted this multi-volume work to be placed."[123] At the end of "The Little Man," striking a hopeful and prophetic note, Ellison leaves a further reminder to those who might wish to imitate him: "Where there's a melting pot there's smoke, and where there's smoke it is not simply optimistic to expect fire, it's imperative to watch for the phoenix's vernacular, but transcendent, rising" (LM, 38).

Notes

1. Alexis de Tocqueville, *Democracy in America*, trans. Harvey C. Mansfield and Delba Winthrop (Chicago: University of Chicago Press, 2000), II.i.1, 403; hereafter cited as *DA*.

2. Tocqueville, *DA*, II.i.10, 434; see also the transcript of "Ralph Ellison's Legacy—July 21, 1999," *Online NewsHour*, available at pbs.org/newshour/bb/entertainment/jan-june99/Ellison_6-21.html, 5.

3. Tocqueville, *DA*, II.i.8, 427; II.i.17, 458–63.

4. Ralph Ellison, "The Little Man at Chehaw Station: The American Artist and His Audience," in *Going to the Territory* (New York: Vintage, 1986), 3–38; hereafter cited in as LM.

5. An earlier version of this paper was delivered at the 2003 American Political Science Association Meetings in Philadelphia. I wish to express my profound thanks to Patrick Deneen, Wilson Carey McWilliams, and Flagg Taylor. For exceptional commentary on *Invisible Man*, see Lucas E. Morel, ed., *Ralph Ellison and the Raft of Hope: A Political Companion to Invisible Man* (Lexington: University of Kentucky Press, 2004).

6. Ralph Ellison, "Brave Words for a Startling Occasion" and "Twentieth-Century Fiction and the Black Mask of Humanity," in *The Collected Essays of Ralph Ellison*, ed. John F. Callahan (New York: Modern Library, 1995), 151 and 84; hereafter cited as ML.

7. Ralph Ellison, "Society, Morality and the Novel," ML, 697–98, 701–2, 704.

8. Ralph Ellison, "Going to the Territory," ML, 611; Ralph Ellison, *Invisible Man*, 2nd ed. (New York: Vintage, 1995), 377, 440–41; Ellison, LM, 14.

9. Ellison, "Society, Morality and the Novel," ML, 704.

10. Ellison, "Going to the Territory," ML, 600–603.

11. Tocqueville, *DA*, II.i.9, 431–32; II.i.11, 439–41; II.i.13, 446–47.

12. Tocqueville, *DA*, II.i.13, 446–49; Ellison, "Going to the Territory," ML, 608–9.

13. Ellison, "Going to the Territory," ML, 609.

14. William Shakespeare, *The Tragical History of Hamlet, Prince of Denmark*, ed. A. R. Braunmuller, Pelican Shakespeare ed. (New York: Penguin Books, 2001), III.ii.358–65.

15. Ellison, *Invisible Man*, 6–7, 13.

16. Ellison, *Invisible Man*, 493, 498–99, 559, 576; Ralph Ellison, "The Art of Fiction: An Interview," ML, 223.

17. Ellison, *Invisible Man*, 498–99.

18. Ralph Ellison, "A Special Message to Subscribers," ML, 351 (emphasis added).

19. Ralph Ellison, "Introduction to *Invisible Man*," ML, 481.

20. Ellison, "Introduction to *Invisible Man*," ML, 481.

21. Ellison, "Introduction to *Invisible Man*," ML, 481.

22. Ellison, "Introduction to *Invisible Man*," ML, 481–82.

23. Ellison, "Introduction to *Invisible Man*," ML, 484.

24. Ellison, "Introduction to *Invisible Man*," ML, 484.

25. Ellison, "Introduction to *Invisible Man*," ML, 484; Ellison, "Society, Morality and the Novel," ML, 696–97.

26. Ellison, "Going to the Territory," ML, 598–99; Ralph Ellison, "On Initiation Rites and Power," ML, 535; Ralph Ellison, "Working Notes for *Invisible Man*," ML, 344; Ellison, *Invisible Man*, 581.

27. Ellison, *Invisible Man*, 49–69; Ellison, "Working Notes for *Invisible Man*," ML, 344.

28. Ellison, "Art of Fiction," ML, 217.

29. Ellison, "Introduction to *Invisible Man*," ML, 482; Ellison, "Society, Morality and the Novel," ML, 714. Tocqueville also says that poetry "is the search for and depiction of the ideal." As to whether democratic people have natural sources of poetry, he says, "Democracy, which closes the past to poetry, opens the future to it. . . . Democratic nations perceive more clearly than all others their own shape, and that great shape lends itself marvelously to the depiction of the ideal." See Tocqueville, *DA*, II.i.17, 458, 460–61.

30. Ellison, "Introduction to *Invisible Man*," ML, 482–83.

31. Ellison, "Going to the Territory," ML, 596–97.

32. To a large extent the same illusions also dominate the narrator in *Invisible Man*, albeit his journey ends not in death but in an ironic "blues-toned laughter." See Ellison, "Introduction to *Invisible Man*," ML, 478, 481.

33. Ellison, "On Initiation Rites and Power," ML, 521–23, 525–27; Ellison, "Going to the Territory," ML, 598–99; Ellison, "Society, Morality and the Novel," ML, 696–97.

34. Ellison, "Introduction to *Invisible Man*," ML, 484.

35. Ellison, "Introduction to *Invisible Man*," ML, 482.

36. Ellison, "Introduction to *Invisible Man*," ML, 483.

37. Ellison, "Introduction to *Invisible Man*," ML, 483.

38. Ralph Ellison, "The World and the Jug," ML, 162.

39. Ralph Ellison, "The World and the Jug," ML, 176.

40. Ellison, "The World and the Jug," ML, 163. "[Wright] is no mere product of his socio-political predicament. He is a product of the interaction between his racial predicament, his individual will, and the broader American cultural freedom in which he finds his ambiguous existence. Thus, he, too, in a limited way, is his own creation" (160). See also pp. 163–64, 177, 185. See Ellison, "Introduction to *Invisible Man*," ML, 481; Ralph Ellison, "That Same Pain," ML, 74–75.

41. Ellison, "The World and the Jug," ML, 167; Ellison, "On Initiation Rites and Power," ML, 540–41; Ralph Ellison, "Indivisible Man," ML, 383–86; Ralph Ellison, "Remembering Richard Wright," ML, 659–75.

42. Ellison, "Art of Fiction," ML, 223–24; Ellison, "Society, Morality, and the Novel," ML, 702, 704, 714.

43. Ellison, "Society, Morality and the Novel," ML, 702.

44. Ellison, "Art of Fiction," ML, 224.

45. Ellison, *Invisible Man*, 194–95, 295.

46. Ralph Ellison, "What America Would Be Like without Blacks," ML, 578–79.

47. For a good survey of current arguments, see Tamar Jacoby, ed., *Reinventing the Melting Pot: The New Immigrants and What It Means to Be American* (New York: Basic Books, 2004).

48. See, e.g., Stanley Crouch, "Goose-Loose Blues for the Melting Pot," in Jacoby, *Reinventing the Melting Pot*, especially 273–75.

49. Ralph Ellison, "Haverford Statement," ML, 429.

50. Ellison, "Society, Morality and the Novel," ML, 703.

51. Ellison puts the African American experience with integration in terms of an overall pattern that includes all former and later immigrants; conversely, for the argument that recent immigrant experiences conform to the pattern of recent African American politics, see Peter Skerry, "'This Was Our Riot, Too': The Political Assimilation of Today's Immigrants," in Jacoby, *Reinventing the Melting Pot*, especially 227–32.

52. See Jacoby, *Reinventing the Melting Pot*, 51, 236–37, 309; Ellison, "What America Would Be Like without Blacks," ML, 580.

53. See Jacoby, *Reinventing the Melting Pot*, 48–49, 308–9.

54. Robert Penn Warren, *Who Speaks for the Negro?* (New York: Random House, 1965), 345–46.

55. Ellison, "What America Would Be Like without Blacks," 580.

56. Ellison, "What America Would Be Like without Blacks," ML, 580. There is perhaps some structural similarity between Booker T. Washington's and Ellison's arguments here in that each defends integration in a nonpolitical area of American society both for its value in itself and for its potential to further full political integration for African Americans. Unlike Washington, however, Ellison does not make a demand for economic integration in the hopes of storming the bastion of political and social integration; rather, he insists on recognition of the *fact* of cultural integration in order to take away the last arguments of opponents of full political and social participation for blacks as being based on a false premise. Yet, as Washington was forced to confront the fact that irrational passions can defeat the hopes placed in the calculus of economic self-interest, so Ellison addresses the various passions that underlie our resistance to our own standards.

57. Tocqueville, *DA*, II.ii.2, 482–84.

58. Tocqueville, *DA*, II.i.9, 432; Ellison, "Haverford Statement," ML, 431. See also Tocqueville, *DA*, II.i.17, 461.

59. Tocqueville, *DA*, II.ii.2, 483.

60. Tocqueville, *DA*, II.ii.2, 484.

61. Tocqueville, *DA*, II.ii.13, 513.

62. Tocqueville, *DA*, II.ii.13, 511–14.

63. Tocqueville, *DA*, II.iii.13, 577–78; Tocqueville may have had something less harmful in mind, but see also I.i.10, 319–20, and I.i.10, 326–48.

64. Ellison, "Haverford Statement," ML, 432.

65. The narrator excites as much vehement opposition from the Brotherhood when he talks about "personal responsibility" as he did earlier at the town leaders' "smoker," when he talked about "social equality." See Ellison, *Invisible Man*, 31, 405, 459, 463–64, 477, 575. See also Ellison, "Art of Fiction," ML, 218–21; Ralph Ellison, "If the Twain Shall Meet," ML, 575; Ellison, "On Initiation Rites and Power," ML, 528; Tocqueville, *DA*, I.i.3, 52.

66. Ellison, "Haverford Statement," ML, 431.

67. Ellison, "Haverford Statement," ML, 431.

68. Ellison, "Going to the Territory," ML, 600–612; Ralph Ellison, "Portrait of Inman Page: A Dedication Speech," ML, 585–90.

69. Ellison, "What America Would Be Like without Blacks," ML, 582.

70. Ralph Ellison, "Some Questions and Some Answers," ML, 299.

71. Ellison, "Indivisible Man," ML, 356.
72. Ellison, "Haverford Statement," ML, 430.
73. Ellison, "What America Would Be Like without Blacks," ML, 580.
74. Ellison, "Some Questions and Some Answers," ML, 300.
75. Ellison, "What America Would Be Like without Blacks," ML, 580; Ellison, "Portrait of Inman Page," ML, 588.
76. Ellison, *Invisible Man*, 200–202.
77. Ellison, "What America Would Be Like without Blacks," ML, 580.
78. Ellison, *Invisible Man*, 577.
79. Ellison, "Going to the Territory," ML, 611; Ralph Ellison, "Homage to Duke Ellington on His Birthday," ML, 681.
80. Ellison, "Going to the Territory," ML, 610.
81. Ellison, "Going to the Territory," ML, 605, 611.
82. Warren, *Who Speaks?* 329; Ralph Ellison, "*An American Dilemma*: A Review," ML, 328–40.
83. Montesquieu, *The Spirit of the Laws*, ed. and trans. Anne M. Cohler, Basia Carolyn Miller, and Harold Samuel Stone (Cambridge, U.K.: Cambridge University Press, 1989), IV.21.5.
84. Ellison, "Going to the Territory," ML, 603; Ellison, LM, 10.
85. Ellison, "The World and the Jug," ML, 164; Ellison, "On Initiation Rites and Power," ML, 531.
86. Ellison, *Invisible Man*, 579–80.
87. Ellison, "Remembering Richard Wright," ML, 661; Ralph Ellison, "Alain Locke," ML, 446.
88. Ellison, "Going to the Territory," ML, 612.
89. Ellison, "On Initiation Rites and Power," ML, 523; Ellison, "Some Questions and Some Answers," ML, 300; Ellison, "The World and the Jug," ML, 177; Ellison, "If the Twain Shall Meet," ML, 574.
90. Warren, *Who Speaks?* 333; Ellison, "Haverford Statement," ML, 431. Ellison also suggests that all debts can be squared by giving credit where credit is due: once recognized, the creators in the underground want to be judged, not as representatives of their race or ethnicity, but by "the excellence of their art." See Ellison, "Going to the Territory," ML, 611.
91. See also Ellison, *Invisible Man*, 498.
92. Ellison, "Going to the Territory," 604–8.
93. Ellison, "The World and the Jug," ML, 178; Ellison, "Some Questions and Some Answers," ML, 300; Ellison, "Going to the Territory," ML, 595.
94. Ellison, "Going to the Territory," ML, 610, 612.
95. Jacoby, *Reinventing the Melting Pot*, 51.
96. Ellison, "Going to the Territory," ML, 610.
97. Ellison, "Going to the Territory," ML, 609–10.
98. Ellison, "Going to the Territory," ML, 609.
99. Ellison, "Going to the Territory," ML, 605; Ralph Ellison, "An Extravagance of Laughter," ML, 622–23, 625; Ralph Ellison, "What These Children Are Like," ML, 545–47.
100. Ellison, "Going to the Territory," ML, 610.
101. Ellison, "Going to the Territory," ML, 605.
102. Ellison, "Going to the Territory," ML, 610.

103. Unlike Tocqueville, Ellison conceives of the American Revolution as a social, as well as a political, revolution, a rejection *tout court* of the old world. See Tocqueville, *DA*, II.ii.1, 481. See also Ellison, "Going to the Territory," ML, 597.

104. Followed through to its conclusion, the existential cast of Burke's remarks will not, of course, fit with the rendering of Nature in our "great documents of state." Ellison's use of Burke is, however, meant for a primarily political purpose, to elaborate the duties that the founders implied along with our rights.

105. Tocqueville, *DA*, II.i.8, 427; II.i.17, 460.

106. Ellison, *Invisible Man*, 574–76.

107. Ellison, "What America Would Be Like without Blacks," ML, 582. For the implications for American novelists, see Ellison, "Brave Words for a Startling Occasion," ML, 152–53; Ellison, "Twentieth-Century Fiction," ML, 86–90, 98–99; Ellison, "Society, Morality and the Novel," ML, 702; Ellison, "Art of Fiction," ML, 223–24.

108. Ellison, "Portrait of Inman Page," ML, 588; Ellison, "Going to the Territory," ML, 595.

109. Ellison, "Twentieth-Century Fiction," ML, 83.

110. Warren, *Who Speaks?* 336ff.; Ellison, "The World and the Jug," ML, 172–76.

111. Ellison, "Society, Morality and the Novel," ML, 703–4.

112. Ellison, "The World and the Jug," ML, 170.

113. Ellison, "An Extravagance of Laughter," ML, 638.

114. Ellison, "The World and the Jug," ML, 171, 173; Ellison, *Invisible Man*, 574.

115. Warren, *Who Speaks?* 328–29.

116. Warren, *Who Speaks?* 350.

117. Warren, *Who Speaks?* 328; Ralph Ellison, "A Stern Discipline," ML, 740.

118. Ellison, "Indivisible Man," ML, 382–83; Ellison, *Invisible Man*, 577.

119. Warren, *Who Speaks?* 334.

120. See Robert Penn Warren, *Democracy and Poetry: The 1974 Jefferson Lecture in the Humanities* (Cambridge, MA: Harvard University Press, 1975).

121. George Orwell, *The Road to Wigan Pier* (New York: Harcourt Brace Jovanovich/Harvest, 1958), 193 (emphasis added).

122. Orwell, *Wigan Pier*, 162.

123. Ralph Ellison, *Juneteenth: A Novel*, ed. John F. Callahan (New York: Random House, 1999); *Online NewsHour*, "Ralph Ellison's Legacy," 7. Ellison writes in his essay "Indivisible Man," ML, 394–95, "Craft to me is an aspect of morality. I don't mean that I've mastered it. . . . Every time I walk into my study or into another room of books down the hall I see the great masters. *They're* the ones I have to measure myself against, not because I want to but because that's what is stuck up there. Those are the standards. *I* didn't create them; they were there. Lord knows it would be much easier if you didn't have to work out of a knowledge of what had gone before."

7

Go Tell It on the Mountain

James Baldwin and the Politics of Faith

Wilson Carey McWilliams

James Baldwin was a constant American despite all his years of expatriation, a native son whose subjects and audiences were primarily American, even when (as in *Giovanni's Room*) he set his story overseas. He was a fervent critic of the American regime precisely because he was an anguished lover, and nothing is clearer in Baldwin's work than the depth of his concern for American political life and culture.

Baldwin's direct involvement in political affairs, however, was relatively slight, skeptical, and infrequent, confined almost entirely to the edge of movements, parties, and events.[1] He practiced a version of what Neal Riemer has called "prophetic politics";[2] he spoke of "political freedom in spiritual terms," Baldwin said, out of a conviction that the "spiritual state" of a nation ultimately controls its institutions and laws.[3] Politics, so understood, is starkly at odds with the prevailing doctrine of contemporary liberalism: Baldwin's politics had "foundations"; except in the narrowest legal sense, religious neutrality is impossible; and most of what passes for politics is only so many shadows on the wall of the Cave.[4]

In Baldwin's view, social categories and institutions—all the distinctions which do and must mean so much in practice—are ultimately incomplete definitions of our identities, at best useful and at worst distortions that obscure or diminish our humanity.[5] Race, obviously, was Baldwin's primary example, but almost as frequently he pointed to gender; similarly, he regarded all ideologies as overly abstract efforts to simplify human complexity.[6] At the same time, conventions are inevitable: the Cave is real, its partial truths and illusions have power, and it is extremely difficult, even "virtually impossible," to step beyond the terms and assumptions of one's society and time. Still, nature tests convention, and society itself is not free from ambivalence:

> The paradox of education is precisely this: that as one begins to become conscious, one begins to examine the society in which [one] is being educated.

> The purpose of education, finally, is to create in a person the ability . . . to ask questions of the universe and then learn to live with those questions. . . . But no society is really anxious to have that kind of person around. What societies . . . want is a citizenry that will simply obey rules.[7]

In American practice, one cannot exist without being "black" or "white," but one cannot inwardly be either without ceasing to exist: a self-definition in terms of race (or in terms of sexual orientation) abridges or rejects one's humanity.[8] Practical politics matters, but—engrossed with the issues as they appear in the half-light of convention—neither the "protest novel" nor protest politics is "profound and tough" enough to get to the human heart of things.[9] The effectual truth is not the *whole* truth, and it is the whole truth that justice demands.[10]

Politics depends on people who excel at the cave art of getting results, but it also needs voices to articulate the human universals, not only our dependence and mortality, but also the recognition of the self in the other (and the other in the self), the fact of commonality, the self as a part of a whole.[11] In one sense Baldwin argued for the proposition—the too-often garbled cornerstone of multiculturalism—that the human is naturally sovereign over the cultural, the theoretical over the experiential.[12] Love, Baldwin's Grail, he saw as the dynamic of a journey that points to the love of all, that "opens the door to that which is greater than oneself" and, ultimately, even greater than humanity itself.[13]

At the same time, Baldwin recognized—in part from first-hand experience—that the impulse to love is dangerous, that it is all too easy to be deceived by one's hopes and illusions, and that human love at its best involves the certainty of loss.[14] Moreover, Baldwin knew that it is only in rare moments of the soul that human beings catch a glimpse of his vision and that our yearning for the extraordinary can endanger the commonplace. Nevertheless, he was persuaded that human fraternity, ultimately beyond human realization, always draws us. Even in his most pessimistic moments, Baldwin emphasized the need to keep the faith, seeking to find words for the too-often voiceless promptings of the spirit.[15] Early on, Baldwin wrote that he left the pulpit to preach the gospel: he became, in other words, an evangelist of the pen.[16]

Yet, while his work had echoes of evangelical politics—Lawrie Balfour calls him "preoccupied with personal transformation"—writing imposes its own discipline on the evangelical mantra, "one soul at a time."[17] Potentially accessible to all literate persons, writing addresses an audience far less specific, less known, and more varied in the states and qualities of soul of which it is composed than that reached by an evangelist's voice or person. And the writer who would speak of high things, consequently, is even more strongly impelled to speak in parables, embedding extraordinary teaching in conventional stories for those "who have ears to hear."[18]

Balfour shrewdly titled her study of Baldwin *The Evidence of Things Not Said*, a paraphrase of the definition of faith in Hebrews 11:1—"the evidence of things not seen"—which itself leaves unsaid the first part of that text, "the assurance [or substance] of things hoped for." The African American heritage, as Baldwin understood it, is premised on an assurance offered by the unseen and unsaid, the word beyond words.[19] *Go Tell It on the Mountain* includes any number of autobiographical elements; it describes a dimension of African American experience with unique power.[20] But it is much more than a record of a time or culture. In one sense a parable about racial identity, the book is also a teaching about human identity, and Baldwin devotes his eloquence and craft to leading his readers beyond the categories of practice, and the evidence of eyes and words, toward the unseen city.[21]

★ ★ ★ ★ ★

Go Tell It on the Mountain describes a day in the life of a Harlem family in 1935, John Grimes' fourteenth birthday, a traditional marker of entry into manhood. And from the beginning, Baldwin signals his own artistry.

The novel is divided into three parts, "The Seventh Day," "The Prayers of the Saints," and "The Threshing Floor," each broadly sermonic and furnished with a scriptural text.[22]

The first, "The Seventh Day," is prefaced by a reference to the last chapter of the last book of the Christian scriptures, as if to mirror that testament's promise that the "last shall be first," a reversal of conventional order and perception. The citation itself, to Revelation 22:17, invites "him that heareth" to join the "Spirit and bride" in yearning for Christ's coming, also promising the "water of life" to "him that is athirst." The following verse in the text (22:18), however, warns against adding to or subtracting from the words of the book, "For I testify unto every man that heareth the words of the prophecy of this book." Baldwin's citation indicates that the effectiveness of a teaching depends on hearers who are able and disposed to discern and receive it; emphasizing that a written doctrine depends on care in writing and attention in reading, Baldwin's subtext is a guide and caution when approaching his own book.

"The Seventh Day" introduces the principal characters in *Go Tell It on the Mountain*, the Grimes family and their church, the storefront Temple of the Fire Baptized. Like "The Threshing Floor," "The Seventh Day" is distinctively John's story, and the major characters in John's version of the family drama—himself; his mother, Elizabeth; and his stepfather, Gabriel—evoke the account of the birth of John the Baptist in the first chapter of Luke.[23] There, the Angel Gabriel silences Zacharias, Elizabeth's husband, for his failure to believe in her miraculous conception of John. Baldwin's Gabriel, however, in part plays the role of Zacharias, unable to see that his stepson,

John, is the child of his spirit because he is fixated on Royal, the child of his body. But unlike Zacharias, Gabriel Grimes is decidedly not silent.

For that matter, John, when we meet him, is no prophet in the wilderness. He knows that his power lies in words, but he intends to use his talent as a writer to *resist* God, to escape the life of "his father and his father's fathers," the poverty and humiliation he associates with the "way of the cross" (*GTM*, 14–15, 35).[24] At the very least, he yearns for some way around "God's injustice," the choice between righteousness and the things of the world (*GTM*, 44). Of course, John has reason to be angry at the oppressiveness of his circumstances, but his rebellion—rejecting the African American heritage as little more than a record of shame—mirrors and validates the prevailing doctrine of white society.

Liberalism, for all its varieties, is united by the conviction that liberty is humanity's defining characteristic and excellence, a good to be preserved and enhanced to the greatest possible extent, even—as F. W. J. Schelling called it—"the one and all of philosophy."[25] Liberty is linked to dominion: political society, which sets limits to the will of individuals, is justified when it adds to our safety and our mastery over nature, pushing back the boundaries of that great constraint, making us, in way one or another, freer than we were before. While the liberal tradition regards self-preservation as an instinctive goal, its strong voice also advises us that without our fundamental liberties, nothing is secure, so that we must defend our rights even at the risk of life, because it is unendurable to be less than free. Generations of young Americans learned the lesson from Patrick Henry:

> Is life so dear or peace so sweet as to be purchased at the price of chains and slavery? Forbid it Almighty God. I know not what course others may take, but as for me, give me liberty or give me death.[26]

The great majority of African Americans trace their descent to ancestors who made the other choice, and in these terms, the verdict of liberalism is that the African American past is founded on a preference for life that is at best understandable but low, and at worst, a mark of dishonor.[27]

In *Go Tell It on the Mountain*, a large part of Baldwin's concern is the effort to help African Americans reclaim their past, rather than feel obliged to reinvent it, to set a truer value on the teachings and human qualities that liberalism deprecates.[28] At the same time, in speaking *of* African Americans, Baldwin is talking, through John, *to* all Americans: African Americans found support and inspiration in the texts and teachings of biblical religion, and Baldwin's broader aim is to rearticulate that second voice of American culture, and in the process, to rededicate all of us to the proposition that all human beings are created equal.[29]

As Baldwin introduces it in "The Seventh Day," the Grimes family's church teaches a gospel that is unyielding and harsh: two teenagers, Ella

Mae and Elisha, the friend of John's heart, humiliatingly are called to the front of the church and warned against sin, even though—Elisha says—"we didn't have nothing on our minds at all," because the pastor caught the scent of temptation to come (*GTM*, 65). "Ain't no such thing as a big fault or a little fault," Sister McCandless explains. "Satan get his foot in the door, he ain't going to rest till he's in the room. You is in the world or you ain't—ain't no halfway with God" (*GTM*, 70). Yet, Baldwin lets his readers see that this stern teaching has its reasons. Initially, he was furious at his pastor uncle, Elisha says, but "the Lord made me see that he was right" (*GTM*, 65). In practice, African American churches were necessarily the champions of the community in its efforts to resist the demoralizations of racism. Facing a world in which the "temptations of the street" were the more alluring when set against the certainty of secular indignity and frustration, churches insisted on moral discipline in the name of immortal destiny.[30] "People say it's hard," Elisha tells John, "but . . . it ain't as hard as living in this wicked world and all the sadness of the world where there ain't no pleasure nohow, and then dying and going to Hell" (*GTM*, 64).

The church's doctrinal militancy, moreover, is amplified by the ways in which the practice of racism is entangled with theoretical tenets of American secularity. In general, liberalism and modernity have been inclined to define human nature and identity in terms of the body, discounting if not rejecting the soul.[31] This view, in turn, encourages us to see social or political reality in terms of appearances, the motion and collision of bodies; thus, it adds *intellectual* authority to the human disposition to group or categorize by eye and, hence, by race. More subtly, these doctrines urge us to be guided by the evidence of our senses and, hence, by experience, a persuasion that still might lead us to regard blacks—disproportionately poor, ill educated, and apt to fall afoul of the law—as somehow inferior. In Shakespeare's Venice, when Brabantio argues that it is against "all rules of nature" for Desdemona to love Othello, "in spite . . . of years, of country, credit, everything," the Doge dismisses the evidence of "these thin habits and poor likelihoods of modern seeming."[32] In modern America, by contrast, it is modernity that occupies the position of authority, and African American churches have reason to "Put on the whole armor of God" for their combat against the "rulers of this present darkness."[33]

Battle and war, however, are simplifiers that call for slogans rather than subtleties. The logic of combat includes a tendency to make oneself the mirror image of one's enemy, a negation rather than an affirmation. Virtually all American churches, for example, know the danger that African American churches encounter with special force: in resisting the doctrine that their members are nothing but bodies with desires, the church becomes preoccupied with the sins of the flesh, neglecting those of the spirit. For African Americans, this includes a temptation to reverse racism—especially potent because, as a general rule of practice, whites *are* the enemy.[34] Gabriel had taught John "that all white people were wicked," with no shortage of historical evidence to support that view, and John—envying whites their advantages and reflecting on the inevitable exclusions of racism—"knew that one day he could hate them if God did not change his heart" (*GTM*, 38–39). And more subtly, the same inclination is evident in Gabriel's preoccupation with his "royal line," the child of his blood as opposed to the child of his spirit.[35]

Baldwin had good reason to expect that the great majority of his readers would agree with—and even anticipate—the foregoing critique of the church. For Baldwin himself, however, the more fundamental criticism was one that most of his readers would not share: in its battle with American society, the church's principal weapon is words, but words used as instruments distort the Word, the "power which outlasts kingdoms," reducing Christ to culture and the quest for truth to ideology.[36]

Religion's higher wisdom, as Baldwin understood it, runs counter to the modern doctrine that the art and science of politics consists of mastering nature and her seasons (as in Bill Clinton's inaugural promise to "force the spring"). It teaches, by contrast, that political action depends on discerning, or even ransoming, the times.[37]

"The Prayers of the Saints" is introduced by a citation from Revelation, in which those "that were slain for the word of God" ask for belated justice: "And they cried with a loud voice, saying, How long, O Lord, holy and true, dost thou not judge and avenge our blood on them that dwell on the earth?" In the succeeding verse, they are told to "rest yet for a little season," warned that their "fellow servants and brethren" must also endure martyrdom but robed in glory and assured of ultimate vindication.[38]

That promise, Baldwin will remind his readers, has found supporting testimony in African American experience. In *Go Tell It on the Mountain*, Florence recalls her mother's memories of slavery:[39]

> For it had been the will of God that they should hear, and pass thereafter, one to another, the story of the Hebrew children who had been held in bondage in the land of Egypt, and how the Lord had heard their groaning, and how His heart was moved; and how he bid them wait but a little season till he should send deliverance. . . . She had only to endure and trust in God. She knew that the big house, the house of pride where the white folks lived, would come down: it was written in the Word of God. They, who walked so proudly now, had not fashioned for themselves or their children so sure a foundation as was hers. They walked on the edge of a steep place and their eyes were sightless . . . and one day the time to forsake evil and do good would be finished, and then only the whirlwind . . . awaited those people who had forgotten God. . . . The word was fulfilled one morning, before she was awake. . . . There was a great running and shouting . . . everywhere outside, and as she opened her eyes to the light of that day, so bright, she said, and cold, she was certain that the judgment trumpet had sounded. . . . [I]n rushed Bathsheba and . . . shouted, "Rise up, rise up, Sister Rachel and see

> the Lord's deliverance. He's brought us out of Egypt just like He promised, and we's free at last!" (*GTM*, 81–84)

That oppression had reasserted itself in new forms only emphasized the lesson. Slave-owning society, false to nature and to humanity, rested on illusion and was doomed to fall by its own error and lie, and as with slavery, so with its successors: one need only remain in readiness, alert but waiting for the time.

★ ★ ★ ★ ★

In fact, "The Prayers of the Saints" is prefaced by a sign, the presence in church of John's Aunt Florence for "John knew that it was the hand of the Lord that had led her to this place, and his heart grew cold. The Lord was riding on the wind tonight" (*GTM*, 72).

Baldwin knew, of course, that most of his readers would confront the temple as outsiders, and he is being characteristically artful: Florence, whose reflections open "The Prayers of the Saints," is the bridge between us and the inner experiences of the faithful.[40]

Her name—one of the few nonbiblical names in John's family—evidently evokes Renaissance humanism and the rejection of "cities that have never been seen," and Florence herself has qualities that secular and modern readers can be expected to like and admire.[41] She is tough, savvy, irreverent about Gabriel's pieties and pretensions, and fiercely independent—self-sufficiency is *her* pretension—and it probably helps white readers identify with her that she is a bit of a racist, despising "common niggers" out of her own ambition and pride (*GTM*, 77, 104). But Florence has cancer and doctors and folk cures have failed her: she is brought to the altar by her recognition that "death's got a warrant out for you" (*GTM*, 110). Just as the fear of death is liberalism's civilizing passion, the fact of death—that inevitable limit to human mastery and freedom—makes even very secular liberals more open to faith.[42]

Gabriel, John's stepfather, has had a more orthodox experience of dependence and rebirth. While his mother lay dying, holding on to life in hope of seeing his birth in Christ, Gabriel—something of a roisterer—had fled into the arms of a harlot. Returning home the next morning, Gabriel encountered a moment of dreadful silence—"the very birds had ceased to sing, and no dogs barked, and no rooster crowed for day" (*GTM*, 117)—a stillness that emphasized his isolation, his vulnerability, and his exposure to the judgment of God.

But Gabriel's surrender to God, which he dates from that day, defines itself as an alliance with God's power:

> Yes, he wanted power—he wanted to know himself to be the Lord's anointed. . . . He wanted to be master, to speak with that authority which could only come from God. (*GTM*, 113)[43]

Gabriel's motto or text, we are told, is "set thine house in order" (2 Kings 20:1), God's command to Hezekiah, given in view of that king's impending death.[44] But Hezekiah's righteous obedience to God wins him an *extended* span, beyond the limits of nature: for Gabriel, the ordered house is shorthand for expanded dominion.

And Gabriel does see himself as a king: he is caught up by the vision of establishing a "royal line" composed of the children of his body (*GTM*, 178), a dream that raises many questions about his faith. Angered, Gabriel speaks of John as the "son of the bondwoman" and not the "rightful heir," adopting Sarah's tone of complaint against Hagar (Genesis 21:10–13).[45] However, in Galatians, Paul argues that the *true* "child of the bondwoman" is one born "after the flesh"; the child of the free woman is one born "by the promise" (Galatians 4:23).[46] Identifying the "rightful heir" with his bloodline, Gabriel reverses Paul's teaching: he sees the body but is blind to the spirit.[47]

In a similar reversal, confronted by God in and through *silence*, Gabriel seeks to fill the world with *words*: "I opened my mouth to the Lord that day and Hell won't make me change my mind" (*GTM*, 119). By the time of the story in *Go Tell It on the Mountain*, Gabriel only rarely occupies the pulpit: he is "a kind of fill-in speaker, a holy handyman." But in his younger days, in the South, he had a "mighty reputation," and in Gabriel's own mind, preaching is his calling, virtually equivalent to "his life as a man" (*GTM*, 58–59, 119).

It is appropriate, then, that Gabriel's prayer includes two sermons, complete with texts. In the first, he brings a sinner to the mercy seat; in the second, his failure to draw the sensual Esther to the altar anticipates his own surrender to his adulterous passion for her, his words proving less powerful than the flesh. Closely examined, however, both of these sermons prove to miss the scriptural point of their respective texts, a lesson Gabriel himself needs: God's cause, like God's love, transcends ours, and the effort to speak for God, as opposed to yearning for God, is inevitably tainted by pride and folly.

The text of the first sermon is Isaiah 6:5: "Woe is me, for I am undone, because I am a man of unclean lips and I dwell in the midst of a people of unclean lips, for mine eyes have seen the King, the Lord of hosts." Gabriel uses it as the basis for a denunciation of sin, especially the sins of the flesh, a praise of God that emphasizes the woe of unrighteous humanity (*GTM*, 126–31). Yet, the text itself goes on to tell us that an angel seared the prophet's mouth with a live coal, purging his sin, suggesting that he must be silenced in order to be redeemed. God then calls the prophet and sends him to speak to the people, foreknowing that he will not be understood. God, in other words, gives the prophet a second, humbled mouth. The lips of the people are not "unclean" in any conventional sense; Israel speaks of God, but in a way that debases His glory, as any human speech inevitably must do. The real defect is in the ear: the people's ears are stopped because, hearing words, they reject or ignore their meaning, the Word beyond words.

Moreover, Isaiah tells us that his vision occurred "in the year King Uzziah died."[48] At the beginning of his reign, Uzziah "set himself to seek God," but a string of military successes made him feel invulnerable, secure because of his army and his technology of war, so that he was "lifted up to his presumption." He claimed the right to enter the sanctuary, contrary to the law, and leprosy "broke out upon his forehead."[49] Uzziah's piety, the text suggests, was only a matter of appearance; his corruption, like leprosy in the scriptural view, was internal, only waiting for its moment to become manifest.[50] The king valued God as an ally of his will to power, but strength and success tempted him to believe that he could command God: inwardly, it was not God he sought, but mastery, and only relative weakness kept that desire under wraps. This, however, is not a teaching Gabriel could be expected to discern.

Gabriel's second sermon is preached on 2 Samuel 18:29, where Ahimaaz answers David's demand for "tidings" by saying "I saw a great tumult, but I knew not what it was." Gabriel uses this remark as an example of the confusion of the unredeemed, and he urges his hearers to know the meaning of "tumult" so they will be able to give proper tidings to the Lord (*GTM*, 148–51). This is a genuinely startling misreading. Ahimaaz is not at all hesitant. He is eager to bring tidings to the king—after all, David's army has won a great victory—and he persists in asking to be sent even after Joab's warning that there will be no reward for these tidings, because the king's son, Absalom, is dead. It is only when he is in David's presence that Ahimaaz recognizes the truth that the king is more loving and forgiving than Ahimaaz recognized and that the victory Ahimaaz saw as grounds for celebration is reason for mourning for the king. And what is true of David is even more true of the Lord: a king knows that in practice there are battles that must be fought, and that the relatively just side is to be preferred, but he laments the necessity; the goal of royalty is the good of the whole, not the triumph of a part.[51] That higher dimension of politics, however, is one that Gabriel (and to a lesser degree, the church), devoted to the God of power and judgment, is all too prone to ignore.

By contrast, John's mother, Elizabeth, who offers the concluding prayer, is the voice of human love. As a child, she was love starved: her mother, for whom she felt little affection, died when Elizabeth was eight. Her father, whom she adored, left her to the care of a sternly respectable aunt, whose pious version of love—very much like Gabriel's—Elizabeth recognized as in reality only "a bribe, a threat, an indecent will to power" (*GTM*, 200). By contrast, Elizabeth knew that

> the kind of imprisonment love might impose was also, mysteriously, a freedom for the soul and spirit, was water in the dry place, and had nothing to

> do with the prisons, churches, laws, rewards, and punishments that so positively cluttered the landscape of her aunt's mind. (*GTM*, 200)

But Elizabeth, echoing the young Augustine, was "in love with love," cherishing love as her own version of pride and power, building her life around her devotion to Richard, John's biological father.[52]

Like Florence, Richard has a nonbiblical name, emblematic of his secularism (and one that, given Baldwin's preoccupations, inevitably suggests Richard Wright). Elizabeth's attraction to him is at least largely explained by the ways in which he is like her father, an individualist of "deadly pride" who taught her "to weep, when she wept, alone; never to ask for mercy; if one had to die, go ahead and die, but never let oneself be beaten" (*GTM*, 198). Richard is at least as prideful and as devoted to independence, defiantly irreverent,[53] cultivating an air of "indifferent aloofness" (*GTM*, 203), and pursuing knowledge as a means to mastery:

> I just decided me one day that I was going to get to know everything the white bastards knew, and I was going to know it better than them, so could no white son-of-a-bitch *nowhere* talk *me* down and never make me feel that *I* was dirt, when I could read him the alphabet, front, back and sideways. Shit—he weren't going to beat my ass, then. And if he tried to kill me, I'd take him with me, I swear to my mother I would. (*GTM*, 216)[54]

Events shatter that confidence. Richard is arrested for a crime he did not commit. He is in the wrong place at the wrong time, and the police sweep him up along with the guilty: "They were all colored, they were all about the same age, and . . . they stood together on the subway platform" (*GTM*, 221). The police are predictably brutal, but the system works, more or less, and Richard is released. Richard, however, is devastated by his inability to control his fate: being freed is as humiliating as his arrest, an exclamation point added to the experience of dependence and vulnerability. His love for Elizabeth is not strong enough to override the blow to his individualist's pride: he commits suicide, a final and futile gesture of independence that overpowers the claims of her love and the obligations of his own.

Elizabeth is left with the lesson that human love at its best is unable to command the world and is sure to be defeated by it. Recognizing the brittleness and desperation of Richard's pose, she sought to make her love his fortress, "the indisputable reality to which he could always repair" (*GTM*, 211), but her love's reality proved inadequate to the test of the world's strength and Richard's illusions.[55] Humanity's strength, and love's, rests on a deeper yearning:

> For the world called to the heart, which stammered to reply; life, and love, and revelry, and, most falsely, hope, called the forgetful, the human heart. Only the soul, obsessed with the journey it had made, and had still to make,

> pursued its mysterious and dreadful end; and carried, heavy with weeping and bitterness, the heart along. (*GTM*, 227)

Elizabeth's soul carried her until John's birth, "the beginning of her life and death," and from there, through Florence, to Gabriel. And after a time, Gabriel, in a moment of "grace and humility," pledged to love and provide for Elizabeth and her son (*GTM*, 245–46). There is no indication that Elizabeth loved him; she was touched by his kindness and she saw in him a means of returning to respectability and providing for her son. And Gabriel "kept the letter of his promise" to care for John, even though predictably "the spirit was not there" (*GTM*, 228). John's coming into the world, however, was Elizabeth's second birth, a travail followed by joy that pointed beyond itself, "toward that moment when she would make her peace with God" (*GTM*, 246–47).

In sum: Baldwin presents his readers with three reflective prayers, each with its thematic motive—the fear of death (Florence), the desire for power (Gabriel) and the love of love (Elizabeth). These are primary dynamics of social and political practice, inevitable concerns of custom and law. Taken together, in fact, they constitute a kind of psychological Augustinian subtext to the unalienable rights mentioned in the Declaration of Independence. All of them have touched and helped to nurture John, but by the end of "The Prayers of the Saints," their inadequacies have been exposed: human life cries for something more. It is no surprise, then, that the section ends with John on the threshing floor or that his cry is "not the cry of the child, newborn, before the common light of earth; but the cry of the man-child, bestial, before the light that comes down from Heaven" (*GTM*, 247).

★ ★ ★ ★ ★

The scriptural preface to "The Threshing Floor" repeats Isaiah 6:5, the text of Gabriel's first sermon, underlining the difference between that preaching and Baldwin's own evangel.

On the threshing floor, John experiences the full force of his rage and agony and fear, his fury at his father and his love for Elisha, and above all, the desolating sense of being utterly abandoned—particularly by his father's rejection—in darkness and alone. All of this is bound up with his dread of the past and fate of his race; the "ironic voice" of temptation tells him to go his own way, to "rise from that filthy floor if he did not want to become like all the other niggers" (*GTM*, 252).

> And he struggled to flee—out of this darkness, out of this company—into the land of the living, so high, so far away. Fear was upon him, a more deadly fear than he had ever known, as he turned and turned in the darkness, as he moaned, and stumbled, and crawled through the darkness, finding no hand,

> no voice, finding no door. *Who are these? Who are they?* They were the despised and rejected, the wretched and the spat upon, the earth's offscouring; and he was in their company, and they would swallow up his soul. The stripes they had endured would scar his back, their punishment would be his, their portion his, their humiliation, anguish, chains, their dungeon his, their death his. (*GTM*, 262–63)

Even at this bleak moment, however, there is a hint of a turn in the road. John is reminded of Paul's account of his travails (2 Corinthians 11:25–27), which he associates with the "dread testimony" and "desolation" of his people (*GTM*, 263). But Paul gloried in these things, assured of the ultimate sufficiency of God's grace and power and of its paradoxical corollary, the proposition that "when I am weak, then I am strong" (2 Corinthians 11:30, 12:9–10). So, it proves for John, at any rate. Despairing of human help and his own power, reduced to his flawed and vulnerable humanity, John has a instant of dazzling insight—"the darkness, for a moment only, was filled with a light he could not bear" (*GTM*, 266)—that leaves him with an abiding truth.[56] Creation, the fundamental nature of things, has power against its contemners. Even what is most shameful in human life and conduct—and "no one's hands are clean"—testifies to something beyond itself.[57]

> Then John saw the river, and the multitude was there. And now they had undergone a change; their robes were ragged, and stained with the road they had traveled, and stained with unholy blood; the robes of some barely covered their nakedness; and some indeed were naked. And some stumbled on the smooth stones at the river's edge, for they were blind; and some crawled with a terrible wailing, for they were lame; some did not cease to pluck at their flesh, which was rotten with running sores. All struggled to get to the river, in a dreadful hardness of heart: the strong struck down the weak, the ragged spat on the naked, the naked cursed the blind, the blind crawled over the lame. And someone cried, "*Sinner, do you love my Lord?*" (*GTM*, 265–66)

Human beings, spiritually blind and crippled, savagely competitive and self-seeking, are universally drawn by a higher end, seeking the river. This unity of human striving testifies to the obedient soldier's courage that underlies the "way of the cross," keeping one's human station up to the sacrifice of life, confident that God and nature will prevail against the illusions of mastery.[58]

> [T]hey moved on the bloody road forever, with no continuing city, but seeking one to come: a city out of time, not made with hands, but eternal in the heavens. No power could hold this army back, no water disperse them, no fire consume them. One day, they would compel the earth to heave upward, and surrender the waiting dead. They sang, where the darkness gathered, where the lion waited, where the fire cried, and where blood ran down: *My soul, don't you be uneasy.* (*GTM*, 267)

Almost immediately, John recognizes that his life has been bought with a price, his ancestors' pilgrimage of faith and suffering, and that his own life—like all human lives—is lived under obligation.[59]

If it needs saying, that John is "saved" means that his life has undergone a turning, that its agony has become a conscious struggle, permanently affected by the memory of his moment in light.[60] In his conversation with Elizabeth, and even more in his exchanges with Elisha and Gabriel, lower motives are quite evidently mingled with spiritual affirmations, but John's new insight remains an insistent whisper.

Talking with Gabriel, John tries and fails to find "the authoritative . . . word" that will "conquer the great division" between him and his stepfather, and "in the silence something died in John, and something came alive." Recognizing that he must speak and that "his tongue only could bear witness to the wonders he had seen," John finds "common testimony" in the text of one of Gabriel's sermons, Job 16:19: "My witness is in heaven and my record is on high" (*GTM*, 271).

Yet, the interpretations of that common text differ: the gap between prophecy and practice can be bridged—the effort to do so is a major office of politics—but it cannot be eliminated. For Gabriel, the text apparently implies a confident appeal to God against men. Job, however, is denouncing those who offer him the comfort of pious words. God's design, Job argues, is beyond human speech, and certainly beyond human ideas of justice, since God knows ("my record is on high") that Job has not merited his afflictions. Consequently, Job observes, one cannot plead with God as one *can* plead for one's neighbor (16:22). By implication, human words, so inadequate for capturing the divine, should primarily be devoted to seeking justice between human beings, just as the recognition of human vulnerability before God should lead us to support and sustain each other. John's politic appeal to Job indicates that he has come full circle, that his words will now proclaim his unity with the humble rather than afford a means to escape them.

The Grimes family's mantelpiece is adorned with two mottoes: the first is an invitation to guests—and especially, to the Guest—to come without warning, assured of a welcome; the second is the familiar words of John 3:16, "For God so loved the world." These sentiments, Baldwin remarks, are "somewhat unrelated," a comment that begs us to ask in what ways they *are* related (*GTM*, 26–27). That inquiry would lead us to John, the cited text, and to the observation (3:13) that establishes its context: no man has ascended to heaven, but God descended to man.[61] Heaven cannot be scaled, that passage suggests; God must be awaited, made inwardly welcome (as in the Grimes' first motto), and recognized as the light of and in this world (3:20–21). Baldwin appears to be arguing that the church, even in hands more unambiguously benign than Gabriel's, is, first of all, too eager to speak with authority and too unwilling to seek and to listen, and second, too indifferent to this world, where human speech and action can make a difference in alleviating pain.[62]

This is, however, no merely secular teaching. The Spirit can be heard, if not bidden, if one listens with the right ears. The recognition of God's love for all His children and for all His creation, the lesson of Jonah, is necessary for any people, but perhaps especially for those, like African Americans, who are justly furious at oppression. The demand for justice—the victorious retribution Ahimaaz is so ready to trumpet—needs to be softened by a desire for reconciliation, and especially by the need to avoid "victories" that make one into the image of one's oppressors and enemies.

If in one sense Baldwin points people of faith—and human beings in general—toward greater politicality, his message is also that they must be guided by the city founded not on victory or utility but the truth. John hears the music on the threshing floor:

> *I, John, saw a city, way up in the middle of the air,*
> *Waiting, waiting, waiting up there.* (*GTM*, 267)

We are all, Baldwin declares, "meant to be witnesses to a truth we will never see," most evidently the high, half-terrifying fact of human equality.[63]

Notes

1. Baldwin, writes Lawrie Balfour, *The Evidence of Things Not Said: James Baldwin and the Promise of American Democracy* (Ithaca, NY: Cornell University Press, 2001), 138, had "virtually nothing to say about political institutions and policies." See also David Leeming, *James Baldwin: A Biography* (New York: Knopf, 1994), 18, 216–230. For that matter, Baldwin's judgments about people and events in political practice were not always fortunate, especially when he strove to avoid seeming irrelevant to younger black militants, although even then he retained a certain ironic detachment: in 1968, he listed Henry James's *The Princess Casamassima* as a book he would recommend to Black Power militants (Leeming, *James Baldwin*, 284–302).

2. Neal Riemer, ed., *Let Justice Roll: Prophetic Challenges in Religion, Politics and Society* (Lanham, MD: Rowman & Littlefield, 1996).

3. James Baldwin, *The Fire Next Time* (New York: Dell, 1963), 88–89. David Leeming's verdict is the more telling because of its balance: Baldwin, he writes, was "not a saint . . . not always psychologically or emotionally stable. But he was a prophet." (Leeming, *James Baldwin*, xii; for Kenneth Clark's similar judgment, see p. 138).

4. On the philosophic impossibility of religious neutrality, see Roy Clouser, *The Myth of Religious Neutrality* (Notre Dame, IN: University of Notre Dame Press, 1991.

5. James Baldwin, *Nobody Knows My Name* (New York: Dial, 1961), 42–43; Balfour, *Evidence of Things Not Said*, 58; Leeming, *James Baldwin*, 352–53, 358. "We are

all under the same mental calamity," G. K. Chesterton wrote, "we have all forgotten our names. We have all forgotten what we really are." See Chesterton's *Orthodoxy* (New York: Dodd Mead, 1908), 97.

6. James Baldwin, *Notes of a Native Son* (Boston: Beacon, 1955), 9; Balfour, *Evidence of Things Not Said*, 95–96; Leeming, *James Baldwin*, 294, 369. Baldwin's arguments, Henry Louis Gates Jr. wrote, were "richly nuanced and self-consciously ambivalent . . . far too complex to serve straight forwardly political ends" ["The Fire Last Time," *New Republic* (July 1, 1992): 38].

7. James Baldwin, "A Talk to Teachers," *Saturday Review* 46 (December 21, 1963): 46.

8. James Baldwin, *The Price of the Ticket* (New York: St. Martin's, 1985), 643; "The world tends to trap and immobilize you in the role you play," Baldwin wrote, "and it is not always easy—in fact, it is always extremely hard—to maintain a kind of watchful, mocking distance between oneself as one appears to be and oneself as one actually is." Baldwin, *Nobody Knows My Name*, 173. See also Balfour, *Evidence of Things Not Said*, 7; Leeming, *James Baldwin*, 268–69, 335, 338, 358, 362.

9. Baldwin, *Notes of a Native Son*, 20, 23, 35–36, 113. Baldwin's examples of protest novelists were Harriet Beecher Stowe and, inevitably, Richard Wright.

10. "Though we do not fully believe it yet, the interior life is a real life, and the intangible dreams of people have a tangible effect on the world" (Baldwin, *Nobody Knows My Name*, 23) The importance of the inner life is underlined in America by the fact that "society is much given to smashing taboos without thereby managing to be liberated from them." (Baldwin, *Nobody Knows My Name*, 23)

11. David Leeming, "An Interview with James Baldwin on Henry James," *Henry James Review* 8 (1986): 47–56; Balfour, *Evidence of Things Not Said*, 56–58; James Baldwin, *The Evidence of Things Not Seen* (New York: Holt, Rinehart and Winston, 1985), 101–2; Baldwin, *Nobody Knows My Name*, 13, 66.

12. As Henry Louis Gates writes, "our histories, individual and collective, do affect what we wish to write and what we are able to write. But that relation is never one of fixed determinism. No human culture is inaccessible to someone who makes the effort to understand, to learn, to inhabit another world." ("'Authenticity' or, the Lesson of Little Tree," *New York Times Book Review* (November 24, 1991): 30).

13. James Baldwin, "To Crush the Serpent," *Playboy* (June 1987): 66ff.; Baldwin, *Nobody Knows My Name*, 113; Leeming, *James Baldwin*, 30, 125, 321, 369, 375.

14. Josh Kun, "Life According to the Beat: James Baldwin, Bessie Smith and the Perilous Sounds of Love," in *James Baldwin Now*, ed. Dwight McBride (New York: New York University Press, 1999), 307–28.

15. Baldwin, *The Fire Next Time*, 105, 119. See also James Baldwin, *Just above My Head* (New York: Dial, 1979); Leeming, *James Baldwin*, 351.

16. Baldwin, *Notes of a Native Son,* 9; Leeming, *James Baldwin*, 146. Balfour points to Baldwin's effort to develop a "moral vocabulary" adequate for citizenship and "democratic ideals." (*The Evidence of Things Not Said*, xi). Of course, Baldwin was often sharply critical of Christianity—although that goes with the prophetic vocation—and notoriously departed from conventional sexual morality. (He was troubled, Baldwin said, by "demons," as well as "the Lord"; see Leeming, *James Baldwin*, 309). Yet Baldwin was a believer, convinced of sin and human shortcoming and

devoted to a morality that was often surprisingly traditional (Balfour, *Evidence of Things Not Said*, 33); for example, when asked by an unmarried graduate student for advice about her unwanted pregnancy, Baldwin told her—Leeming says that he "ordered" her—to "carry and keep" the child (*James Baldwin*, 340–41). He spoke of himself as bearing witness to a truth learned "in the church where I was raised," as devoted to the Bible as a text (along with gospel songs), and as being definitively "in the hands of the Living God" (Baldwin, *Notes of a Native Son*, 113; Leeming, *James Baldwin*, 309, 367, 370).

17. Balfour, *Evidence of Things Not Said*, 23.

18. Mark 4:1–32.

19. On the general point, see Toni Morrison, "Unspeakable Things Unspoken," *Michigan Quarterly Review* 28 (1989): 1–31.

20. Citations to *Go Tell It on the Mountain* (orig. 1953) refer to the Modern Library edition (New York, 1995); hereafter cited as *GTM*.

21. Leeming, *James Baldwin*, 84–85.

22. The Prayers of the Saints is further divided into three chapters, each identified as the prayer of a member of the Grimes family, of which the second (and longest) is Gabriel's prayer, making it central among the book's subdivisions.

23. John's stepbrother Royal and his stepsisters Sarah and Ruth are essentially secondary characters in John's imagination and in Baldwin's story.

24. Balfour, *Evidence of Things Not Said*, 146–47n52. See also Baldwin, *Nobody Knows My Name*, 168–69. John's literary talent evidently links him to Baldwin, as do many details in the story. It is also notable that Baldwin frequently gave his central characters the name "John," for example, in his story "Peace on Earth" (Leeming, *James Baldwin*, 29) and in the more autobiographical "Death of the Prophet" [*Commentary* 9 (March 1950): 257–61], to say nothing of Giovanni in *Giovanni's Room* (New York: Dial, 1956). The choice of a name, especially in broadly autobiographical fiction, is suggestive, since Baldwin repeatedly wrote about and in terms of a search for a name beyond conventional names, as in *Nobody Knows My Name* or Baldwin's *No Name in the Street* (New York: Dial, 1972). James is the apostle who speaks of the importance of deeds; John—whether we think of John the Baptist (prophecy), John the Apostle (the word beyond words), or John of Revelation—is associated with a vision beyond appearances: I suspect that just as James or Jimmy was Baldwin the person we see, identity in practice, Baldwin thought of John as a kind of inward identity, the person who sees.

25. F. W. J. Schelling, "Philosophische Untersuchungen über das Wesen der menschlichen Freiheit und die damit zusammenhängenden Gegenstände," in *Sammtliche Werke* (Augsburg: Cotta, 1860), 6:351.

26. Speech to the Virginia Convention, March 23, 1775, in William Wirt, *Sketches of the Life and Character of Patrick Henry* (Philadelphia: Thomas, Cowperthwait & Co., 1838), 141–42. Mark Twain has Tom Sawyer forget Henry's peroration during his school's exercises—implausibly, since a glory seeker like Tom would have cherished that line if he forgot everything else, but significantly, if Twain wanted to raise questions about America's devotion to freedom. See *The Adventures of Tom Sawyer* (Berkeley: University of California Press, 1982), 155.

27. A judgment evidently reflected in Eldridge Cleaver's late-sixties demeaning of his own parentage in *Soul on Ice* (New York: Dial, 1968), 210: "A Slave who dies of natural causes cannot balance two flies in the Scales of Eternity."

28. Horace Porter, *Stealing the Fire: The Art and Protest of James Baldwin* (Middletown, CT: Wesleyan University Press, 1989), 99; Leeming, *James Baldwin*, 86–87, 89. Baldwin never obscured the lamentable aspects of African American experience or culture; he only insisted that there was a vital "something more" (*Notes of a Native Son*, 121).

29. Cornel West, *Keeping Faith* (New York: Routledge, 1993), 72–73, 85, 290–91.

30. Balfour, *Evidence of Things Not Said*, 68, 123–24. This effort is evident in religion's worst manifestations: Gabriel calls on the Lord as he beats his son, Royal, precisely because he resists the lesson of secularity offered by his sister, Florence: "You can't change nothing, Gabriel. You ought to know that by now" (Baldwin, *GTM*, 56).

31. The identity of a human being, Locke wrote, "consists . . . in nothing but a participation in the same continued life . . . [in] the same organized Body"; in this respect, human identity is "like that of other Animals" (*Essay on Human Understanding*, II, xxvii).

32. *Othello*, Act I, scene 3.

33. Ephesians 6:11–12.

34. James Baldwin, *The Evidence of Things Not Seen*, 78; Baldwin, *Nobody Knows My Name*, 36; Baldwin, *Notes of a Native Son*, 165.

35. For Baldwin personally, spiritual paternity was a major theme, whether in relation to his stepfather or to Richard Wright (*Nobody Knows My Name*, 153, 160.) It is significant, of course, that in *GTM*, Richard is John's biological father.

36. Baldwin, *Nobody Knows My Name*, 183. See also H. Richard Niebuhr, *Christ and Culture* (New York: Harper Brothers, 1951).

37. Ecclesiastes 3:1; Ephesians 5:16. See also Jacques Maritain, *Ransoming the Time* (New York: Charles Scribner, 1941). For those who would change the world, contra Marx, the first task is to understand it.

38. Revelation 6:9–11.

39. Baldwin's stepfather's mother, like the mother of Florence and Gabriel, had been born a slave and lived the last years of her life in Baldwin's home (Leeming, *James Baldwin*, 4).

40. On the seductive quality of Baldwin's writing, see Balfour, *Evidence of Things Not Said,* 36; Leeming, *James Baldwin*, 101.

41. The quotation, of course, is from Machiavelli, *The Prince*, ch. xv.

42. Alexis de Tocqueville, *Democracy in America* (New York: Knopf, 1980), I, 309–10; Hobbes put the "Fear of Death" first among the "Passions that conduce to Peace" (*Leviathan*, Pt. I, ch. 13).

43. His own stepfather, Baldwin wrote, saw himself as the "good friend of Great God Almighty." Baldwin, *No Name in the Street*, 3–9. See also Baldwin, *Notes of a Native Son*, 87–92.

44. Baldwin, *GTM*, 33; it is also, appropriately, a text that occurs to Florence (Baldwin, *GTM*, 78). It was the favorite text of Baldwin's stepfather, and one that Baldwin himself used in his own last sermon, where the "house" in question was Western civilization (Leeming, *James Baldwin*, 31).

45. The metaphor is strikingly inappropriate, since Gabriel's complaint—unlike Sarah's—is against John's paternity: Elizabeth is also the mother of Gabriel's "rightful heir."

46. In fact, Paul describes himself as a mother—"in travail of birth until Christ be formed in you" (Galatians 4:19). Notably, Gabriel appeals to Paul's teaching in his first great sermon (Baldwin, *GTM*, 128).

47. By contrast, Baldwin saw his stepfather as his father "in every sense except the biological or literal one" [*The Devil Finds Work* (New York: Dial, 1976), 12–16].

48. Isaiah 6:1

49. 2 Chronicles 26:5, 16, 19.

50. The fact that lepers had to cover their lips because their breath might pollute the community (Leviticus 13:45) is an indication of the view that leprosy bespeaks an inner corruption.

51. On the necessities of political practice, see the account that follows Gabriel's text (2 Chronicles 19:1–8).

52. The citation of Augustine, of course, is from his *Confessions*, Bk. 3, ch. 1.

53. His response to Elizabeth's appeal to the love of Jesus is to "tell that puking bastard to kiss my big black ass" (Baldwin, *GTM*, 211).

54. The first person italics underscore Richard's individualism: he resents the indignities of race, but his protest is personal, not political.

55. Elizabeth, fearing to add to Richard's burdens, did not tell him she was pregnant, leaving him ignorant of an obligation that just might have bound him to life (Baldwin, *GTM*, 226).

56. "The light and the darkness had kissed each other, and were married now, forever, in the vision of John's soul." (Baldwin, *GTM*, 266–67).

57. Baldwin, *Notes of a Native Son*, 44.

58. Baldwin, *GTM*, 286–87; Jeremiah 31:8–12; compare the implicit contrast of Socrates' courage with that of Achilles in Plato's *Apology*, 28D–29A.

59. Leeming, *James Baldwin*, 89; Bertrand de Jouvenel, *Sovereignty*, trans. J. F. Huntington (Indianapolis: Liberty Fund, 1997), 317.

60. John's plea to Elisha is almost certainly Baldwin's own proclamation to his readers: "no matter what happens to me, where I go, what folks say about me, no matter what anybody says, you remember—please remember—I was saved. I was *there*" (Baldwin, *GTM*, 290). Leeming writes that Baldwin's early "salvation" was "the preface to a life of searching on the universal threshing floor of personal and societal pain" (*James Baldwin*, xiii). John's emphasis suggests that Baldwin's experience might better be described as a foundation for that life.

61. See also John 1:18.

62. Defending himself against Florence's attack on his pretensions and misbehaviors, Gabriel declares that "God sees the heart." Florence responds that God "ought to see it" because "He made it. But don't nobody else see it, not even your own self. *Let* God see it—He sees it all right, and He don't say anything"; Gabriel, with unconscious irony, answers, "All you got to do is listen"(Baldwin, *GTM*, 280). Similarly, Sister McCandless, also a great talker, says that "all you got to do is *listen* to the Lord" (Baldwin, *GTM*, 272).

63. James Baldwin and Margaret Mead, *A Rap on Race* (Philadelphia: Lippincott, 1971); G. K. Chesterton, *What I Saw in America* (New York: Dodd Mead, 1922), 18.

8

Vexed Genealogy

Octavia Butler and Political Memories of Slavery

Lawrie Balfour

> I see her shape and his hand in the vast networking of our society, and in the evils and oversights that plague our lives and laws. The control he had over her body. The force he was in her life, in the shape of my life today. The power he exercised in the choice to breed her or not. . . . In his attempt to own what no man can own, the habit of his power and the absence of her choice.
>
> —Patricia J. Williams

> It is a hard thing to live haunted by the ghost of an untrue dream.
>
> —W. E. B. DuBois

Memory Politics[1]

In a 1989 interview, Toni Morrison remarked about *Beloved*, "I thought this has got to be the least read of all the books I'd written because it is about something that the characters don't want to remember, I don't want to remember, black people don't want to remember, white people don't want to remember. I mean it's national amnesia."[2] Clearly, Morrison's prediction about her book's reception has not been borne out, and recent demands for reparations provide just one indication of a growing willingness among many African Americans to call public attention to slavery.[3] Yet, the observation is telling insofar as it suggests a multiplicity of reasons for not wanting to remember suggested by the phrase "national amnesia" and indicates why controversies about the presence of the slave past are so difficult to resolve. They are fraught, in quite different ways, for different citizens. Thus, Patricia Williams' meditation on the legacy of her great-great-grandparents, the one a slave and the other her master, offers up a reminder that getting the facts straight about this past requires of many Americans a willingness to become involved, personally, in a wrenching paradox. Investigating the forced coupling that eventually led to Williams' own birth may enable her to understand the workings of white supremacy more thoroughly but at the cost of coming face-to-face with the interplay of possession and dispossession at work in her history.[4] At the same time, W. E. B. DuBois's sympathetic musing about the hold of Lost Cause ideology in white Southern imaginations suggests that revisiting the past may be equally, albeit differently, demanding for many whites. That the vision of a slaveless Confederacy distorts the record makes it no less compelling to its believers.[5] And this "untrue dream" holds not only for those Americans who march out under the Confederate battle flag but also for those who believe in America as the locus for an already realized liberalism: for both groups, it is black Americans who appear as the dispossessors; for both, the flourishing of American democracy requires, in Ralph Ellison's words, "getting shut" of them.[6]

The perspectives represented by the epigraphs, and the gap between them, ought to be of signal importance for political theory because they help to illuminate an impasse in contemporary debates about racial justice. Contending narratives about the meaning and relevance of the past emerge repeatedly to justify divergent positions on questions of racial justice in the post–civil rights era. The political currency of claims of "reverse discrimination," which elide the distinction between race-conscious remedies for generations of injustice and the injustice that engendered the need for such remedies in the first place, and the popularity of California's Proposition 209, which framed the abolition of affirmative action as a matter of "civil rights," provide just two examples of the ways in which history is selectively appropriated in American political imaginations. What Michel-Rolph Trouillot defines as "formulas of erasure" have served to minimize the horrors of slavery by emphasizing "paternalism" or to deny the links connecting slavery and Jim Crow and thereby to discredit claims to present relevance.[7] Yet, the conviction that African Americans have something to offer as bearers of a "diverse" perspective suggests that the success of these strategies is qualified. Americans have not simply forgotten their history. Rather, as Benedict Anderson observes, they have been trained "to remember/forget," to remember the Civil War as an instance of fratricide, for example, and forget the slavery at the root of the conflict.[8] This "kind of memory . . . that forgets though it still remembers" matters politically;[9] as beneficiaries of collective injustice, white Americans, by and large, resist memorializing the disreputable past not only because it is painful but also because it asks something of them. Thus, Sheldon Wolin concludes, "temporal distance and historical accommodations have so far removed them from [the injustice] that they do not feel responsible, only uneasy."[10] And in such a context, the presence of those citizens whose racial identity serves as a reminder of truths many Americans would rather forget continues to be figured as a "problem."

To call attention to the ways in which selective memories of historical injustice are politically mobilized is also to call attention to the limits of conventional theorizing. Just as the abstract formulation of a "national amnesia" disguises what is different and simplifies what is complex in the suppression of memories of slavery, the demands of theoretical argument can work against confrontation with live meanings of the past. "The great intellectual advantage of telling stories," observes Judith Shklar, "is that it does not rationalize the irrationality of actual experience and of history. Indecision, incoherence, and inconsistency are not ironed out or put between brackets. All our conflicts are preserved in their inconclusiveness."[11] By working and reworking through concrete particulars, literature not only provides a medium for creative engagement with the past but it also discloses what is hidden or excluded by abstract analyses. It can, furthermore, raise pointed questions about how those abstractions preserve relations of power.[12]

The virtue of literary approaches to understanding slavery's legacy goes beyond a capacity to render the messiness against which analytical approaches array themselves, however. It resides as well in a capacity to arouse. Well-crafted stories provoke the imagination as much by what is left unexplained as by the details. In their gaps and silences, one encounters what Peter Euben, drawing on Walter Benjamin, calls their "amplitude."[13] And at a moment when conventional tellings of American history allow most Americans to keep their distance from slavery and, relatedly, to insulate themselves from recognizing the pervasiveness of racial injustice as a fundamental crisis, fictional renderings of slavery's stories may be what is needed to "fa[n] the spark of hope in the past."[14] Octavia Butler's novel *Kindred* (1979) offers one such rendering.

Variously described as science fiction, "grim fantasy," neo–slave narrative, and "memory machine,"[15] *Kindred* witnesses the experiences of a twentieth-century African American writer, Edana (Dana) Franklin, who is transported, repeatedly and against her will, from twentieth-century Los Angeles to a plantation in antebellum Maryland. Free from the strictures of theoretical argument, from the demand for logical and logistical plausibility, Butler offers what Charles Maier calls "contrapuntal history."[16] Her account of Dana's sojourns enables readers to examine multiple stories about the life and afterlife of slavery without offering a synthetic resolution to the fissures and paradoxes the narrative reveals. Eschewing the impulse to tidiness, the novel both relies upon and discloses the "human intelligence" that, according to Morrison, distinguishes truth from fact and exposes the lifelessness of the latter.[17] By foregrounding the experiences of an African American woman and the slaves she comes to know, furthermore, Butler illuminates connections between past and present from perspectives rarely heard in political theory. She calls attention to the ways in which conventional, linear histories of slavery reinforce white privilege. Yet, *Kindred* does not simply substitute black truth for white, female-centered history for male. The deftness with which the story is presented reinforces Dana's authority as critical observer of American history without relying on an unexamined notion of authenticity.[18] By rendering slavery both more and less alien than her readers assume it to be, Butler conveys the necessity and the sheer difficulty, for all Americans, of coming to terms with the past. Butler's novel discredits efforts to deny the lingering effects of slavery, both materially and psychologically, in American public life. It breathes life into the injunction to remember by telling a story that one does not easily forget.

"This Alien Time"[19]

Kindred begins in 1976, when Dana is abruptly removed from her new house in Los Angeles to a Maryland plantation in the early nineteenth century. Her initial trip to the past, like the five that follow, is occasioned by cries for help from Rufus, a white boy prone to self-destruction. In each case, Dana returns to save him. He summons her whenever his life is in peril, and she is only able to return to the twentieth century when she perceives an immediate threat to herself. Complicating her feelings about being held captive to Rufus's needs and to the imperatives of slave society is her realization that the boy is her ancestor; the failure to keep him alive, at least until the birth of his daughter, Hagar, means the obliteration of Dana's own existence. Further complicating her attempts to keep some distance between her sense of herself as a free woman and as the slave she must pretend to be to survive the trips to Maryland is Dana's growing entanglement with the people of the Weylin plantation. With each successive trip to the past, Dana's implication in the alien world deepens. Her relationship to Alice, the free black woman whom Rufus enslaves and who becomes Hagar's mother, is particularly fraught because of the two women's triangular relationship with Rufus—Dana's survival depends on her complicity in Rufus's repeated rape of Alice—and their striking physical resemblance; they are, in Rufus's eyes, "two halves of the same woman" (229). When Dana eventually manages to kill Rufus and to return permanently to 1976 (on the Fourth of July), her left arm becomes stuck in the wall of her house and is painfully amputated. What political sense might a reader make of a story so fabulous? In this section, I will attempt to sketch a response through an exploration of the dislocations enacted by the text,[20] the dismemberments at the heart of it, and, finally, the notions of agency and responsibility that issue from it.

The dislocation most obviously recalled by Dana's involuntary removal from California is the massive forced migration of the Middle Passage, and the tradition the novel invokes is that of the slave narrative. Although Butler is best known as a writer of science fiction, *Kindred* wastes no space explaining the mechanisms of Dana's time travel. As Robert Crossley notes in the introduction, Butler's account conjures the image of slave ships in lieu of a time machine.[21] The cursory descriptions of Dana's movements across time, furthermore, echo the *Narrative of the Life of Frederick Douglass,* in which the author dispenses with the details of his flight from slavery to freedom in a pair of deliberately undescriptive sentences.[22] Yet, *Kindred* does not exactly follow the slavery-to-freedom trajectory of many slave autobiographies, and it offers nothing so straightforward as a brief for abolition. Teasing out the political implications of Dana's story is more complicated.

Kindred is a historical narrative and a narrative about history. "*Kindred* questions all forms of historical knowledge," Christine Levecq argues, "by demonstrating the inescapable shaping or silencing of the past by perception, ideology, and language. But this skepticism does not stand in the way of a very realistic account of life under slavery,"[23] or, I would add, life in the post–civil rights period as well. Thus, Sandra Govan remarks, "Without turning to an actual slave narrative, there is probably no more vivid depiction of life on an Eastern Shore plantation than that found in *Kindred*."[24] Butler's choice of Maryland in the early nineteenth century is not accidental; it recalls the travels of Harriet Tubman and Frederick Douglass across the line from slavery to freedom and allows her to bring to life a world of tangled relationships between slaves and free blacks that was distinct from life in the North or lower South. Writing about the upper South in the post-Revolutionary period, Ira Berlin observes that "the simultaneous expansion of freedom and of slavery defined black life . . . and united free and slave as in no other region of the United States."[25] The juxtaposition of past and present also enables Butler to suggest the lingering traces of slave society in the regular indignities Dana endures in Los Angeles without minimizing what is appalling in easy appropriations of the past. Dana's freedom in 1976 is a qualified one. Supporting herself by going to the "slave market," where temporary workers seek work (52), Dana is viewed by her employers as one among the "nonpeople rented for a few hours, a few days, a few weeks. It didn't matter" (53). She is dependent on the caprices of her dispatcher for survival ("Home meant no money" [52]) and endures regular taunting about her sexuality as the price of employment (54–57). Even Kevin, the white man and fellow writer/temp who becomes Dana's husband, displays the continuing association of black women with service and subservience when he repeatedly asks her to type his manuscripts and finds her refusal outrageous (109). Here, too, the ambiguity of Butler's description is productive: it signals continuity even as the very fact of Dana and Kevin's marriage indicates the enormity of the gap between the slaves' time and their own.

Despite the care with which Butler details the historical contexts of her story, *Kindred* explicitly questions the value of conventional retellings of history. In Dana's trips back to Los Angeles, she reads every book related to slavery (fiction, nonfiction, textbooks, "even *Gone with the Wind,* or part of it") and finds them wanting. None serves as a helpful map of the world she unwillingly comes to know so intimately. Indeed, the map of Maryland that she takes with her on her third journey proves to be of little assistance. Although Dana does find, in the testimonies of survivors of German concentration camps, descriptions that resonate with her experiences in Maryland, Butler is careful not to make facile connections between slavery and the Holocaust or comparisons with different instances of suffering (116–17). Rather, she indicates the challenge of grasping what Avishai Margalit calls the "sensibility" of the past.[26] Even as *Kindred* informs, it undermines the idea that publication of previously unknown or unacknowledged "facts" is enough to understand the past or to effect change in present circumstances. Instead, Butler's account of Dana's forays back and forth in time suggests how historical understanding is enlarged through the adoption of what might be called a genealogical orientation. *Kindred*, according to Ashraf Rushdy, offers readers a "palimpsest narrative" in which the author "explore[s] the political underpinnings of racial identity by showing how the original markings of 'race' in antebellum America continue to exert deleterious power over people of African descent in contemporary American society."[27] Like Michel Foucault's notion of genealogy "operat[ing] on a field of entangled and confused parchments, on documents that have been scratched over and recopied many times,"[28] Dana's travels to her past give the lie to the simple chronology recorded in the family Bible. By presenting Dana herself as a product of stories that have been (incompletely) erased and written over, Butler challenges progressive histories in which past injustices eventually and inevitably give way to greater freedom. Still, while Dana's story dramatizes the effects of the past in the present, while her experience of dislocation leaves its marks, I hesitate to describe hers as "a body *totally* imprinted by history."[29] For her insertion into her own family history raises critical questions about the ways in which "the past is shaped, or constructed, by the present."[30]

For example, the great surprise of Dana's return to the past is that Rufus, whose name is included without comment in her family Bible, is white (28). Yet, the discovery no more explains Dana to herself than does Shane Phelan's experience of "coming out" in which, armed with the newly revealed truth of her identity, Phelan revisits her life history looking for buried evidence of innate lesbianism.[31] Butler's treatment of Dana's story resonates with Phelan's critique of her own: both demonstrate the illusoriness and the dangers of the "search for origins." In Butler's case, the story is designed to challenge black nationalist preoccupations with purity of lineage and politics.[32] But the timing of the novel to coincide with American bicentennial celebrations equally undermines self-congratulatory renderings of the American national narrative. "A bicentennial," Wolin writes, "might be thought of as an official story that narrates a past to support an image of collective identity that confirms a certain conception of the present."[33] Butler's bicentennial, by contrast, offers a countermemory that challenges prevailing conceptions of descent. Her relentless troubling of the idea of home, which she uses alternately to describe Dana's house in Los Angeles and the Weylin plantation, further provokes a confrontation with the difficulty of sorting out "real" from imagined histories and shifts attention to the ways in which those histories are used.

It is fitting that Dana's travels across time are signaled by dizziness. Untethered from the certainties of the present, she encounters a deep epistemological divide between her own experiences and those of the slaves. This sense of vertigo is exacerbated by Dana's apprehension that time moves at different paces in the two periods—the sojourns in the past span more than twenty years, from Rufus's childhood to his assumption of control over the plantation, while Dana ages less than a month in the twentieth century. Against the unreality of these shifts in time, the concreteness of Butler's description and its lack of sentimentality remind the reader of the material realities of American slavery. Although a veteran of the casual labor market, Dana is unprepared for the direct experience of the institution for which the "slave market" is named. On Dana's second trip, for instance, Butler explores contemporary Americans' inability to grasp the physicality of whites' power over the both slaves and free blacks in the antebellum world. When Dana witnesses the whipping of a black man by white patrollers who have caught him visiting his wife without permission, she is overwhelmed by the smell of sweat and cries of shame and sound of labored breathing (36). Despite years of exposure to graphic television and movie violence, she is probably more shocked by the scene than the child who is there with her. Her experiences thus not only expose the reader to the everyday brutality of slavery but also warn that the effort to know what slavery was cannot be perfectly realized.

This becomes painfully apparent in Dana's attempts to tell Kevin about those experiences. The gap between her efforts to make sense of her travels and his willingness to believe is revealing. As the story becomes, in Kevin's words, "crazier and crazier," it seems "more and more believable" to Dana (46). As they argue, he pits his "facts" against hers with the confidence that his view will prevail; even the evidence of the physical scars she carries back with her is inadequate proof. When he sees first-hand the world Dana describes, moreover, Kevin sees it differently. Arguing about how to interpret the whipping that Dana (but not Kevin) has just witnessed, he challenges her outrage and attempts to assure her with what Trouillot might call a "formula of banalization": "One [whipping] is too many, yes, but still, this place isn't what I would have imagined. No overseer. No more work than people can manage" (100).[34] This breach between them is further demonstrated by his relative lack of uneasiness about the fact that he and Dana are tacitly allowed to sleep together in the Weylin house, not as married partners but as master and concubine (97). Even at the conclusion of the novel, when Dana and Kevin are closer than ever, they do not reach complete mutual understanding about the meaning of what they have encountered (246). Although Kevin's commitment to Dana is so strong that he intertwines his own fate with hers by reaching out to her and, thus, accompanying her when she is called back to the past, his responses to her claims reproduce a pattern of white incapacity to believe what black Americans are saying about the conditions of their lives. It suggests, furthermore, the particular difficulties those Americans who have historically been insulated from systematic abuses of power have in accepting that the abuses exist.[35] And it dramatizes the circumstances under which the slave narratives appeared, their "authenticity" always suspect and their status as truth only confirmed through the endorsement of prominent whites.[36]

If Dana's dislocations indicate the challenges of producing a truthful account of the past, her arm's amputation signals Butler's ambition to convey the multiple dismemberments—of individual bodies and of families and communities—enacted by American slavery.[37] *Kindred* begins in injury. "I lost an arm on my last trip home," Dana reports in the opening line of the novel (9). The marks of her time in Maryland prompt Dana to recall photographs she had once seen of slaves whose backs were defined by thick scars and to reconsider the distance she once felt existed between herself and them (113). Dana's wounds prompt readers to consider the afterlife of slavery in what Hortense Spillers describes as "a kind of hieroglyphics of the flesh whose severe disjunctures come to be hidden to the cultural seeing by skin color."[38] Crucially, the deftness of Butler's approach enables her to resist two perils of bringing slave stories to present notice: her attention to the ways in which the characters shape their circumstances even as they are shaped by them discredits the impulse to reduce them to their wounds, and the matter-of-factness of her style dampens any temptation to idealized or romantic identification with their suffering.[39] The symbolism of Dana's lost arm, for example, demonstrates the permanence of the harms of the past and deflates dreams of wholeness. At the same time, Butler uses the story of Dana's amputation to examine and discredit reductive allegories that domesticate the meanings of the past.[40] In the prologue of the novel, which begins when Dana is hospitalized after her amputation, she is asked repeatedly to tell the police who "hurt" her arm. What is striking about this formulation is both the euphemism—for the arm is *gone*, not merely hurt—and the police officers' confidence that Kevin must be responsible. Despite the fact that her injuries are fantastic, not easily explainable, Dana's words are intelligible to her would-be protectors only as long as she corroborates their interpretation, only as long as she fits the role of the battered wife.

Dismemberment is evident not only in the physical harms Dana endures but in the psychological violence of slavery. Dana finds signs of this violence everywhere: when she hears slaves refer to themselves as "niggers"; when she watches slave children make up a game in which they are participants in a mock slave auction; and at the moment when she recognizes her own adjustments to the expectations of antebellum life. "I never realized how easily people could be trained to accept slavery" (101), Dana concludes, echoing Douglass's comment that "you have seen how a man was made a slave."[41] The damage is not limited to black Americans. Despite Dana's efforts, Rufus develops from an irresponsible little boy into a tyrant. Slavery, in Butler's words, "left its unlikable marks on him" (32). Watching the ways that Rufus and his family are shaped by the conventions of slave society, Dana worries that Kevin, too, would be "in another kind of danger if he accompanied her to the past. A place like this would endanger him in a way that I didn't want to talk about" (77). Her fears are realized when he does make the journey and is forced to spend five years in the nineteenth century before Dana can help return him to the present. Although not nearly as physically disfigured as his wife, Kevin returns from his trip to the past with a mysterious scar on his forehead and a new expression on his face; it "was like something I'd seen, something I was used to seeing on [Rufus's father,] Tom Weylin. Something closed and ugly" (194).

Kindred also speaks to the past and present meanings of the dismemberment of family, the "kinlessness" enforced by the slave system.[42] The novel offers a vivid accounting of the caprice with which slaves were separated from their families, the luck embodied in a child whose muteness means she will not be sold away. And Butler's exploration of Dana's vexed genealogy suggests that the recovery effort itself produces a kind of dismemberment. "Reclaiming that from which one has been disinherited is a good thing," writes Patricia Williams. "Self-possession in the full sense of that expression is the companion to self-knowledge. Yet claiming for myself a heritage the weft of whose genesis is my own disinheritance is a profoundly troubling paradox."[43] The ambiguity of "kindred" as a metaphor conjures up the romance of the family but simultaneously undermines it. This ambiguity is represented on the cover of the book, which spells the title "KiNdre d." Marking absence and suggesting, through the missing letter, the unspoken dread that is summoned by slavery's memory, the title undercuts the sentimental picture of the family. Butler resists the temptation to elide the difference between the idea of family and the idealization of that idea. Instead she confronts readers with the complexity of family relationships by describing Dana's genuine affection for Rufus, which somehow persists, despite the ease with which he sacrifices her safety to satisfy his own desires.[44] She exposes as well the way in which the notion of family has been used to euphemize the reality of slave relations, as when Dana hears Rufus refer to a slave as "Aunt Sarah." (In an ironic twist of which Rufus is probably unaware, his presumption of familiarity is in fact an accurate rendering of his familial connection to a woman whose "man" was the father-in-law of Rufus's own father.) Most powerfully, the portrait of Rufus's attentiveness to Alice, the free black woman he loves so much that he rapes her, enslaves her, and has her husband sold, indicates the interrelation of black and white lives, of the simultaneous growth of love and denial of the human personality of the beloved, under slavery. The notion of kin thus speaks directly to white Americans, especially those who insist that this is not their story.

Although Butler carries her examination of the links between slavery and familial dismemberment into the twentieth century, *Kindred* is not a narrative about the pathologies of black matriarchy. Rather, it undermines investment in the purity of family lines and discredits the use of racially inflected appeals to family as justification for exclusion. Both Dana and Kevin are orphans, but their ties to their surviving family members become broken or strained when they announce their plans to marry. Butler's juxtaposition of the outraged racism of Kevin's sister against Dana's uncle's disappointment does not equate the two responses. Yet, by exposing the racial terms in which family loyalty is to be displayed, and the swift move from deviation to expulsion, Butler prompts the reader to consider whether calls for family unity are any less treacherous when their aim is to fight power rather than to retain it.[45]

Despite the obvious damage done by the dismemberments Butler describes, it would be wrong to read *Kindred* as an exercise in victimology. On the contrary, the novel offers a portrait of constrained agency and a reflection on the difficulties of acting ethically under conditions of unequal power. Some of that work is done by rehearsing the obvious but generally unacknowledged point about the invisible role of black labor in the nation's creation.[46] Even in the tiny world of the Weylin plantation, it is the slaves who produce the wealth, maintain the household, and soothe the pains and hide the weaknesses of their masters. Further, Butler's depictions of relationships among the slaves and their complex responses to their condition convey what Toni Morrison calls their "interior lives" and demonstrates how, far from waiting for anything so unlikely as assistance from above, they developed their own practices of redress.[47] This is perhaps most evident in the description of Sarah. In Sarah, Dana immediately recognizes someone who "had done the safe thing—had accepted a life of slavery because she was afraid." While she likes Sarah, depends on her kindness, and finds occasional glimmers of the deep rage Sarah harbors against the family that sold her children away, Dana nonetheless thinks of the older slave in epithets: "the house-nigger, the handkerchief-head, the female Uncle Tom" (145). Butler's exploration of Sarah's story enables her to expose Dana's sense of easy superiority as a delusion and to counter a politics of rectitude in which any form of accommodation to one's circumstances is taken as betrayal. The counternarrative here is aimed at black political ideologies grounded in an inadequately complicated understanding of the past.[48] Butler is asking that her readers consider how the presumed will-lessness of the women and men who lived in bondage lingers in their own imaginations. That Dana herself is susceptible to such assumptions reinforces the importance of telling the story otherwise.

Butler attempts to do so, revealing a complicated network of responsibility that connects past and present and by implicating Dana for her own part in her history. Dana's efforts to keep Rufus alive make his rape of Alice possible; her role in his death likely means that the slaves on the Weylin plantation will be sold and families separated. Dramatizing the complex interplay of contingency and will, Dana's trips to the past take place by accident as Rufus's mistakes (drowning, setting fire to curtains, initiating fights he cannot win, and so forth) pull her back in time. And her perception that she alone is able to save him exposes a paradox: "I was the worst possible guardian for him—a black to watch over him in a society that considered blacks subhuman, a woman to watch over him in a society that considered women perennial children" (68). Her failure to protect Rufus from corruption, even as she protects him from death, reinforces Dana's sense of inefficacy. Compromised though her position may be, however, Dana makes choices. Responsibility requires that she improvise. She not only nurses Rufus after his bouts of self-destruction, but she also helps to heal Alice after Rufus has her brutally beaten, despite the fact that the healing makes Alice available to Rufus. At the same time, Dana is never wholly compliant; she challenges the limitations of the situation by slashing her wrists, by running away, by teaching some of the slaves to read, and, ultimately, by killing Rufus.

Where Dana's situation is defined by hard choices qualified by relative powerlessness, Rufus's power is dissembled through the attribution of exaggerated agency to the blacks in his life and the disavowal of his own. In his exchanges with Dana, for example, Rufus simultaneously endows her with superhuman responsibilities—for saving him, for saving his father, even for determining whether or not Rufus will sell his own children—and reminds her that she has no rights against him or any white man. Of his theft of Alice, he says that he has been driven to his deeds by her resistance to his advances. This tension between proclaimed equality and unequal power is brutally realized at a moment when the reader knows that Rufus has been secretly preventing Dana from reuniting with Kevin, and still he declares, "You want Kevin the way that I want Alice. And you had more luck than I did because no matter what happens now, for a while he wanted you too. Maybe I can't have that—both wanting, both loving. But I'm not going to give up what I can have" (163). Rufus's recognition in Dana of a human being with feelings like his own thus becomes a justification for his unwillingness to accord Dana—or Alice—any independence from him. It vivifies the questions Saidiya Hartman poses: "What do reciprocity, mutuality, and the recognition of the captive's humanity mean in the context of slavery? In other words, who is protected by such notions—the master or the slave?"[49]

In her portrayal of the Weylin plantation as a relatively "humane" site of slavery, Butler raises further questions about the ways in which ethical formalism can be used to preserve and entrench relations of unequal power. The vacuity of such formalism is illustrated by an early exchange between Rufus and Dana, when Rufus—with genuine sincerity—points out that Dana's refusal to call him "Master" is no less an affront to his sense of self-respect than is his own habit of calling her "nigger" instead of "black" (30). Part of the power of the exchange resides in Dana's recognition, and the reader's, that there is a logic to Rufus's objection, even as it appalls. The flattening effect of formally egalitarian language is further exposed when Rufus insists to Dana that his father is too "fair" to mete out arbitrary punishment; he is right insofar as Weylin's beatings are always connected to some proscribed activity. But he also inadvertently highlights the perversity of a world that is governed by laws and bound by moral limits in which the mistreatment of blacks by whites is the norm, a world in which the same man who feels duty-bound to honor a promise given to Dana sees it equally as his obligation to beat her mercilessly when she forgets her "place" (134). It is a world in which the family that has informally enslaved Dana can demand repayment from her husband for her "keep" (187), and one in which promises to slaves are actually fulfilled in order to preserve the sanctity of a white man's word (181). The novel exposes a frame of reference in which blacks have responsibility without standing, and white men's standing allows them to define their responsibilities as they please. It suggests as well the continuing imprint of what Williams describes as the habit of power on white consciousnesses. As Dana notes when Rufus apologizes for betraying her, again, "He was always sorry. He would have been amazed, uncomprehending if I refused to forgive him. I remembered suddenly the way he used to talk to his mother. If he couldn't get what he wanted from her gently, he stopped being gentle. Why not? She always forgave him" (218).

Slavery and the Democratic Imagination

To underscore the ways in which *Kindred*'s rendering of the life and afterlife of slavery both challenges and enriches political reflection, I conclude by reading the novel against two recent attempts to come to terms with the political significance of past injustices: Jeremy Waldron's "Superseding Historic Injustice" and Thomas McCarthy's "*Vergangenheitsbewältigung* in the USA: On the Politics of the Memory of Slavery." Waldron's essay begins with the affirmation of the continuing importance of crimes of the past, and it is exemplary in its effort to resist the antimnemonic stance associated with the social contract tradition.[50] "To stand on the premise that the past cannot be changed," he writes, "is to ignore the fact that people and communities live whole lives, not just a series of momentary events, and that an injustice may blight, not just hurt, such a life."[51] Furthermore, Waldron explicitly recognizes the present pain, on the one hand, and self-satisfaction, on the other, that issue from public denials of the crimes of the past and the links between mistreatment in the past and present social arrangements. Despite the concerns that animate the essay, however, it concludes with a breezy dismissal of claims to restitution as simplistic, "unpleasant" equivalents of the playground cries of "first come, first served" and "we were here first" (28).[52] When contrasted with the richer moral picture conjured by Butler, it becomes clear how Waldron's rendering deflects difficult questions about the significance of large-scale injustices at the core of liberal democratic societies and, thereby, insulates today's citizens from a profound confrontation with those injustices.

One of the virtues of reading the novel and essay together is that it highlights the *narrative* choices made by the theorist. Superficially, both Butler and Waldron engage in a version of what Waldron calls "winding the film back"(12). Yet, Butler's deliberately fantastic telling forces the reader to consider the multiple and possibly contradictory demands the past makes on the present, demands that are elided in the attempt to tell the story within the limits of reason alone. Waldron's return to the past, in contrast, comes by way of counterfactuals. Committed to the view that "hypothetical rational choice is essential to our normative thinking about justice" (20), Waldron's essay asks how circumstances might be different if the original injustice—in this case, the theft of aboriginal lands—had not taken place:

> What would the tribal owners of that land have done with it, if wrongful appropriation had not taken place? To ask this question is to ask how people would have exercised their freedom if they had had a real choice. Would they have hung on to the land and passed it on to future generations of the tribe? Or would they have sold it—but this time for a fair price—to the first honest settler who came along? And, if the latter, what would he have done with it? Sold it again? Passed it on to his children? Lost it in a poker game? (9)

In this version of the past, present circumstances are the result of a chain of discrete, readily isolable decisions. There are no amputations, no calls from beyond the grave, but the abstraction is, in its own way, weirder than anything in *Kindred*.[53] Beyond the difficulties that inhere in assuming that *we* must engage in this kind of narrativizing in our considerations about justice, lie the unanswered questions raised by the description. For example: What does it mean to speculate about what "tribal owners" and "honest settlers" would have chosen to do apart from a telling of how these characters came to be recognizable as "tribal owners" and "honest settlers" in the first place? Although Waldron recognizes the absence of choice that defined the situation, the thinness of the description distorts the ways in which choice was compromised or denied and, thereby deflects the challenges posed by aboriginal claims today. Butler's portrait of the perpetually and differentially compromised situations of her characters and the complex social networks in which they act, by contrast, calls attention to what rationalist reconstructions of history omit.

Although Waldron admits that counterfactual arguments are problematic on a variety of counts, the rest of his essay raises further troubling questions about how responsibility is to be defined. On the one hand, it exaggerates the autonomy of the actors it describes by neglecting the role of relations of power in constituting them and shaping their decisions. On the other, it also understates their agency, especially the agency of the men and women who have profited from the wrong. Waldron's inquiry into whether entitlements can be "overtaken by circumstances," for example, describes the "changes" that intervene between the original theft of aboriginal lands and the present situation as though they were acts of God. Populations may multiply, ecological problems may or may not develop, new generations may find themselves more attached to the land than their ancestors, and it all appears to happen outside the realm of human responsibility. These are just "facts" in Waldron's view. They just happened. The ways these developments are intimately related to a complicated network of dislocations and dismemberments of the kind Butler describes remains beyond consideration.

Relatedly, Waldron's essay reveals how the commitment to formal equality that is so crucial to liberal theory undermines the aspiration to think historically about the demands of justice. In considering claims for restitution, Waldron emphasizes that it is crucial to "address the present circumstances in a way that respects the claims and needs of everyone" (27). This formulation pits those who have "innocently" benefited from past injustices against men and women whose claims can only be firmly established through speculation. "The present circumstances are the ones that are real," he writes. "It is in the actual world that people starve or are hurt or degraded" (27). But how to separate the hurt and degradation and even starving of today from crimes on the scale Waldron describes? Are all "claims and needs" to be treated as equals when it comes to assessing responsibility for the past? Butler offers no simple answer. Yet, her account of Rufus's sincerely felt "claim" to the title of "Master" and "need" for Alice's submission provides just one illustration of how easily privilege can be smuggled into ostensibly fair trade-offs.

Kindred's contribution to political reflection emerges in another way when contrasted with McCarthy's exploration of the presence of the past. Drawing parallels between the German "Historians' Debate" about the significance of Nazism and American debates about the legacy of slavery, McCarthy argues for the importance of historical education to shape citizens' conceptions of their identities and their responsibilities vis-à-vis the past.

He identifies a "lag in historical consciousness" between the discrediting of racist historiography—and the Lost Cause narratives it undergirds—among professional historians in the United States and the impact of those scholarly developments on the public imagination. Motivated by Americans' failure to muster the political will necessary to dismantle racial hierarchies, McCarthy's essay describes a political culture in which, to paraphrase Benjamin, Americans are capable of amazement at the fact that racial injustices are "still" possible in the twenty-first century.[54] Americans, particularly white Americans, refuse to acknowledge connections between current racial inequalities and the unjust practices of the past. "In the absence of widespread public familiarity with the causal background to contemporary racial problems," McCarthy reasons, "the political-cultural resources for resisting racist reframings of them are seriously impoverished."[55]

At one level, *Kindred* constitutes precisely the kind of reframing McCarthy would endorse. Butler documents antebellum life in order to dispel misinformation about the nature of slavery, and, by literally inserting the past into the present, she dramatizes the linkages between the enslavement of African Americans and present circumstances.[56] That Dana herself is educated through the experience and comes to a deeper understanding of herself and her society suggests Butler's interest in expanding readers' understanding of the past. At another level, however, *Kindred* raises troubling questions about the political efficacy of "historical enlightenment." Even as Butler corrects the record, she asks how much political mileage is to be gained by substituting for the distorted histories an account of "the way things really were." Ignorance, she recognizes, is not the whole of the problem. For example, when Kevin describes his sister's outraged response to the news of his impending marriage to Dana, he surmises that "she didn't even believe the garbage that she was handing me" (110). Knowing that her position is indefensible does not soften Kevin's sister's investment in protecting a world in which interracial marriage is unthinkable. And other characters similarly refuse to acknowledge what they know to be true. By exploring the self-justificatory mechanisms by which the characters defend their interests and attempt to camouflage their anxieties, Butler raises questions about how the stories of the American past have been produced and reproduced and to what effect.[57] She asks her reader to consider not only the falsity of the mythology that reduces a character like Sarah to will-lessness but also the character of the society that sustains such myths. Without attention to that context, righting the historical record has its own hazards. For to engage with slave narratives is, as Saidiya Hartman warns, to risk becoming numb to, narcissistically identifying with, or finding titillation in the horrors the narratives describe.[58] Even to revisit the past, as Butler does, without the presumption that there is a single fact of the matter, is not to define the politics that issues from that journey.[59] Thus, while *Kindred* affirms the importance of historical knowledge as a component of political change, it also insists that simply to tell the story is not enough. What is demanded is "repetition with a difference."[60]

In *Kindred*'s epilogue, Dana and Kevin return to Maryland and try to find the site of the Weylin plantation. Visits to the Maryland Historical Society provide some concrete evidence—a newspaper article about a fire that destroyed the house, notices of slave sales—of the fates of the men and women still living on the Weylin plantation when Dana left for the last time. But the slaves not listed in those notices and the plantation itself are like the "empty place" where Dana's arm once was (10). Like Dana's phantom limb, their memories throb. Although Dana and Kevin know that they cannot get satisfaction for their questions and they rightly worry about the dangers of letting Rufus's world overwhelm their own, they agree that their future depends on the effort to touch the past. As Deborah McDowell puts it, "getting 'beyond' slavery" requires "remembering it, paradoxically burying it and bearing it."[61] And the tensions that inhere in this conclusion point Butler's readers, finally, toward a trio of not readily compatible ideas at the heart of the narrative: that the horrors of slavery are unbelievable, profoundly and often unequally inaccessible in certain respects; that coming to terms with the past will not miraculously release Americans from it; and that this history must nonetheless be revisited, touched, and remembered, for the sake of the fragile, impermanent, always compromised health of American democracy.[62]

Notes

1. This chapter does not make precise distinctions between "memory" and "history," both because the edges of the terms are blurred in practice and because I aim to resist the impulse to privilege one over the other. For a helpful account of the stakes of the history/memory controversy and the variety of meanings attached to the terms, see Dominick LaCapra, *History and Memory after Auschwitz* (Ithaca, NY: Cornell University Press, 1998), 8–42.

2. Toni Morrison, "The Pain of Being Black," interview by Bonnie Angelo, *Time* 133 (May 22, 1989): 120–23.

3. As Martha Biondi, "The Rise of the Reparations Movement," *Radical History Review* (fall 2003): 8, points out, African American arguments for reparations constitute a political tradition that stretches back to the nineteenth century, but "the reparations movement has never enjoyed greater popularity among African Americans or mainstream black leadership than now."

4. Patricia J. Williams, *The Alchemy of Race and Rights: Diary of a Law Professor* (Cambridge, MA: Harvard University Press, 1991), esp. chs. 2 and 12. W. E. B. DuBois's image of the "two passing figures of the present-past"—one a former slave owner whose sons have died in battle and the other a former slave whose own son, the child of that same owner, died at the hands of lynchers—is as affecting an image as any of the ways in which the possessors and the dispossessed of American racial history re-

mained bound together after the war [*The Souls of Black Folk*, ed. David W. Blight and Robert Gooding-Williams (1903; repr. Boston: Bedford Books, 1997), 54–55].

5. Although DuBois is describing the longings of white Atlantans at the turn of the twentieth century, recent political events provide ample evidence of the continuing hold of the "untrue dream." The skirmishes over the nominations of John Ashcroft and Gale Norton to cabinet positions, for example, included debates about their indebtedness to "Lost Cause" interpretations of the Civil War. Furthermore, Trent Lott's open nostalgia for the segregationist world suggests that DuBois's comment has not lost its acuity.

6. Ralph Ellison, "What America Would Be Like without Blacks," in *Going to the Territory* (New York: Vintage, 1986), 105.

7. Michel-Rolph Trouillot, *Silencing the Past: Power and the Production of History* (Boston: Beacon Press, 1995), 96–97.

8. Benedict Anderson, *Imagined Communities: Reflections on the Origin and Spread of Nationalism*, rev. ed. (London: Verso, 1991), 201. See also David W. Blight, "Quarrel Forgotten or a Revolution Remembered? Reunion and Race in the Memory of the Civil War, 1875–1913," in *Union and Emancipation: Essays on Politics and Race in the Civil War Era*, ed. David W. Blight and Brooks D. Simpson (Kent, OH: Kent State University Press, 1997), 151–79.

9. Sheldon S. Wolin, "Injustice and Collective Memory," in *The Presence of the Past: Essays on the State and the Constitution* (Baltimore: Johns Hopkins University Press, 1989), 34.

10. Wolin, "Injustice and Collective Memory," 34.

11. Judith N. Shklar, *Ordinary Vices* (Cambridge, MA: Harvard University Press, 1984), 230.

12. For a helpful distinction between the function of abstraction per se and racially "idealizing" abstraction, see Charles Mills, *The Racial Contract* (Ithaca, NY: Cornell University Press, 1997), 76.

13. J. Peter Euben, "Platonic Noise," *Political Theory* 31 (February 2003): 66.

14. Walter Benjamin, "Theses on the Philosophy of History," in *Illuminations*, ed. Hannah Arendt, trans. Harry Zohn (New York: Schocken Books, 1969), 255.

15. As Robert Crossley notes in his introduction to Octavia Butler, *Kindred* (Boston: Beacon Press, 1979), xii, Butler herself has said that, since there is "absolutely no science fiction in it," *Kindred* is better understood as a "grim fantasy." For studies of the novel as "memory machine," "neo-slave narrative," and historical novel, respectively, see Lisa Yaszek, "'A Grim Fantasy': Remaking American History in Octavia Butler's *Kindred*," *Signs* 28 (summer 2003): 1053–66; Ashraf H. A. Rushdy, *Remembering Generations: Race and Family in Contemporary African American Fiction* (Chapel Hill: University of North Carolina Press, 2001); Sandra Y. Govan, "Homage to Tradition: Octavia Butler Renovates the Historical Novel," *MELUS* 13 (spring–summer 1986): 79–86.

16. Charles S. Meier, "Overcoming the Past? Narrative and Negotiation, Remembering, and Reparation: Issues at the Interface of History and the Law," in *Politics and the Past: On Repairing Historical Injustices*, ed. John Torpey (Lanham, MD: Rowman & Littlefield, 2003), 301.

17. Toni Morrison, "The Site of Memory," in *Inventing the Truth: The Art and Craft of Memoir*, ed. William Zinsser (Boston: Houghton Mifflin, 1987), 113.

18. See Ann DuCille, "The Occult of True Black Womanhood," in *Skin Trade* (Cambridge, MA: Harvard University Press, 1996), 81–119.

19. Butler, *Kindred*, 221. Subsequent references to this text will be noted parenthetically in the body of the paper.

20. For an attempt to use "magical realism" to effect "dramatic dislocations in conventional wisdom" about race and law in the post–civil rights U.S., see Lani Guinier and Gerald Torres, *The Miner's Canary: Enlisting Race, Resisting Power, Transforming Democracy* (Cambridge, MA: Harvard University Press, 2002), 25.

21. Crossley, "Introduction," xi.

22. See Frederick Douglass, *Narrative of the Life of Frederick Douglass, An American Slave*, ed. John W. Blassingame, John R. McKivigan, and Peter P. Hinks (1845; repr. New Haven, CT: Yale University Press, 2001), 74. Douglass's *Narrative* was, according to Crossley, one of the texts Butler consulted in her research for the book ("Introduction," xx). For further discussion of Butler's references to Douglass and of the links between Dana and Douglass, see Christine Levecq, "Power and Repetition: Philosophies of (Literary) History in Octavia E. Butler's *Kindred*," *Contemporary Literature* 41 (fall 2000): 523–53.

23. Levecq, "Power and Repetition," 527–28.

24. Govan, "Homage to Tradition," 94.

25. Ira Berlin, *Many Thousands Gone: The First Two Centuries of Slavery in North America* (Cambridge, MA: Belknap/Harvard University Press, 1998), 256.

26. Avishai Margalit, *The Ethics of Memory* (Cambridge, MA: Harvard University Press, 2002).

27. Rushdy, *Remembering Generations*, 8.

28. Michel Foucault, "Nietzsche, Genealogy, History," in *Language, Counter-Memory, Practice: Selected Essays and Interviews*, ed. Donald F. Bouchard, trans. Donald F. Bouchard and Sherry Simon (Ithaca, NY: Cornell University Press, 1977), 139.

29. Foucault, "Nietzsche, Genealogy, History," 148 (emphasis added).

30. Angelyn Mitchell, "Not Enough of the Past: Feminist Revisions of Slavery in Octavia E. Butler's *Kindred*," *MELUS* 26 (fall 2001), 55.

31. Shane Phelan, "(Be)Coming Out: Lesbian Identity and Politics," *Signs* 18 (summer 1993): 774.

32. Rushdy, *Remembering Generations*, 100–101.

33. Sheldon S. Wolin, "Introduction," *The Presence of the Past: Essays on the State and the Constitution* (Baltimore: Johns Hopkins University Press, 1989), 3.

34. Trouillot, *Silencing the Past*, 96.

35. "In effect," observes Charles Mills, *Blackness Visible: Essays on Philosophy and Race* (Ithaca, NY: Cornell University Press, 1998), 147, "whites have been a disadvantaged epistemic community."

36. See William L. Andrews, *To Tell a Free Story: The First Century of Afro-American Autobiography, 1760–1865* (Urbana: University of Illinois Press, 1986).

37. My claim for the importance of the "*dis-membering* of slaves from their families, their labor, their selves" as a central theme in *Kindred* was inspired by Mae G. Henderson's reading of *Beloved*. Mae G. Henderson, "Toni Morrison's *Beloved*: Re-Membering the Body as Historical Text," in *Comparative American Identities: Race, Sex, and Nationality in the Modern Text*, ed. Hortense J. Spillers (New York: Routledge, 1991), 62–86 (emphasis in the original). For an illuminating exploration of

the relationship between dismemberment and political corruption, see J. Peter Euben, *The Tragedy of Political Theory: The Road Not Taken* (Princeton, NJ: Princeton University Press, 1990).

38. Hortense J. Spillers, "Mama's Baby, Papa's Maybe: An American Grammar Book," *Diacritics* (summer 1987): 67.

39. The novel thus cautions against indulging in the pleasure/pain of "memory-envy." See Geoffrey Hartman, "Public Memory and Its Discontents," *Raritan* 13 (spring 1994): 39–40.

40. Although Butler does not make this connection explicitly, the novel also stands as a warning about what gets lost when a democratic impulse is institutionalized as policy.

41. Douglass, *Narrative*, 50.

42. Spillers, "Mama's Baby, Papa's Maybe," 74.

43. Williams, *Alchemy of Race and Rights*, 217.

44. Elizabeth Ann Beaulieu, *Black Women Writers and the American Neo-Slave Narrative: Femininity Unfettered* (Westport, CT: Greenwood Press, 1999), 118–32, develops this theme further, exploring the ways in which Dana serves as a "mother" to Rufus.

45. For a critique of political appeals to the trope of family, see Paul Gilroy, "It's a Family Affair," in *Black Popular Culture*, ed. Gina Dent (Seattle: Bay Press, 1992), 303–16.

46. For an account of black labor's role in securing the economic achievements of the nineteenth-century United States, see W. E. B. DuBois, *Black Reconstruction in America: An Essay toward a History of the Part Which Black Folk Played in the Attempt to Reconstruct Democracy in America, 1860–1880* (1935; repr. Cleveland, Ohio: Meridian, 1964).

47. Morrison, "Site of Memory," 110; Saidiya V. Hartman, *Scenes of Subjection: Terror, Slavery, and Self-Making in Nineteenth-Century America* (New York: Oxford University Press, 1997), 49–78.

48. In a 1997 interview, Butler recounts the exchange that inspired the novel. Arriving at Pasadena City College at a point when the Black Power movement was a powerful presence on campus, she met another student who "was still blaming [his parents] for their humility and their acceptance of disgusting behavior on the part of employers and other people. He said, 'I'd like to kill all these old people who have been holding us back for so long. But I can't because I'd have to start with my own parents.' When he said *us* he meant black people, and when he said *old people* he meant older black people" [Octavia E. Butler, "An Interview with Octavia E. Butler," by Charles H. Rowell, *Callaloo* 20 (1997): 51 (emphasis in the original)].

49. Hartman, *Scenes of Subjection*, 53.

50. See Wolin, "Injustice and Collective Memory," 32–46.

51. Jeremy Waldron, "Superseding Historic Injustice," *Ethics* 103 (October 1992): 7. Subsequent references to this essay will be noted parenthetically in the body of the text.

52. This kind of dismissal might be compared to the divide in public opinion about reparations for American slavery in which, according to Michael Dawson and Rovana Popoff in "Reparations: Justice and Greed in Black and White," *The DuBois Review* 1 (2004): 47–91, most white Americans "see the quest for reparations as a manifestation of black greed."

53. For a compelling account of the ways in which narrative structure, and the process of "disaggregation" in particular, can obscure the operation of racial power, see Kimberlé Crenshaw and Gary Peller, "Reel Time/Real Justice," in *Reading Rodney King/Reading Urban Uprising*, ed. Robert Gooding-Williams (New York: Routledge, 1993), 56–70.

54. Benjamin, "Theses on the Philosophy of History," 257.

55. Thomas McCarthy, "*Vergangenheitsbewältigung* in the USA: On the Politics of the Memory of Slavery," *Political Theory* 30 (October 2002): 641.

56. See, e.g., Melvin L. Oliver and Thomas M. Shapiro's discussion of the "sedimentation of racial inequality" in *Black Wealth/White Wealth: A New Perspective on Racial Inequality* (New York: Routledge, 1997).

57. One way to think about the difference between McCarthy and Butler is to consider a distinction Robert Gooding-Williams makes between "demystification" and "demythification." McCarthy's aim is to demystify American racial history, to reveal the actual causal chains between past and present injustices that are occluded in public discourse about race. While Butler might be said to share McCarthy's interest in such a correction, she also recognizes the limitations of what he calls "historical enlightenment." In "demythifying" that history, she calls critical attention to the ways in which racialized understandings of the past operate in American lives. See Robert Gooding-Williams, "'Look, A Negro!'" in *Reading Rodney King/Reading Urban Uprising*, ed. Robert Gooding-Williams (New York: Routledge, 1993), 158.

58. Hartman, *Scenes of Subjection*, 4. See also Mark Reinhardt's account of the pleasures of reliving the horrors of slavery and segregation and the responsibilities that fall to those of us "who still traffic in slave narratives" in "Who Speaks for Margaret Garner? Slavery, Silence, and the Politics of Ventriloquism," *Critical Inquiry* 29 (autumn 2002): 81–119.

59. As Wendy Brown explains in *Politics out of History* (Princeton, NJ: Princeton University Press, 2001), 119, "A genealogical politics has no necessary political entailments."

60. George Shulman, "American Political Culture, Prophetic Narration, and Toni Morrison's *Beloved*," *Political Theory* 24 (May 1996): 306.

61. Deborah E. McDowell, "Negotiating between Tenses: Witnessing Slavery after Freedom—*Dessa Rose*," in *Slavery and the Literary Imagination*, ed. Deborah E. McDowell and Arnold Rampersad (Baltimore: Johns Hopkins University Press, 1989), 155.

62. Earlier versions of this chapter were presented at the Collegium for African American Research and at the annual meeting of the American Political Science Association. I am grateful for the comments of participants in both sessions and, particularly, for the suggestions of Wendy Brown, Roxanne Euben, Donald Moon, and George Shulman.

9

"Hello Babies"

Eliot Rosewater and the Art of Citizenship in the Graduation Speeches of Kurt Vonnegut

D. A. Hamlin

> I have only this to say, basically: This is the end—this childhood's end for certain.
>
> —Kurt Vonnegut, graduation speech at Fredonia College[1]

Kurt Vonnegut has told readers that one of his favorite songs is "Class of '57" by the Statler Brothers, so much so that he reprinted the lyrics in *Palm Sunday*.[2] An elegy of disappointment about life after graduation, the song should be our national anthem, according to Vonnegut. Such a change would tell the world that American commencement ceremonies are the beginning of the path to underachievement if one is lucky, disaster if one is not. Vonnegut's graduation speeches reveal a philosophy that somewhere amid the celebration, one generation should give the next one the bad news. Really bad news, usually. "My wife begged me to bring you light," he told the graduating class at Bennington College in 1970, "but there is no light. Everything is going to become unimaginably worse, and never get better again."[3] As an artist, Vonnegut sees his role as something like a canary in a coal mine, warning fellow citizens about noxious times to come. Thus, he told the American Physical Society, "The most useful thing I could do before this meeting is to keel over."[4]

Even as a moment marking achievement, graduation is also a time of subsurface dread. Those commencement smiles that later show up in celebratory photographs mask complicated anxiety. Graduates realize that the four years they have been allowed to themselves for training and self-discovery are over, and society replaces this indulgence with expectations. By taking a degree, most of them have accomplished no more than what was expected of them. They receive their diplomas with sunny hopes, to be sure, but also with conflicted emotions, and more often than not, mortgagelike debt. To pay it off, many graduates head directly to law or business school, where it is possible to dig the hole exponentially deeper. They also understand that in America, the future for them is increasingly

Darwinian; they must contribute or crawl out of the way. The air is close in a commencement hall, thick with smiling apprehension. As their speaker, Vonnegut breathes this atmosphere, a canary with a mortarboard.

A commencement address is a form of intergenerational dialogue, and the diploma itself is recognizable as a *wampeter*, Vonnegut's term for "an object around which the lives of many otherwise unrelated people may revolve."[5] Traditionally, the commencement speaker has earned a legitimate standing to address graduates by virtue of experience and achievement in the world they are poised to enter. The grandiose verb most often used to describe this transfer of insight is "impart," which suggests that the information the speaker will bestow—presumably the last kernel of knowledge one will absorb while at college—is important enough to warrant the reflection of newly polished minds. As a storyteller, Vonnegut recognizes that the address is somehow intended to be the "snapper of a college education," the kind of revelation at the end that is essential to a reader's understanding of the whole tale.[6] It need not be solemn, for often the most sought-after speakers are the ones who can entertain if not edify. Yet, the role of the speaker is signaled most succinctly when we recognize which audience within the audience the speaker has been brought to address. Speakers like Bill Cosby are hired for the laughter, but most of the jokes will be about how much money the parents have just spent with the strong possibility that their offspring will return to, instead of leave, the nest. This is in spite of the reality of student loans, and without speaking at all to the weakness of an economy that generally offers too few jobs. Such speakers josh the graduates and wink at their mothers and fathers. Also listening to a speaker are the educators and administrators of the institution itself. Serious, high-level players like Colin Powell are a testament, more than anything, to the marketable prestige of the school. U.S. presidents often announce major policy positions from the podium of a commencement stage. When the bearers of real-world gravitas speak to the graduates, the representatives of the college or university are the ones who beam like parents. But the primary audience, nominally if not in fact, is the graduating class. Gowned in rented academic regalia, seated on folding chairs, their very presence marks them as a final but transient product.

In the early 1970s, Kurt Vonnegut became a perennial student favorite as a graduation speaker, if only because his ironic pacifism spoke humanely to a wartime generation. Over the years, his commencement voice reached such a level of familiarity that the lyrics of "Everybody's Free to Wear Sunscreen," a hit pop song in 1999, were widely reported to be one of Vonnegut's graduation addresses, despite the fact that he had never delivered such a speech.[7] Closer to the truth, however, is that rather than being strictly ironic, Vonnegut's message to graduates has been consistently earnest. His speeches are infused with the humanistic politics that established their relationship to him as readers. Indeed, many of Vonnegut's works are featured prominently on college syllabi. Graduates know that he will make them laugh, but they listen for his insight. In that, Vonnegut assumes the traditional role of the commencement speaker more powerfully than most, even as he subverts that position by telling them that citizenship in their society will be disappointing and lonely. But though they will be stuck with inept, deteriorating, and sometimes cruel institutions, without much possibility for change, Vonnegut also tells graduates that only they can deny themselves satisfying lives of good simple purpose.

"Help Is Not on the Way"

Vonnegut has said that his motives are political, that writers should be "agents for change."[8] They should educate and warn. Scientists are poor democratic educators because they have little concern for history or the soul, much less the question of political equality. Science and technology can change the world with immediacy and dramatic results. Such change is ultimately superficial, however, because while scientists and engineers can bring the future to us, their contributions come without the moral clarity necessary for humane progress. Artists can do this in a democracy. They can see things coming, and they can effect change through the subtle influence of language and stories. Vonnegut sees the writer's political role as an evolutionary contribution, without survival-of-the-fittest tough love. Yet, the effect is late and slow, generational at best, so the moral of the story must come decades in advance. Thinking carefully and long-term, a writer who wants to serve democratic politics must operate with faith in the educational possibilities of storytelling. In his fiction, Vonnegut has often returned to a basic theme, in his own words, "people who behaved decently in an indecent society."[9] Certainly Vonnegut would carry this understanding of his role in society to the podium at a commencement ceremony. At that moment, it is no longer possible to change their parents or influence the professionals who run the university, but it may not be too late for the graduates.[10] The special relationship Vonnegut has to the young is often noted.[11] In the commencement speech at Bennington College, the first one he ever delivered, he told the graduates that his own youthful optimism was transformed into fully matured pessimism when he was their age; learning of events such as Hiroshima and German extermination programs had darkened a view of progress that had already been staggered by his experiences as a prisoner of war in Dresden during the Allied massacre of a civilian population in 1944. A desire to avoid making war seem attractive to future generations was a primary concern in *Slaughterhouse-Five*.[12] In a typical commencement address, he effectively melts the generational barrier by simply welcoming the graduates into the dispirited reality of adulthood. "We are all experiencing more or less the same lifetime now," he told the graduating class at Fredonia College.

One of the matters Vonnegut is pessimistic about is liberalism, even though it is a way of life that would seem to be inherently optimistic.[13] Human beings, free of mind and with minimal restraints, are presumed capable and motivated enough to operate sturdy institutions. When they are adequately grounded in education and culture and briefed on the issues, citizens will have the sensibilities to know when to leave each other alone and when to form bucket brigades for the problems they face in common. This kind of democratic faith pretty much fills out the definition of Vonnegut's concept of *foma*—"harmless untruths, intended to comfort simple souls."[14] In their primary and secondary school careers, American students are suckled on *foma*. They advance through an educational system that labors to establish in them, explicitly or through osmosis, that their lives are defined by opportunity. Higher education assumes that this belief has sufficiently taken hold: thus, the only political education a college student is generally required to endure, if any at all, is a refresher on the existence of Congress, the president, and a Supreme Court to occasionally call the tie. Most of what they will learn of politics reflects how political scientists bring their training to bear on issues of policy. Yet, what college students are *not* required to consider are the dire limitations of democratic life, the dismaying sense of uselessness in the life of an American citizen. This is where Vonnegut likes to fill in the gaps on the reading list.

Vonnegut typically deflates commencement platitudes early on, as he did in the speech at Fredonia College, where he mocked conventional advice about making money and winning love, also reminding his listeners not to murder or put things in their ears. His initial tone often suggests that commencement speakers, including him, should not be taken too seriously. "I am about to make my own ancestral guess as to what life is all about, what young people should do with it," he announced at Hobart and William Smith Colleges. "I will again issue the caveat that I am as full of baloney as anybody, and that anybody who says for sure what life is all about might as well lecture on Santa Claus and the Easter Bunny and tooth fairies, as well."[15] That he subverts the commencement tradition so immediately demonstrates his faith in the form, revealing a belief that any speaker who addresses graduates dishonestly is failing in a responsibility to tell them how blasé citizenship in America can be, and that's on a good day. The bad days are painful and fruitless. "If I lied to you about that," he told the graduates at Bennington, "you would sense that I had lied to you, and that would be one more cause for gloom. We have enough causes for gloom." A Kurt Vonnegut commencement address often employs this dampening voice, for he makes sure the graduates have some idea of what they have no chance of accomplishing. Bleak as it sounds, however, Vonnegut's message balances futility with hope, what the critic Robert Scholes called Vonnegut's capacity to "put bitter coating on sweet pills."[16] Vonnegut himself is conscious of the need to form some kind of harmony of perspective, telling the graduates at

Fredonia College that his stance before them could be captured by paraphrasing Friedrich Nietzsche's line that only a person of great faith can be a skeptic.

The bitter taste of Vonnegut's pessimism is rooted in a rejection of another tenet of liberal faith, the idea of progress. In two of his earliest novels, *Player Piano* and *Cat's Cradle*, he warned that our scientific achievements and engineering feats may bring expanded knowledge and efficiency, but this is a kind of technical advancement, not enlightenment. That is why when he spoke to graduates at the Massachusetts Institute of Technology, he reminded them that the science they perform is a combination of their expertise and somebody else's agenda. "It can make quite a difference not just to you but to humanity: the sort of boss you choose, whose dreams you help come true."[17] Like Mark Twain, Vonnegut excoriates the relationship of politics to technology, although to give credit where it is due, he told his audience that he would grade the work of the designers at Auschwitz and Birkenau with an A+: "They surely solved all the problems set for them."[18] The development of the atomic bomb, he told the graduates at Agnes Scott College, was simply the reality of Mary Wollstonecraft Shelley's prescience.[19]

Vonnegut also douses graduates with realism. "Pollyanna is not your graduation orator today," he said to his audience at Agnes Scott College, admitting that he does not see the good in everything. "So I will comment, as briefly and efficiently as possible, on the perfectly horrible news CNN has been giving us about the Balkans and that high school in Colorado." Speaking at Bennington College only days after the Kent State shootings, Vonnegut suggested that establishing a Reserve Officers' Training Corps, or ROTC, unit at Bennington would bring important insight about military types and their weapons. "There is a lesson for all of us in machine guns and tanks: Work within the system." When it comes to solving the world's problems, he advised those same graduates to "skylark" for a while instead, because they do not yet have the wealth or power to fix things and because the notion that they should save the world at this point in their lives is a "great swindle." Nevertheless, Vonnegut does not want them thinking that some cosmic or spiritual force will bail us out in the end. He told the graduates at Hobart and William Smith Colleges that even extraordinary natural phenomena, like the comet Kahoutek, are but a fizzling signal that

> We can expect no miracles from the heavens, that the problems of ordinary human beings will have to be solved by ordinary human beings. The message of Kahoutek is: "Help is not on the way. Repeat: help is not on the way."

Perhaps the most bitter of all the pills Vonnegut offers graduates is that their lives as Americans will feel empty. "No matter how old we are, we are going to be bored and lonely during what remains of our lives," he told graduates at Fredonia College.

> We are so lonely because we don't have enough friends and relatives. Human beings are supposed to live in stable, like-minded extended families of fifty or more. . . . When we or our ancestors came to America, though, we were agreeing, among other things, to do without such families. It is a painful, unhuman agreement to make. Emotionally, it is hideously expensive.[20]

Human beings need such ties, he explained at Hobart and William Smith Colleges, "almost as much as they need B-complex vitamins and a heartfelt moral code." He later advised the future political leaders in that same audience, "You would be very shrewd indeed if you recognize that the people are in fact crying out not so much for money as for relief from loneliness." The reality of living in a society that is not psychologically or emotionally appropriate to their needs ends up making people homesick; young people identify with Hesse, Vonnegut wrote elsewhere, because this homesickness is acknowledged in his works.[21] "I sure wish I could wave a wand," Vonnegut told graduates at Agnes Scott College, "and give every one of you an extended family—make you an Ibo or a Navaho—or a Kennedy." At Syracuse, he declared the entire audience to be members of *Generation A*, a new extended family, albeit a family limited to one ceremony on one day.[22] It is even worth remembering here that the subtitle of *Slapstick* is "Lonesome No More!"[23]

In short, things can be so bad that Vonnegut has said that he thinks the planet should be renamed "Triage."[24] With all the tragic choices we have to make about the wounded and dying, earth must manage on its own, with no help on the way, bowling alone in the universe.

But Scholes' insight holds true in that, despite the limits and bleak realities the future holds for graduates, Vonnegut invariably tempers his pessimism with humanist hope. In fact, every reason for pessimism represents a reason for possibility, because for Vonnegut, young people in commencement settings are at least for that moment the very definition of possibility. The graduation ceremony is thus an optimistic event with a skeptical coating, the very opposite of what most of its participants take it to be. The taste of his words may be bitter at first, but there is an essential sweetness inside, and his speeches are an effort to bring it to the graduates. "I would like to do that now, to have the bitterness of my pessimism melt away, leaving you with mouthfuls of a sort of vanilla fudge goo," he told the Bennington graduates.

> But I find it harder and harder to prepare confections of this sort—particularly since our military scientists have taken to firing at crowds of their own people. Also—I took a trip to Biafra last January, and that was a million laughs. And this hideous war in Indochina goes on and on.
>
> Still—I will give you what goo I have left.

The "goo" has a familiar ring to it, however, for there is a voice in Vonnegut's fiction that sounds a lot like the voice coming from the podium during one of his commencement speeches. It is the voice of Eliot Rosewater.[25] *God Bless You, Mr. Rosewater* is subtitled *Or Pearls before Swine*, revealing Vonnegut's sense of hopelessness for the misfits and ne'er-do-wells Rosewater attempts to help with his millions.[26] But this sentiment is not reflected in Vonnegut's attitude toward graduates. The attitude Vonnegut shows in a graduation speech is more like the attitude of Eliot Rosewater when asked to perform a baptism for twins born to one of his pathetic social projects. The baptismal rite Eliot improvises for the occasion reflects a desire to factually inform the infants, while at the same time encouraging them to adopt a simple but useful approach to the maintenance of their humanity:

> Hello babies. Welcome to earth. It's hot in the summer and cold in the winter. It's round and wet and crowded. At the outside, babies, you've got about a hundred years here. There's only one rule that I know of, babies: God damn it, you've got to be kind.

In tone and purpose, a Kurt Vonnegut commencement speech is an Eliot Rosewater baptism, a chance to speak usefully to a particular audience. For Vonnegut, graduates at a commencement ceremony are newborns: he takes the opportunity to baptize them with an honest appraisal of the world they are entering, and he throws in a little advice on how to be a human being.

"Hello Babies"

When Eliot Rosewater gets his chance to address an audience that is dear to him, a gathering of science fiction writers, he speaks with characteristic effusion. "I love you sons of bitches," he tells them. Rosewater adores the writers of science fiction because he sees their attention channeled toward understanding the ordinary and the cataclysmic, pondering questions at once minute and awesome, typically attempting to make sense of today by formulating tomorrow in their heads. A college student does the same thing all in one dorm-room bull session. Graduates are an audience that Vonnegut understands, toward whom he exhibits great warmth. They are still in a place, intellectually and emotionally, where they are more open to possibility, and the information graduates have spent four years accumulating is still fresh enough to be called knowledge. Despite anxiety about what comes next, it is still a moment of dreams coming true and dreams commencing. To Rosewater, science fiction writers are like poets, more sensitive to important changes, and beyond the average person in their willingness to speculate about the direction of a society's path. Vonnegut sees this in graduates: they may be holding at a social weigh station, but graduates also occupy a position from which they can envision the future—if only their own futures—with a peculiar opportunity to move from theory to practice.

More traditional graduation speeches attempt to "impart" wisdom, with copious and banal references to the promise of the future. Vonnegut welcomes graduates not so much to the world of tomorrow as to the reality of today, a reality that one cannot expect to change radically in the future. Appreciating the ceremonial moment, Vonnegut initiates them as though they were immigrants who have just been naturalized. The metaphor is appropriate, for what he really welcomes graduates to is the task of citizenship. In this sense, a Vonnegut graduation speech echoes the letter Eliot Rosewater leaves in a safety deposit box for his successor to the leadership of the Rosewater Foundation. Both messages offer a critique of America: the audience is coming into something valuable, and the speakers want them to understand where the wealth comes from, and how it operates in a "stupid and savage" class system.[27] Relative to the rest of the world, to be an American is to inherit vast political and economic riches, an unlimited reach of opportunity. The great American objective is to achieve and acquire. For Vonnegut, however, the goal is a new kind of citizenship. The new American is committed to decency and affection toward others, informed by a factual base of scientific and historical knowledge, satisfied with less-than-glorious contributions to society, psychologically rewarded for being useful, and able to bond with other Americans, even if what holds them together is a common desire to feel less empty. In the minds of many, these apparently small efforts garner a reward that is unimpressive as a measure of American accomplishment and status. True, it may not seem like much, but for Vonnegut it is everything, because it is possible.

God Bless You, Mr. Rosewater suggests that in America, to concern oneself with decency toward the less fortunate is a sign of insanity. Sen. Lister Ames Rosewater would rather consider his son a drunk than entertain the idea that Eliot's desire to help the downtrodden is a rational and worthy purpose. As a result of her sympathies for the dregs of society, Sylvia Rosewater suffers a mental collapse not once but twice. Her psychiatrist identifies this concern as the root cause of a peculiar affliction, *samaritrophia*, "the suppression of an overactive conscience by the rest of the mind." Eliot is most certainly sick, his illness embedded in an accidental wartime atrocity and in his role in the accidental death of his mother, whom Eliot describes as a "wise and amusing woman, with very sincere anxieties about the condition of the poor." Vonnegut's own position on the matter is not that being decent is insane; the problem, rather, is an unweaning desire to fix everything up for the lazy and unlucky. Eliot's experiment fails because there are limits to what love and money can accomplish. The message Vonnegut brings to graduates amplifies this reality. He wants them to understand that it is unwise and unhealthy to help others from a belief that others can always be helped or that they can always learn to help themselves. Even Eliot seems to understand the complexity of the situation, to some extent, as evidenced by the graffiti he leaves in public bathrooms: "If you would be unloved and forgotten, be reasonable." The new citizen Vonnegut envisions will live in conscientious equilibrium, prepared to help but not beyond the bounds of reasonableness where concern deteriorates into pathological do-goodism. For Vonnegut, decency is a political virtue. The decency of a citizen may not be able to transform society, but it is still a good idea simply because we need it. Decency is the only rule Rosewater sets out for the babies, and it is the primary admonition Vonnegut foists upon graduates. *God damn it, you've got to be kind.* According to Kilgore Trout, the main lesson Eliot learned from his time spent among the losers of Rosewater County, Indiana, is that "people can use all the uncritical love they can get." Trout continues,

> It's news that a man was able to *give* that kind of love over a long period of time. If one man can do it, perhaps others can do it, too. It means that our hatred of useless human beings and the cruelties we inflict upon them need not be parts of human nature. Thanks to the example of Eliot Rosewater, millions upon millions of people may learn to love and help whomever they see.

Vonnegut told his audience at Agnes Scott College that just by making the effort required to graduate, "you have made our little planet, our precious little moist, blue-green ball, a saner place than it was before you got here." While admitting that he is a humanist, in commencement speeches Vonnegut has also expressed his admiration for the Seven Spiritual Works of Mercy, the Seven Corporal Works of Mercy, and the Sermon on the Mount.[28] The theme of his address to the graduates at Southampton College was to not give up on humanity, to be smart and make power listen.[29] At Bennington, he begged the graduates to cling to the "most ridiculous superstition of all," that humanity is at the center of the universe. Eliot Rosewater is often referred to as a saint of one kind or another. Vonnegut shared with the graduates at Syracuse what he once told a worried pregnant woman: decency in an indecent society is a kind of sainthood, for the decent among us make living worthwhile. "Perhaps many of us here, regardless of our ages or power or wealth, can be saints for her child to meet." His consistent message to graduates is that it is possible to be decent and honorable in America. You do not have to be crazy to be a saint.

In preparing Eliot for the court hearing on his mental capacity to head the Rosewater Foundation, Kilgore Trout argues that Eliot's attempt to sustain the abandoned and distraught was a sane, valuable endeavor. Eliot's failure was valiant because it engaged a looming crisis for industrial societies. "The problem is this: How to love people who have no use?" This is a matter of tragic importance to Vonnegut, a nagging theme he also explores in *Player Piano*. The most troubling aspect of human worthlessness is the inevitability of the affliction. He sees it as nothing less than an ultimate concern. Trout sums it up for Eliot: "So—if we can't find reasons and methods for treasuring human beings because they are human beings, then we might as well, as has so often been suggested, rub them out." No wonder Vonnegut raises the issue with graduates on the day they leave the world of curriculum, a day like no other if only because their expulsion is so immediate. "This is Eden," he clarified for the graduates at Rice, "and you're about to be kicked out. Why? You ate the knowledge apple. It's in your tummies now."[30]

College is perhaps the last truly democratic structure in the lives of those who have shared it. From there it is unequal parcels of promise and despair, setback and success. The real world has computers to do the thinking and machines to do the work, so their lives will be an inescapable struggle to avoid redundancy. In America, if they become useless, they will be reviled, and they know it. Given his belief that writers have a role to play in society, Vonnegut is acting on his own advice. Making all those graduation speeches is one way to be useful. Eliot's desire to be useful is most efficiently captured in his obsession with volunteer fire departments. To Kilgore Trout, it is one more sign that Eliot is sane and well applied in his work, because these volunteers are "almost the only examples of enthusiastic usefulness to be seen in this land." Besides water, they bring comfort and pity. "There we have people treasuring people as people." Speaking at Rice, Vonnegut abruptly dismissed the notion that their expensive college degrees will return the investment by bringing them the kind of money Eliot Rosewater was handed through the accident of birth. Instead, the richness of their destinies will more likely be found in the use they make of themselves locally, although they will receive much less money and only the occasional gesture of gratitude. "Please love such a destiny, if it turns out to be yours—for communities are all that is substantial about what we create or defend or maintain in this world." He borrows from Twain a definition of the most satisfying object of human efforts: *the good opinion of one's neighbors.* "To earn their good opinions, you should apply the special skills you have learned here, and meet the standards of decency and honor and fair play set by exemplary books and elders." To the graduates of Southampton College he offered "a truly modern hero," Ignaz Semmelweis, the nineteenth-century Hungarian obstetrician who labored to convince his colleagues that they should wash their hands when moving from patient to patient. Proved right, his reward was to be shunned by the highest levels of his medical community. Nevertheless, Vonnegut implored his audience to be more interested in humanity than in winning, even though the good opinion they deserve may come many years late, if at all. "Save our lives and your lives too," he told them. "Be honorable."

At Rice, Vonnegut said a decent and useful citizen is "informed, reasonable, and capable." This, too, seems like a new American by definition, because there are few expectations that any citizen must meet even those standards. Perhaps more important, this different kind of citizen is *happy* because she is decent and useful. As Tocqueville observed, in critical ways citizenship is a psychological matter. The chance to remain connected in America was weak almost from the beginning and now may be broken beyond repair. It is hard enough to be a human being. Vonnegut argues that an American is unmoored, "an experiment not only with liberty but with rootlessness, mobility, and impossibly tough-minded loneliness."[31] Eliot Rosewater exhibits this problem as he wanders around the country, stepping away from Greyhound buses just long enough to locate another volunteer fire department. Yet, when he finds his way to Rosewater County, he finds himself. His drinking continues, but he is happy because he is useful, attached as he is to what his father calls "the sniveling camaraderie of whores, malingerers, pimps, and thieves." Indeed, his patrons are sometimes loathsome as they strain for his handouts. But they belong to him, and he to them. No longer a loose craft, he is tied to their needs, thus fulfilling his own need for a steady, worthwhile role in the very place where his family's immense fortune was born. For Vonnegut, the only people with a chance to make a difference are the ones who are useful. And the truly useful new citizens are like volunteer firefighters, who Eliot believes are the only ones competent to make a revolution. From individual points in the community, each volunteer responds to the call of immediate need with bravery and skill to stop the destruction and empathy to comfort the distressed. Eliot Rosewater is delighted to have found an extended family based on need, but he is happier still to be part of an extended family of servers.

Vonnegut tells graduates that no matter what kind of troubles and grief await them, they do not have to be alone. They can always belong to some kind of community, they can always be of some kind of use. American political life creates lonely citizens who are homesick for a life of dignity and purpose. Vonnegut does not want the graduates to feel any lonelier and lost than their institutions will inevitably make them. And if they concentrate solely on the great pressures of civilization, they have no chance of making a difference in the long run because the momentum of humanity is taking the species and the planet to destruction. Vonnegut confronts those hopeful faces so that they can avoid useless pain and go straight to the arenas where they can be both useful and happy. So, he tells them to look for people as well as jobs. "And don't try to make yourself an extended family out of ghosts on the Internet," he told graduates at Agnes Scott College. "Get yourself a Harley, and join Hell's Angels instead." If the community an individual needs does not exist, he should invent it. Alcoholics Anonymous demonstrates that a community based on the needs of one can ultimately have a profound effect on generations of similarly bereft souls. Twelve-step programs recognize, as grievers have always known, that we are weaker alone than we are just sitting with weaklings like ourselves. "So I recommend," he told the graduates at Freedonia College, "that everybody here join all sorts of organizations, no matter how ridiculous, simply to get more people in his or her life."

An American citizen can be kept from making a big difference, but she cannot be kept from a meaningful citizenship, for when it is most useful, citizenship is an act of imagination. Even as Vonnegut tells graduates to approach politics with skepticism, he encourages them to trust their intuition. Eliot Rosewater makes this point clearly. "I'm going to love these discarded Americans," he tells his wife Sylvia, "even though they are useless and unattractive. *That* is going to be my work of art." Elsewhere, Vonnegut has spoken of the brilliance of one of his teachers, a man who offered an explanation for what an artist does. "The artist says, 'I can do very little about the chaos around me, but at least I can reduce to perfect order this square of canvas, this piece of paper, this chunk of stone'"[32] In this way, a citizen is an artist, with the power to bring order to chaos on a limited but satisfying scale. Of course, this is an artist's version of citizenship, but it offers a potent definition of what a citizen does. A new kind of citizen will renounce any delusion that she can save the planet, working instead to perfect the canvas of her own role in the community. Great achievements are often individual achievements, Vonnegut told the graduates at Agnes Scott College, but they "make us feel proud to be part of the human race." In speech after speech, Vonnegut requests that each graduate turn to another and say the name of one teacher who made it splendid to be part of a class. Teaching is the noblest profession in a democracy, he said. "And only well-informed, warm-hearted people can teach others things they'll always remember and love. Computers and TV's can never do that." Eliot understands that thoughtful citizens are like artists, but he also knows that the only citizenship that makes a difference is born of affection for one's countrymen, no matter how useless and scorned they may be.

Ultimately for Vonnegut, the role and purpose of a citizen turns on love. Long known is the understanding that infants deprived of love are emotionally ruined and that they will grow into fragile, warped, and often destructive human beings. Much of what Vonnegut says to graduates suggests a belief that unnurtured citizens turn out the same. An unloving spirit of individualism inhabits the free enterprise system affirmed by Eliot's father. "We must be hard," he urges from the floor of the Senate, "for we must become again a nation of swimmers, with the sinkers quietly disposing of themselves." Graduates know that it is this world they stand to enter, and they have known it for as long as they have known they are Americans. Although the need to feel loved is deeply rooted in the need for family, political life in America does not begin to provide for the corresponding emotional needs of a citizen. Americans are like Eliot Rosewater: rich enough not to care about each other or the world, unhappy if we do not, suspected of lunacy if we do. But we need to *feel* as if we matter because, as Vonnegut and the comet Kahoutek remind us, we really do not matter in the big picture. We can only matter to each other. Perhaps this is why Vonnegut so often rocks the cradle in a commencement speech. "We need you because we hope to survive as a species," he told his audience at Southampton College, "and you are in possession of or can get possession of solid information which, properly understood and put to use, can save us as a species." Vonnegut's new citizen would be capable of civic love, an honorable duty that is accomplished most fully with useful acts of imagination. For Vonnegut, the purpose of humanity is described most eloquently by his son Mark, in the epigraph to *Bluebeard*. "We are here to help each other get through this thing, whatever it is."[33]

The psychiatry in *God Bless You, Mr. Rosewater* suggests that the desire for utopia is a sexual perversion. On the other hand, *Player Piano* argues that revolution is futile. Like his fiction, Vonnegut's graduation speeches are a dour but compassionate critique of American life, for citizenship itself is a sweet pill with a bitter coating. He directly advises his audience that the violent pathology of American politics makes even a simple protest dangerous. Beware the extremes of political faith, he tells them, and beware the American obsession with individual achievement, because individualism is a root cause of alienation. Seek family instead. The message from the speaker to the graduates is that while he does not like the chances of humanity, there is reason for faith in their American future. Vonnegut's advice to graduates is the same as Eliot Rosewater's lesson to us all: useful and decent political behavior is both improvised and artistic. He calls for simple acts of love and acceptance, the treasuring of people more than ideology. When dozens of mothers claim him as father to their children, Eliot endorses false paternity in order to confer a true and honorable gift. "Let their names be Rosewater from this moment on," he commands the lawyer who administers the vast proceeds of the Rosewater Foundation. "And tell them that their father loves them, no matter what they may turn out to be." Vonnegut said as much to the graduates at Southampton College:

> I give you my word of honor that we love you and need you. We love you simply because you are of our species. You have been born. That is enough.
>
> *But God damnit, you've got to be kind.*

Notes

1. All references to the speech at Fredonia College are found in Kurt Vonnegut, *Palm Sunday* (New York: Dell Publishing, 1981), 173–82.
2. Vonnegut, *Palm Sunday*, 151–53.
3. All references to the speech at Bennington College are found in Kurt Vonnegut, "Address to the Graduating Class at Bennington College," *Wampeters, Foma & Granfalloons* (New York: Dell Publishing, 1974), 159–68.

4. Vonnegut, "Address to the American Physical Society," *Wampeters, Foma & Granfalloons*, 92.

5. Vonnegut, preface, *Wampeters, Foma & Granfalloons*, xv.

6. Vonnegut, "Religion," *Palm Sunday*, 196.

7. The song "Everybody's Free to Wear Sunscreen," was arranged musically by Baz Luhrmann over a spoken track read by Australian actor Quindon Tarvor (Baz Luhrmann, *Something For Everybody*, Capitol ASIN B00000634X). The speech was never, in fact, a speech. It was originally a column written by Mary Schmich for the *Chicago Tribune*, offered in the form of a high school graduation speech ("Advice, Like Youth, Probably Just Wasted on the Young," *Chicago Tribune*, June 1, 1997, Metro section, 1). The most consistent rumor, fueled of course primarily on the Internet, was that it was a speech given by Vonnegut at the Massachusetts Institute of Technology (MIT). Vonnegut began his commencement address at Agnes Scott College that spring in the spirit of the hoax: "I hope you are all wearing sunscreen."

8. Kurt Vonnegut, "Playboy Interview," *Wampeters, Foma & Granfalloons*, 237.

9. Kevin Alexander Boon, ed., *At Millennium's End: New Essays on the Work of Kurt Vonnegut* (Albany: State University of New York Press, 2001), viii.

10. For my understanding of this aspect of Vonnegut's thought, I am indebted to my teacher, Wilson Carey McWilliams.

11. See, e.g., Vonnegut, "Playboy Interview," 237–85; Greg Mitchell's interview "Meeting My Maker: A Visit with Kurt Vonnegut Jr. by Kilgore Trout" in *Conversations with Kurt Vonnegut*, ed. William Rodney Allen (Jackson: University Press of Mississippi, 1988), 133–55; Jerome Klinkowitz, "Why They Read Vonnegut," *Critical Essays on Kurt Vonnegut*, ed. Robert Merrill (Boston: G. K. Hall, 1990), 67–73; Harry Reasoner, "Kurt Vonnegut," in *Conversations with Kurt Vonnegut*, 15–19.

12. Kurt Vonnegut, *Slaughterhouse-Five, or The Children's Crusade*, 25th Anniversary ed. (New York: Delacorte Press/Seymour Lawrence, 1994), 11–14.

13. One excellent examination of this is Michael J. Gargas McGrath's essay, "Kesey and Vonnegut: The Critique of Liberal Democracy in Contemporary Literature," in *The Artist and Political Vision*, ed. Benjamin R. Barber and Michael J. Gargas McGrath (New Brunswick, NJ: Transaction Books, 1982), 363–83.

14. Vonnegut, preface, *Wampeters, Foma & Granfalloons*, xv.

15. All references to the speech at Hobart and William Smith Colleges are found in Vonnegut, *Palm Sunday*, 195–210.

16. Vonnegut, preface, *Wampeters, Foma & Granfalloons*, xxv.

17. All references to the speech at MIT are found in Kurt Vonnegut, *Fates Worse Than Death* (New York: Berkeley Books, 1992), 117–20.

18. In particular, see Mark Twain, *A Connecticut Yankee in King Arthur's Court* (New York: Oxford University Press, 1996), which offers an introduction written by Vonnegut.

19. All references to the speech at Agnes Scott College are found in Kurt Vonnegut, "Graduation Speech at Agnes Scott College," available at www.vonnegutweb.com/vonnegutia/commencement/agnesscot.html.

20. For a more detailed discussion on this problem, see Vonnegut, "Playboy Interview," 237–85.

21. Kurt Vonnegut, "Why They Read Hesse," *Wampeters, Foma & Granfalloons* (New York: Dell Publishing, 1974), 113.

22. All references to the speech at Syracuse are found in Kurt Vonnegut, "Graduation Speech at Syracuse University," available at www.vonnegutweb.com/vonnegutia/commencement/syracuse.html.

23. Kurt Vonnegut, *Slapstick, Or Lonesome No More* (1976; repr. New York: Seymour Lawrence, 1999).

24. Vonnegut, *Palm Sunday*, 76.

25. All references to *God Bless You, Mr. Rosewater* are found in Kurt Vonnegut, *God Bless You, Mr. Rosewater* (1965; repr. New York: Dell Publishing, 1998).

26. In "Playboy Interview," Vonnegut provides an unflinching assessment of precisely the kind of lost causes that are the object of Eliot Rosewater's good intentions: "There are people, particularly dumb people, who are in terrible trouble and never get out of it, because they're not intelligent enough. And it strikes me as gruesome and comical that in our culture we have an expectation that a man can always solve his problems. There is that implication that if you just have a little more energy, a little more fight, the problem can always be solved. This is so untrue that it makes me want to cry—or laugh. . . . When I think about a stupid, uneducated black junkie in this city, and then I run into some optimist who feels that any man can lift himself above his origins if he's any good—that's something to cry about or laugh about. A sort of braying, donkeylike laugh. But every laugh counts, because every laugh *feels* like a laugh" (258).

27. Vonnegut, *God Bless You, Mr. Rosewater*, 9.

28. Vonnegut, "Graduation Speech at Bennington College," and "Graduation Speech at Agnes Scott College."

29. All references to the speech at Southampton College are found in Kurt Vonnegut, "Graduation Speech at Southampton College," available at www.vonnegutweb.com/vonnegutia/commencement/southampton.html.

30. All references to the speech at Rice are found in Kurt Vonnegut, "Graduation Speech at Rice University," available at www.vonnegutweb.com/vonnegutia/commencement/rice.html.

31. Vonnegut, *Fates Worse Than Death*, 35.

32. Vonnegut, *Palm Sunday*, 321.

33. Kurt Vonnegut, *Bluebeard* (1987; repr. New York: Delacorte Press, 1999).

10

The American Mystery Deepens

Hearing Tocqueville in Don DeLillo's *White Noise*

Patrick J. Deneen

> When the old God leaves the world, what happens to all the unexpended faith?
>
> —Don DeLillo, *Mao II*

In an interview that appeared shortly after the publication of *White Noise*, Don DeLillo stated, "I never set out to write an apocalyptic novel."[1] He also denied that he intended to write a comic novel, although he admitted that a novel set at a college with a Department of Hitler Studies had undeniable comic possibilities.[2] And, while many of DeLillo's admirers and detractors have suggested that DeLillo is among the preeminent American authors of "postmodern" fiction, this is not in fact a description or title to which DeLillo lays claim. A question arises: in *White Noise*—a novel about Jack Gladney, professor of Hitler studies, his family, their dramatic encounter with an "airborne toxic event," their traumatic struggle with their fear of death that impels Jack and his wife Babette to seek out an experimental drug therapy to alleviate their fear, and its culmination in Jack's attempted murder of the inventor of the drug—what kind of novel did DeLillo believe that he was writing?

As with all of DeLillo's fiction, it is preeminently a novel about America: not merely by and primarily for Americans, but *about* America—its past, its promise, its pathologies, its "magic and dread" (*WN*, 19). As such, like many of America's great novels about America, it is a novel about "the American mystery": broadly speaking, it attempts to solve the riddle, or mystery, of America (*WN*, 60).[3] The book might therefore properly be understood to be a mystery novel. DeLillo gives us indications that the novel contains classic elements of a mystery story: it tells of disappearances of people—the elderly brother and sister named Treadwell, who are eventually found to have been abandoned at the local mall; and it tells of Jack's culminating attempt to overcome his fear of death through the murder of Willie Mink, inventor of Dylar, a drug that is created in the attempt to inhibit the part of the brain that gives rise to the fear of death. Again and again, DeLillo includes discussions of plots: in response to a question in his course "Advanced Nazism" about the plot to kill Hitler, Jack replies, "All plots tend to move deathward. This is the nature of plots. Political plots, terrorist plots, lovers' plots, narrative plots, plots that are part of children's games. We edge nearer to death every time we plot" (*WN*, 26).[4] The novel, like a classic mystery, signals that it will attempt to solve a question, a riddle, even a crime that has proven resistant to solution.

The most difficult mystery of the novel is to discern the mystery. If all plots move deathward, no main character of the novel dies, kills, or is killed. A crime is committed in the novel—Jack Gladney attempts to kill Willie Mink, inventor of Dylar and the man with whom his wife Babette commits adultery in order to procure the drug—but that crime is not committed until the *conclusion* of the novel, and we know Jack is the would-be murderer. Motive(s), opportunity, and weapon are all accounted for in the course of the story. There is the absence of any desire to "solve" this particular, even spectacular crime: perhaps not unsurprisingly, in a novel in which government is present only in shadowy form (men in Mylex suits who appear and disappear without warning) and dismissed for its weakness (*WN*, 135), no authority appears aware of the attempted murder, much less interested in tracking down the source of Mink's gunshot wounds. The "mystery" does not seem to involve the apparent criminal actions of the book's main characters.

Jack, as narrator, points to "the American mystery." America is the mystery that the novel attempts to solve, or at least to understand. America is a mystery to itself: its people are, in some senses, incapable of understanding themselves and the nation that has formed their character, their dreams, and their fears. DeLillo has said that all of his fiction is fundamentally about the mystery of America: "It's no accident that my first novel was called *Americana*. This was a private declaration of independence, a statement of my intention to use the whole picture, the whole culture. America was and is the immigrant's dream, and as the son of two immigrants I was attracted by the sense of possibility that had drawn my grandparents and parents."[5] To write about America requires a "private declaration of independence" since, for DeLillo, one cannot really see and understand the American mystery without a degree of distance *from* America. DeLillo has suggested that the American mystery remains shrouded and inaccessible except to a few Americans who are fortunate enough to have, or are capable of achieving, even temporary distance from America, a distance manifested most ably by the writer: "The writer is the person who stands outside society, independent of affiliation and independent of influence. The writer is the man or woman who automatically takes a stance against his or her government. There are so many temptations for American writers to become part of the system and part of the structure that now, more than ever, we have to resist. American writers ought to stand and live in the margins, and be more dangerous. Writers in repressive societies are considered dangerous. That's why so many of them are in jail."[6] America is a mystery, DeLillo suggests, above all because Americans cannot perceive the American mystery, indeed, cannot truly perceive America. *White Noise* is an attempt, then, to break through the "white noise" at once produced by America and obscuring it from itself.[7]

America can only be seen and understood from "outside" America. Many commentators on *White Noise* have concentrated upon apparent French influences on DeLillo, particularly the apparent similarity between DeLillo's descriptions of increasingly "simulated" and refracted American phenomena and Jean Baudrilliard's theories of "simulacra" as a definitive feature of modernity and postmodernity.[8] If it can be speculated that such French influences deeply inform DeLillo's apparent postmodern sensibility, those postmodern theorists—and the literary interpreters who employ them to analyze DeLillo—stop short of capturing what seem to be a particularly premodern, or "post-postmodern" (now understood as antimodern), set of concerns that appear to animate DeLillo. These concerns—fundamentally critical of continuities between modernity and postmodernity, including especially the view that there is no human nature that requires the recognition of natural limits and restraints—give rise to the view that the modern condition is approaching the point of its own self-destruction, thereby opening the possibility of a "post-postmodernism" that would amount to a rejection of modernity itself.[9] What commentators of DeLillo's work overlook, then, is the novel's similarity not finally with French postmodernism but with the overarching analysis and even echoes of specific arguments advanced by the greatest French critic of the form of modernism that he believed would find its ultimate fruition in democratic America—Alexis de Tocqueville. Tocqueville's magisterial and unsurpassed analysis of American democracy, *Democracy in America*, limns a portrait of the self-destructive future of America in at least three areas that find full expression in *White Noise*. These three areas, which will be the focus of this essay, arguably comprise core themes of both Tocqueville's analysis of democracy and DeLillo's novel. They are (1) the rising individualism, privatism, isolation, and anomie of democratic man; (2) the restlessness, materialism, and solipsism that arise as a response to the fear of death felt with particular keenness by democratic man; and (3) the decline of religious belief and the pressing need for its sustenance and reaffirmation in a democratic age.[10]

Tocqueville wrote that the prospect of democracy advancing across the canvas of human history filled him with a form of "religious terror" (*DA*, 6).[11] Democracy contained inherent proclivities that, in the end, threatened to create a mediocre, crass, materialistic, politically inactive shadow of a more ennobled and difficult form of self-governance. "To instruct democracy," Tocqueville wrote, "a new political science is needed for a world altogether new" (*DA*, 7). In response to his own "religious terror," he recommended instead a "salutary fear"—one that promotes "watchfulness and combativeness" rather than torpor (*DA*, 673). Writing a century and a half later about Jack Gladney—a character whose existence is defined by all-consuming fear, a fear that is more the culmination of the very democratic proclivities detected by Tocqueville than a response to their possibility—DeLillo suggests that the triumph of that "new world" may require instead an *old* political science, one that can be discerned "half entangled in the debris of the world that is falling" (*DA*, 673).

★ ★ ★ ★ ★

> Individualism is a reflective and peaceable sentiment that disposes each citizen to isolate himself from the mass of those like him and to withdraw to one side with his family and friends, so that after having thus created a little society for his own use, he willingly abandons society at large to itself. . . . Aristocracy had made of all citizens a long chain that went from a peasant up to a king; democracy breaks the chain and sets each link apart. . . . Not only does democracy make each man forget his ancestors, but it hides his descendants from him and separates him from his contemporaries; it constantly leads him back toward himself alone and threatens finally to confine him wholly in the solitude of his own heart.
>
> —Alexis de Tocqueville, *Democracy in America*

> The family process works toward sealing off the world.
>
> —Don DeLillo, *White Noise*

Jack Gladney's family is at once intimate and diffuse. The Gladneys appear to be the picture of the modern American nuclear family: Jack and his wife, Babette, live together and raise four children—Heinrich, Steffie, Denise, and Wilder—in a snug house in the small college town of Blacksmith. Yet, during the course of the novel, we learn that this family is at once far from "normal"—at least according to the classic 1950s definition of the nuclear family—and yet, increasingly "normal" in its representation of the changing form of the American family. Babette is Jack's fourth wife—although it is his fifth marriage, since Jack remarried his first wife after his third marriage and directly before his marriage to Babette—and none of the children is the offspring Jack and Babette together. Heinrich is the son of Jack and his second wife, Janet Savory; Steffie is the daughter of Jack from his remarriage with his first wife, Dana Breedlove; Denise and Wilder are Babette's children from two previous marriages. We also learn that both Jack and Babette have other children from previous marriages who do not live with them: Mary-Alice is Jack's daughter from his first marriage to Dana

Breedlove; Bee, who visits the family briefly, is Jack's daughter from his third marriage to Tweedy Browner; and Wilder has an older brother, Eugene, who lives with his father in Australia. The "normal"-appearing Gladney family is a composite of half- and step-brothers and -sisters from numerous previous marriages. The seeming solidity of the family unit pictured in *White Noise* in fact masks a profound instability: each of the children has been moved from place to place, from marriage to marriage, as each child's respective parents and subsequent step-parents have decided that a particular combination did not work and parted, in most cases amicably, in search of better arrangements. Each of the children—with the exception of the very young and still-innocent (hence "wild") Wilder—knows that the particular constellation formed by the marriage of Jack and Babette could also potentially change at any time. The seemingly traditional Gladney family is defined by insubstantial and shifting commitments.[12]

The family comes together during several key moments of the novel—often in the automobile, either attempting to escape from the airborne toxic event of Nyodene Derivative or on one occasion when the family eats together in the car—although their main form of communal life is a tradition on Friday nights of watching television together (*WN*, 16, 64). By requiring the children to watch television with "parents or step-parents," Babette hopes that the custom will "de-glamorize the medium [of television] in their eyes, to make it a wholesome sport" (*WN*, 16). This form of communal life is, of course, wholly atomistic: one watches television largely oblivious of other people even in the same room. Living together, the Gladney family members nevertheless live in disjunction from one another and even in disjunction from their own successive activities. Jack, for instance, concludes an evening of communal television watching by reading "deeply in Hitler well into the night" (*WN*, 16). A family evening devoted often to the viewing of disaster footage—incongruously intended to impart some kind of "family values"—is followed by lengthy reading of racist and fascist ideology. Even the most intimate relationship portrayed in the novel—between Jack and Babette—may be less secure than it appears. Jack—while claiming that he and Babette tell each other everything (*WN*, 29)—discovers only much later that his wife has been taking an experimental drug that she procured through sexual favors with its inventor, Willie Mink. He, in turn, withholds from her his plot to kill Mink, and it appears at the conclusion of the novel that he has not, nor will he ever, tell her of the attempted murder. Each lies about wishing to be the one to die before the other.

The atomism of the family is appropriately captured in the family's inability to sustain a conversational topic; words cascade in profusion, but without continuity or direction. The locus of "misinformation," a typical conversation among Gladney family members reveals them to be incapable of exploring the nominal topic. Consider the following conversation, which begins with Denise asking her mother about the drug she suspects Babette to be taking:

> "What do you know about Dylar?"
> "Is that the black girl who's staying with the Stover's?"
> "That's Dakar," Steffie said.
> "Dakar isn't her name, it's where she's from," Denise said. "It's a country on the ivory coast of Africa."
> "The capital is Lagos," Babette said. "I know that because of a surfer movie I saw once where they travel all over the world."
> "*The Perfect Wave*," Heinrich said. "I saw it on TV."
> "But what's the girl's name?" Steffie asked.
> "I don't know," Babette said, "but the movie wasn't called *The Perfect Wave*. The perfect wave is what they were looking for."
> "They go to Hawaii," Denise told Steffie, "and wait for these tidal waves to come from Japan. They're called origamis."
> "And the movie was called *The Long Hot Summer*," her mother said.
> "*The Long Hot Summer*," Heinrich said, "happens to be a play by Tennessee Ernie Williams."
> "It doesn't matter," Babette said, "because you can't copyright titles anymore."
> "If she's an African," Steffie said, "I wonder if she ever rode a camel."
> "Try an Audi Turbo."
> "Try a Toyota Supra."
> "What is it camels store in their humps?" Babette said. "Food or water? I could never get that straight."
> "There are one-hump camels and two-hump camels," Heinrich told her. "So it depends on which kind you're talking about."
> "Are you telling me a two-hump camel stores food in one hump and water in the other?"
> "The important thing about camels," he said, "is that camel meat is considered a delicacy."
> "I thought that was alligator meat," Denise said.
> "Who introduced the camel to America?" Babette said. "They had them out west for a while to carry supplies to coolies who were building the great railroads that met at Ogden, Utah. I remember my history exams."
> "Are you sure you're not talking about llamas?" Heinrich said.
> "The llama stayed in Peru," Denise said. "Peru has the llama, the vicuña and one other animal. Bolivia has tin. Chile has copper and iron."
> "I'll give anyone in this car five dollars," Heinrich said, "if they can name the population of Bolivia."
> "Bolivians," my daughter said. (*WN*, 80–81)

As with television programming, transitions between topics are almost nonexistent.[13] Mimicking the "jump-cut" style of music videos or highly edited films or television programming—a style that has only become more prevalent since DeLillo wrote *White Noise*—members of the Gladney family respond to conversational cues almost without regard to the previous statement or even subject. Their responses reflect a narcissism and even solipsism that is not surprising given the dominance of television and media in their lives and the realistic expectation that even the most profoundly intimate familial bonds might be severed at any moment. Such conversations may be the purest examples of "white noise" in the book.

The Gladney family appears to be almost without friends and neighbors. Aside from Babette, Jack's main conversational partner is Murray Siskind, a visiting professor of "American environments" who has only that very year, and only temporarily, joined the faculty of Jack's college. Babette appears to have no friends aside from Jack; her interaction with other people consists primarily of reading tabloids to Mr. Treadwell and teaching an occasional class on posture in the basement of a nearby Congregational Church (*WN*, 5, 27). Heinrich's main external contact is through a correspondence with a convicted murderer, with whom he plays chess and exchanges some personal information (he knows, for instance, the circumstances of the murder that the prisoner committed). Heinrich briefly befriends another boy named Orestes Mercator, whose ambition is to break a record of consecutive days spent in a container with poisonous snakes, but he loses respect for Mercator when the attempt does not come off. Only Murray seems to visit the family, if infrequently; otherwise, no one outside the immediate family other than ex-wives, half- or step-siblings, or grandparents enters within the closed circle of the Gladney nuclear family. In one passing scene, Steffie relays a phone message that another family—the Stovers—want to visit.

> "We don't want them," Babette said.
> "Keep them out," Denise said.
> *What do I say?*
> "Say anything you want."
> "Just keep them out of here."
> "They're boring."
> "Tell them to stay home." (*WN*, 43)

Dinner parties or adult gatherings do not seem to exist.[14] The Gladney family, like most of the people described in the book, appears to be isolated from other families, and its members seem isolated from each other.

Murray Siskind, in spite of his apparent perceptiveness and even brilliance, mistakes both the Gladney family intimacy and even the nature of the town to which he has moved as traditional in nature. In the very first conversation between Murray and Jack, Murray praises small-town life in contrast to the (New York) city life from which he has come. "I like it here. I'm totally enamored of this place. A small-town setting. I want to be free of cities and sexual entanglements. Heat. This is what cities mean to me. . . . I can't help but being happy in a town called Blacksmith," he said. "I'm here to avoid situations. Cities are full of situations, sexually cunning people"

(*WN*, 10–11). Later, Jack echoes this sentiment, evoking a Rousseauean "country" suspicion toward the corruption that one finds in cities: "It is the nature and pleasure of townspeople to distrust the city. All the guiding principles that might flow from a center of ideas and cultural energies are regarded as corrupt, one or another kind of pornography. This is how it is with towns" (*WN*, 85).

Murray is alternately attracted and repelled by the intimate nature of small-town life. On the one hand, like many city dwellers, he suspects without any evidence that people in small towns are narrowminded bigots. Speaking of the fix-it abilities of Murray's landlord, Murray and Jack have the following exchange:

> "He's very good with all those little tools and fixtures and devices that people in cities never know the name of. The names of these things are only known in outlying communities, small towns and rural areas. Too bad he's such a bigot."
>
> "How do you know he's a bigot?"
>
> "People who fix things are usually bigots."
>
> "What do you mean?"
>
> "Think of all the people who've ever come to your house to fix things. They were all bigots, weren't they?"
>
> "I don't know."
>
> "They drove panel trucks, didn't they, with an extension ladder on the roof and some kind of plastic charm dangling from the rearview mirror?"
>
> "I don't know, Murray."
>
> "It's obvious," he said. (*WN*, 33)

On the other hand, Murray praises the virtues of small-town life that are presumably born of the same intimacy—and even parochialism—that nurtures the bigotry that he assumes to be pervasive among the blue-collar denizens of Blacksmith and which, one might assume, can only be sustained in relatively small communities. A few pages after the preceding discussion of Murray's landlord, on an occasion in which Jack and Babette have one of their many encounters with Murray in the local supermarket, Murray now finds the intimacy of small-town life praiseworthy for its ability to nurture memory:

> In cities no one notices specific dying. Dying is a quality of the air. It's everywhere and nowhere. Men shout as they die, to be noticed, remembered for a second or two. To die in an apartment instead of a house can depress the soul, I would imagine, for several lives to come. In a town there are houses, plants in bay windows. People notice dying better. The dead have faces, automobiles. If you don't know a name, you know a street name, a dog's name. 'He drove an orange Mazda.' You know a couple of useless things about a person that become major facts of identification and cosmic placement when he dies suddenly, after a short illness, in his own bed, a comforter and

> matching pillows, on a rainy Wednesday afternoon, feverish, a little congested in the sinuses and chest, thinking about his dry cleaning. (*WN*, 39)

Echoing an observation of Hannah Arendt, Murray seems to recognize the *polis*, or small community, as a form of "organized remembrance."[15] Cities are locales of anonymity and forgetfulness: it is in an anonymous motel—the aptly named Roadway Motel (*WN*, 304)—in a dilapidated section of Iron City that Jack will shoot Willie Mink, and either no one will hear the shots, or they will simply not care.

Yet, Murray's suppositions about Blacksmith prove to be fundamentally mistaken. The people of the town are not small-minded bigots. Not only do we never encounter any such "typical" yokels, but in the continuation of the passage in which Jack reflects on the small-town suspicion of the city's corruption, we are given a significant piece of information about the absence of strained relationships between the "town and gown" that one might expect in such a small town. Jack muses,

> But Blacksmith is nowhere near a city. We don't feel threatened and aggrieved in quite the same way other towns do. We're not smack in the path of history and its contaminants. If our complaints have a focal point, it would have to be the TV set, where the outer torment lurks, causing fears and secret desires. Certainly little or no resentment attaches to the College-on-the-Hill as an emblem of ruinous influence. The school occupies an ever serene edge of the townscape, semidetached, more or less scenic, suspended in political calm. Not a place designed to aggravate suspicion. (*WN*, 85)

The townspeople are altogether tolerant toward, or perhaps oblivious of, the presence of a group of Jewish intellectuals who make up the Department of American Environments, as they seem to be unaware of the Department of Hitler Studies, which shares the same building. Neither of these incongruous undertakings chagrin the townspeople, reflecting a toleration that is, at least in the case of a Department of Hitler Studies—a program in which the study of Hitler "is not a question of good or evil" (*WN*, 63)—perhaps less praiseworthy than the suspicions directed toward "corrupt" academic enterprises that one might otherwise expect to find in a town like Blacksmith.[16]

Alternatively, Blacksmith appears to evince none of the forms of "organized remembrance" that Murray believes makes it distinct from the anonymity of cities. Shortly after Murray's semilyrical paean extolling Blacksmith as a locus of memory and familiarity, it is discovered that the Treadwells have disappeared. No neighbors have seen them leave: of the six nearby houses, two are empty and up for sale—indicating a fairly high turnover among the residents of neighboring houses—and neighbors in the other four houses do not "know anything about the Treadwells' movements over the past few days" (it is worth recalling that Mr. Treadwell is blind and

Mrs. Treadwell is older, and more frail) (*WN*, 57–58). Eventually the Treadwells are found,

> alive but shaken in an abandoned cookie shack at the Mid-Village Mall, a vast shopping mall out on the interstate. Apparently they'd been wandering through the mall for two days, lost, confused and frightened, before taking refuge in the littered kiosk. They spent two more days in the kiosk, the weak and faltering sister venturing out to scavenge food scraps from the cartoon-character disposal baskets with swinging doors. . . . No one knew at this point why they didn't ask for help. It was probably the vastness and strangeness of the place that made them feel helpless and adrift in a landscape of remote and menacing figures. (*WN*, 59)

While it is not clear how they made their way to the mall on the outskirts of town, it is suspected that a grandniece brought them and forgot to pick them up. Since the residents of Blacksmith are unable to remember even living relatives, one suspects Murray may be mistaken to believe that even residents of a modern small town can easily remember endearing details about deceased strangers.

Blacksmith is a palimpsest: an older form of writing lingers beneath the newer inscriptions that more obviously cut across its surface. Its older homes—Victorian buildings with large porches—reappear constantly throughout the novel, but the nineteenth-century communal life in which they were erected has vanished like the Treadwells and the neighbors who have moved away. Like many small towns, its once-vibrant town center—to which, presumably, inhabitants once walked in order to buy essentials and which formed a public space where they could greet neighbors or meet for informal or political discussions—has been replaced by nondescript "dry cleaning shops," "opticians," and "real estate firms" that feature photos of "looming Victorian homes . . . [that] have not changed in years." Blacksmith is a "town of tag sales and yard sales, the failed possessions arrayed in driveways and tended by kids" (*WN*, 59).

Blacksmith's very name reflects a past that is past. A relic of a time when economic transactions were largely local, when family ownership was the dominant model and autonomy was achieved through self-sufficient economic arrangements rather than lifestyle choices, the name "Blacksmith" reflects a basic technological past that has been since superceded by a more fluid, unbounded, and sophisticated technological present. A blacksmith works with the rudimentary, natural elements of the planet—coal, air, fire, and metal—earthy and chthonic ingredients that go into making basic and necessary commodities like nails, horseshoes, and hand weapons like daggers and swords. Among the most basic of the arts or technologies, its practice was symbolized in antiquity by the god Hephaestus—the most homely and, because of his lameness, even most "human" of the gods. A blacksmith must work in a rooted place—the bulkiness of his equipment, most especially the anvil, accentuates its immobility (like that of the god who practiced its craft).

By contrast, Blacksmith is in certain senses no longer a "locality" as such. A highway now cuts through the center of the town—it is the same highway over which Jack and Murray pass during a lengthy walk in a culminating discussion that leads Jack to the attempted murder of Willie Mink, and across which Wilder miraculously rides his tricycle in the final chapter of the novel (indicating that it passes a few short blocks away from Jack's house). The town can be accessed easily by strangers and easily exited by residents; it is probably most often bypassed by the constant flow of Americans moving between once vast and almost nontraversable spaces. Automobiles loom large in the novel: the very opening scene of the novel begins with the description of the beginning of a new semester at College-on-the-Hill: "The station wagons arrived at noon, a long shining line that coursed through the west campus" (*WN*, 3).[17] The family attempts to escape the airborne toxic event in the automobile, and a number of family conversations and meals occur in the automobile. It is by means of a stolen automobile that Jack is able to arrive at the Roadside Motel where he can attempt to kill Willie Mink.

The limitations and boundaries of Blacksmith have been transcended in even more profound ways. Each of the section titles of the novel—"Waves and Radiation," "The Airborne Toxic Event," and "Dylarama"—reveal a world in which natural boundaries are ceasing, or have ceased, to exist, whether understood in terms of territorial boundaries or natural limits. The television is a key "character" in the novel, and the way that it has transformed human life is captured ably by one of the New York émigrés: "For most people there are only two places in the world. Where they live and their TV set. If a thing happens on television, we have every right to find it fascinating, whatever it is" (*WN*, 66). The world as experienced by characters in *White Noise* is at once immediately constrained and conceptually expansive: "where they live" has been reduced to the narrowest set of relationships in the nuclear family, while television brings into that constrained space the most expansive panorama of human experience that is encountered in more intimate terms than can be expended toward the people in their immediate proximity. While the Treadwells' days-long disappearance goes unnoticed by the neighbors that remain nearby, Steffie Gladney must leave the room whenever "something shameful or humiliating seemed about to happen to someone on the screen" (*WN*, 16). Disasters and catastrophes worlds away prove more engrossing than the diurnal, normal, "boring" local relations that wither in Blacksmith.

The airborne toxic event is the most obvious form of "contamination" and borderlessness that characterizes modern Blacksmith. The noxious cloud of contaminants—"packed with chlorides, benzenes, phenols, hydrocarbons, or whatever the precise toxic content"—is unleashed when a tank car is punctured in the rail yard (*WN*, 127). Railroads—as the precursor of automobiles and roads—had already begun to nationalize the American economy in the nineteenth century, requiring the replacement of local "blacksmiths" by a large-scale metal industry that in turn facilitated the industrialization of the American economy and led to the rise of urban centers—for example, the suggestively named "Iron City" of *White Noise*.[18] Nyodene D is a byproduct of insecticides and, therefore, at first glance, a "foreign" substance in the small town of Blacksmith in which the only previous mention of agriculture is a defunct family farm, now a tourist site: "the most photographed barn in America" (*WN*, 12). However, given that most Americans purchase food in supermarkets—described by Murray as "like being at the crossroads of the ancient world, a Persian bazaar or boom town on the Tigris," the location of "exotic fruits, rare cheeses . . . products from twenty countries" (*WN*, 169)—that has been produced by massive agribusiness conglomerates that use such chemical agents to increase the yield and thereby the profit, the "contaminants" are already in Blacksmith, in its most sterile and modern edifices.

While Nyodene D therefore represents precisely the form of contamination toward which Jack believes Blacksmith to be resistant—"we're not smack in the path of history and its contaminants"—such forms of "contamination" have already long existed in Blacksmith (*WN*, 114). The railroads, highways, automobiles, the mall outside of town, the supermarket, television, all represent the infiltration of "external," globalized culture within the traditional, once confining limits of Blacksmith.[19] Everything "enters" Blacksmith—there is a porousness to the old town that is even less membranous than the careful filter that surrounds the capsule of Dylar.[20] Borders of all kinds have fallen, and boundaries have dissolved. We understand that subatomic particles bombard us—"neutrinos go through the earth" (34)—accounting for the sense that Americans are "environed" by "waves and radiation."[21] Heinrich refuses to believe the evidence of his senses as he and Jack drive through a rainstorm. In an uncanny replica of a Socratic dialogue (in which Heinrich plays the part of the Protagorean sophist, and he's accused of being a sophist by Jack [*WN*, 24]), Heinrich asks Jack how he can be certain the substance splattering against their windshield is rain. "How do you know it's not sulphuric acid from factories across the river? How do you know it's not fallout from a war in China?" (*WN*, 24). Even the Nyodene D cloud threatens to spread due to weather that is descending from Canada. The global perspective that encroaches from every direction leads to a radical doubt of common sense and of the *sensus communis*, or the cultivation of memory that can be passed from generation to generation.

This loss of cultural memory is remarked upon in a later section of the novel in which the Greeks are again directly invoked—here again by Heinrich.

> We think we're so great and modern. Moon landings, artificial hearts. But what if you were hurled into a time warp and came face to face with the ancient Greeks. The Greeks invented trigonometry. They did autopsies and dissections. What could you say to an ancient Greek that he couldn't say "Big deal." . . .
>
> Would you know a flint if you saw one? If a Stone Ager asked you what a nucleotide is, could you tell him? How do we make carbon paper? What is glass? If you came awake tomorrow in the Middle Ages and there was an epidemic raging, would you know how to stop it, knowing what you know about the progress of medicine and diseases?

Heinrich's discussion is ironic, occurring at the outskirts of the town of Blacksmith. Clearly, there was a time in the not-so-distant past when the knowledge of how to make things was necessarily handed down from one generation to the next. Now, because of the extensive division of labor in the highly advanced technological economy of twentieth-century America, such knowledge has been lost to all but very few indeed—such knowledge is not even available to those who manufacture such items—and perhaps is only available to those who willfully resist the modern permission to forget such older knowledge. Revealingly, while there are varying rumors about the particular ailments caused by exposure to Nyodene D, among the purported symptoms is a sense of déjà vu, or a form of false remembrance: "it affects the false part of human memory" (*WN*, 116). To this extent, Nyodene D strikingly causes a similar "ailment" as television: we remember things that did not happen to us, all the while forgetting things we ought to remember.[22]

★ ★ ★ ★ ★

> The inhabitant of the United States attaches himself to the goods of this world as if he were assured of not dying, and he rushes so precipitately to grasp those that pass within his reach that one would say he fears at each instant he will cease to live before he has enjoyed them. He grasps them all but without clutching them, and he soon allows them to escape from his hands so as to run after new enjoyments. . . . He who has confined his heart solely to the search for the goods of this world is always in a hurry, for he has only a limited time to find them, take hold of them, and enjoy them. His remembrance of the brevity of life constantly spurs him. In addition to the goods he possesses, at each instant he imagines a thousand others that death will prevent him from enjoying if he does not hasten. This thought fills him with troubles, fears, and regrets, and keeps his soul in a sort of unceasing trepidation that brings him to change his designs and place at every moment.
>
> —Alexis de Tocqueville, *Democracy in America*

> The idea of death, the fear of it, haunts the human animal like nothing else; it is a mainspring of human activity—activity designed largely

> to avoid the fatality of death, to overcome it by denying in some way that it is the final destiny for man.
>
> —Ernest Becker, *The Denial of Death*

All plots move deathward, and a book about the "American mystery" is also of necessity a book about death as well. Death hovers constantly as an implicit and explicit subject in *White Noise*: DeLillo's working title for the novel was *The American Book of the Dead*.[23] There are references in the book to the *Tibetan Book of the Dead* and to the *Egyptian Book of the Dead*. Each of these ancient books treats human behavior in this life in preparation for death as well as describes human existence in the afterlife. By comparison, *The American Book of the Dead* mostly dwells upon Jack and Babette's fear of death rather than on their actual deaths. Among the few textual influences upon *White Noise* that DeLillo has acknowledged is Ernest Becker's book *The Denial of Death*.[24] Becker maintains that the desire to deny death, or overcome the fear of death, functions as the wellspring of most human activity. Everything from Jack's efforts of accumulation—weight, titles, wives, possessions through shopping—to his obsessive efforts to unburden himself of material items (*WN*, 210–11, 249–50), from his efforts to increase his stature by associating himself with Hitler to his hope in the wonder-working power of technology, appears to be driven by an effort to deny or overcome his fear of death. Yet, none of these efforts or beliefs serves to allay that fear.

Jack and Babette are obsessed by death, wondering repeatedly who will die first. Babette's infidelity to Jack is committed in an effort to secure access to an experimental drug that will alleviate her all-consuming fear of death; Jack, too, fearing the consequences of his exposure to Nyodene D (he, a middle-aged man, is told that the contaminant will kill him in twenty or thirty years, and if not by then, at least at that point they'll have a better idea of when) craves the drug that will allay his fears. More than death itself, it is the fear of death that haunts them constantly. Still, in a book that was originally to have been entitled *The American Book of the Dead,* there's very little actual death in the course of the book (of the acquaintances of the Gladney family, only Mr. Treadwell's sister dies, although Jack then proceeds to relate the deaths of several other people who appear in obituaries [*WN*, 99]). Death is an obsession, but its existence in the form of graveyards, ceremonies for the dead, customs surrounding the treatment or remembrance of the dead, or physical memorials to the dead is almost nonexistent.

Therefore, among the most striking scenes in the book that links the themes of locality and memory to the theme of death occurs when Jack impulsively visits the local cemetery. He is returning from the airport on the outskirts of Iron City and pulls off the "expressway" onto a local road where there is a small graveyard with a sign that reads:

The Old Burying Ground
Blacksmith Village

The Old Burying Ground gives little evidence of recent visits—only three small flags planted near grave markers indicate to Jack that "someone had preceded me to this place in this century" (*WN*, 97). The cemetery, while close to the "expressway," is almost without evidence of living human presence: memory, in the form the visits to the gravesides of past generations known to us either in remembrance or solely through stories, has been lost. Because the "village" is as dead as the entombed deceased, there is no longer the possibility of "organized remembrance." The dead are simply forgotten, too silent and hidden away from the kaleidoscopic activity of the living to be heard or recalled amid the "white noise."

Jack is here beyond the roar of the traffic and the din of the factories across the river: it is thus one of the few spaces explicitly pointed out in *White Noise* in which there is no noise.[25] Here Jack reflects on the connection between the living and the dead, imagining that the dead engage in a level of activity that may possibly exceed that of the living, and which may therefore raise questions about what is to be feared more—life or death:

> The power of the dead is that we think they see us all the time. The dead have a presence. Is there a level of energy composed solely of the dead? They are also in the ground, of course, asleep and crumbling. Perhaps we are what they dream. (*WN*, 98)[26]

For the first time, it is here in the cemetery that Jack seems, at least momentarily, to lose his fear of death. Here he imagines a kind of plotlessness: "May the days be aimless. Let the seasons drift. Do not advance the action according to a plan" (*WN*, 98). The Old Burying Ground is thus a place in which Jack seeks not to plot: rather than all plots leading deathward, here all deaths lead to plots. Here Jack abandons the dream of control that lies behind the activity of plotting, instead surrendering himself to the natural rhythms of the wind, of the seasons, of life, and of death. If plots are human machinations aimed at control and manipulation, then Jack's encounter with final human powerlessness inspires him to surrender fond human attempts to plot our escape from death. Among the plots, plotting ceases for a time.

Jack reneges on this surrender following his exposure to the airborne toxic event, which stokes a renewed fearfulness of death and gives rise to his hope or belief that Dylar can allay his fears. The opposite attitude to this momentary surrender of control among the gravestones occurs in his culminating conversation with Murray, who insists that one can distinguish between people who are "killers and diers" (*WN*, 290). Jack responds, "Plot a murder you're saying. But every plot is a murder in effect. To plot is to die, whether we know it or not." "To plot is to live," he said (*WN*, 291). In the midst of that conversation, the two men explore a vast range of human activities, all of which seem to be fundamentally driven by the desire to come to terms with death. "How do we deal with this crushing knowledge?" asks Murray. "We repress, we disguise, we bury, we exclude" (*WN*, 288). We create families; we extend our lives through technology; we devise complex and gorgeous religious systems; we build civilizations (here nodding to Freud) (*WN*, 284–90). Jack has sought refuge and protection through Hitler, one man who is "larger than death" (*WN*, 287). "On one level you wanted to conceal yourself in Hitler and his works. On another level you wanted to use him to grow in significance and strength" (*WN*, 287–88).

Prompted by Murray to become a "killer" rather than a "dier"—to overcome his desire to disappear in the mantle of Hitler (a disappearance symbolized by the sunglasses he wears in the persona of J. A. K. Gladney) and, instead, become more like Hitler in his willingness to kill other humans—Jack formulates a plot to kill Willie Mink, both out of the desire for revenge against the man who had sex with his wife, as well as in an effort to procure Dylar for himself. If, in the Old Burying Ground, Jack for the first and only time surrenders his inclination to plot and finds relief from his fear through such surrender, then at the conclusion of the novel Jack also finds momentary relief from his fear, now through an opposite embrace of the sense of control and power that comes through plotting and decisive action.

In his momentum toward becoming a killer, Jack begins carrying a pistol with him to school: "The gun created a second reality for me to inhabit. . . . It was a reality I could control, secretly dominate" (*WN*, 297). Jack's actions toward fulfillment of his plot become phantasmagoric and dreamlike and are marked above all by a general and uncharacteristic embrace of lawlessness. It begins with his theft of a neighbor's—the Stovers'!—automobile. He breaks traffic rules and runs a toll without paying. Through this lawlessness in the pursuit of his plot, he begins to feel Promethean, or Icarian, power: "This must be how people escape the pull of the earth, the gravitational leaf-flutter that brings us hourly closer to dying" (*WN*, 303). As Jack encounters Willie Mink in the motel room, he notices suddenly that he is surrounded by noise, at first "faint, monotonous, white," continuously building as he moves to shoot Willie—"white noise everywhere"—and finally crescendoing as Jack wounds Willie, when "the sound snowballed in the white room, adding on reflected waves" (*WN*, 306, 310, 312). In exact contrast to his experience in the cemetery—where silence, plotlessness, and the earthly and subterranean reign—in the German section of Iron City, a German-made gun in hand, Jack is surrounded by noise, liberated from "gravity" and the weight of the fear of death, becoming, he believes, for the first time a Hitlerian killer rather than a plotless dier. The fascist impulse to rule, to control human beings and nature by means of will and force, here coincide in the form of lawlessness, modern technology (the Zumwalt pistol), the infiltration of "foreign" toxic substances into the lives of the main characters (the "white noise," and more profoundly, German influences),[27] and, finally, the dream of overcoming the fact or fear of death by means of seemingly heroic action (here echoing the arguments of Ernest Becker).

Nothing Jack does, however, finally releases him from his fear of death. In this sense, Jack is "human, all-too-human": so long as Jack, Babette, Willie Mink, and any other person remains human, the fear of death necessarily remains. With great insight, DeLillo recognizes that the real human challenge is not finally to overcome mortality—there is budding confidence that immortality daily becomes a more realistic possibility during this or the next generation—but rather, to overcome the *fear* of death.[28] Even the technological mastery over natural forms of death—whether the solution to the symptoms of aging or the conquest of all known forms of disease—would not result in the overcoming of death, but merely the absence of nearly all causes of death except accidental ones. The technological and scientific solution for the causes of natural death would not solve the brute problem of death: our seemingly immortal existences might end mundanely as a result of a fall down the stairs or a tumble from a bicycle. In the condition of seemingly natural immortality, it is likely that humans would become ever *more fearful* of death—now in the form of accidental death—and instead organize their lives with the utmost trepidation and fearfulness, avoiding every potential danger that might lead to their now unnecessary deaths.[29] A pharmaceutical substance like Dylar—not aimed at our immortality, but instead at the erasure of that most fundamentally human quality that distinguishes us from all other creatures, namely, the knowledge of the fact of our own deaths—would be even more necessary than any other drugs for longevity in order to make humans truly at home in the world. The point of ultimate mastery points to the extinction of the human creature—and thus reveals the fundamental similarity between the Hitlerian drive for mastery and the aim of self-negation that lies behind the dream of Dylar.

There is only one character in the entire book who is wed to the human condition—ironically enough, a scientist. Winnie Richards, an infrequent presence only in Part Three of *White Noise*, is the biochemist whom Jack consults in order to gain information on Dylar. Upon hearing Jack's surmise that it may be a drug aimed at overcoming the fear of death, Winnie responds,

> I think it's a mistake to lose one's sense of death, even one's fear of death. Isn't death the boundary we need? Doesn't it give a precious texture to life,

> a sense of definition? You have to ask yourself whether anything you do in this life would have beauty or meaning without the knowledge of a final line, a border or limit. (*WN*, 228–29)

Much of the novel has pointed to the porous nature of all borders and boundaries—understood often enough as the ability of modern phenomena like automobiles, like radio signals, like clouds of toxic gas to move physically from one space to another without regard to boundaries or limits that once presented nearly insurmountable obstacles to such freedom of motion. The titles of Parts One and Two of *White Noise*—"Waves and Radiation" and "The Airborne Toxic Event"—each point to the modern capacity of innumerable substances to "enter" human ecologies and to overcome seemingly natural limits. The final section of the novel—"Dylarama"—points to the possibility of overcoming the final boundary or limit, not now one that is spatial or physical in nature, but rather temporal and psychic: the fear, or knowledge, of our own deaths. Winnie points out that the maintenance of such a "boundary," "a border or limit," may well be most fundamentally what makes human excellence possible. Perhaps because of the very existence of such a limit, humans pursue meaning within the confines of a natural human lifespan, through beauty or love, learning, friendship, or art. Perhaps even the effort to concoct a pharmaceutical that will overcome our fear of death is a form of such an attempt to fashion meaning, although now with self-contradictory implications. Winnie's suggestion calls into question Jack's fruitless search to overcome his fear rather than to attempt to see death "as less strange and unreferenced" because of his obsession with "self, self, self" (*WN*, 229). Winnie's worldview exists in direct opposition to Jack's increasing efforts to achieve control and mastery over the world and other humans: revealingly, he parts with Winnie by observing, "You're more than a fair-weather friend—you're a true enemy" (*WN*, 230). Winnie, in pointing to the necessity for "a border or limit," in a similar fashion to Jack's momentary perception of the limits of human life amid the graves in the Old Burying Ground, represents the true alternative to the modern attempt at mastery that is almost universally embraced by the characters in *White Noise*.

★ ★ ★ ★ ★

> The short space of sixty years will never confine the whole imagination of man; the incomplete joys of this world will never suffice for his heart. Alone among all beings, man shows a natural disgust for existence and an immense desire to exist: he scorns life and fears nothingness. These different instincts constantly drive his soul toward contemplation of another world, and it is religion that guides it there. Religion is therefore only a particular form of hope, and it is as natural to the human heart as hope itself. Only by a kind of aberration of the intellect and with the aid of a sort of moral violence exercised on

> their own nature do men stray from religious beliefs; an invincible inclination leads them back to them. Disbelief is an accident; faith alone is the permanent state of mankind.
>
> —Alexis de Tocqueville, *Democracy in America*

> When men have become accustomed to foreseeing from very far what should happen to them here below, and to nourishing themselves on hopes for it, it becomes difficult for them always to arrest their spirits at the precise boundaries of life, and they are very ready to cross these limits to cast their regard beyond. I therefore do not doubt that in habituating citizens to think of the future in this world, one would bring them little by little and without their knowing it to religious beliefs. Thus the means that permit men up to a certain point to do without religion is perhaps, after all, the only one remaining to us to lead the human race by a long detour back toward faith.
>
> —Alexis de Tocqueville, *Democracy in America*

> Out of some persistent sense of large-scale ruin, we kept inventing hope.
>
> —Don DeLillo, *White Noise*

Jack's plot does not come off.[30] Shortly after shooting Willie Mink, Jack is shot and suddenly seems to awaken from the power-induced hallucination that has driven him this far. Jack piles Mink and himself into the Stover's car and searches for an Iron City hospital. Eventually, he finds one—with a neon cross above its entrance—where he has a remarkable conversation about religion with a German nun.

Critics universally agree that this conversation is important. Yet, many critics typically understand the scene to reveal the falsity of religion in the modern age. Religion, like the "most photographed barn in America," or the Dylar-induced, false déjà vu experiences of Steffie and Denise, is simply yet another example of the pervasiveness of postmodern simulacra, that is, the infinite play of simulations behind which no reality ultimately lies (*WN*, 12). As John N. Duvall argues,

> Jack Gladney lives in a world of simulations, modelings of the world tied to no origin or source. The clearest example is SIMUVAC. . . . But SIMUVAC is just the edge of the wedge. At the Catholic hospital in the Germantown section of Iron City, where Jack takes Mink after both are shot, Jack discovers what amounts to SIMUFAITH.[31]

The one apparently explicit moment in which religion is discussed in the novel apparently reveals the falsity of such belief, the ultimate meaninglessness of belief in the modern age.

Modern American culture in *White Noise* appears to be relentlessly secular. There are two mentions of churches in the course of the novel, and they have been converted from a space of worship to buildings with convenient meeting rooms. Babette teaches an adult evening class on posture, and eventually eating and drinking, at the local Congregational Church.[32] The second mention of a religious building provides an even more striking incongruity: Jack holds his international Hitler conference in the college chapel (perhaps the juxtaposition is not so jarring as it first appears, since Jack stresses that the meeting is held in the "starkly modern chapel") (*WN*, 274). Holy spaces seem to have been emptied out to make room for instruction in the mundane or the obvious, or for academic explorations that are incapable of discerning evil in their subject matter.

Religion in its "traditional" form seems to be absent except for emptied or "converted" religious buildings, but faith and religious experience appear repeatedly in the course of the narration. These forms of "modern" faith serve as the backdrop against which the conversation of faith and religion between Jack and the German nun unfolds. All of these religious "moments" occur in the central chapter of the book, chapter 21, which also comprises the whole of Part Two of the book (the center of the three parts). The central location of these modern "religious" experiences points to the centrality of the religious theme. Even the novel's organization resembles a triptych painting, an older religious art form in which three panels would be connected both physically and thematically, with a special emphasis upon the painting in the central panel. Religion is "present" in this central chapter and section, even as God seems to be wholly absent. Thus, the novel appears to be a sustained reflection on how to understand the passing of the old God, on the enduring forms of religious belief, and in particular on what form faith will take in His absence. "When the old God leaves the world, what happens to all the unexpended faith?"[33]

While many critics have understood Jack to be wholly secular in orientation, twice in this central chapter Jack experiences moments of what can only be understood as spiritual epiphanies.[34] These two "religious" moments occur in connection with the two ways that life is encountered in the novel, as discussed earlier: they occur either in relation to the intimately private world of family life or in connection to the relentless spread of modern toxic substances in a porous and borderless world. After finding refuge from the airborne toxic event, Jack finds himself gazing at his sleeping children. A kind of religious awe overcomes him:

> In those soft warm faces was a quality of trust so absolute and pure that I did not want to think it might be misplaced. There must be something, somewhere, large and grand and redoubtable enough to justify this shining reliance and implicit belief. A feeling of desperate piety swept over me. It was cosmic in nature, full of yearnings and reachings. It spoke of vast forces. (*WN*, 154)

This description almost echoes an earlier sense of awe in response to the first glimpse of the airborne cloud of Nyodene D:

> Our fear was accompanied by a sense of awe that bordered on the religious. It is surely possible to be awed by the thing that threatens your life, to see it as a cosmic force, so much larger than yourself, more powerful, created by elemental and willful rhythms. (*WN*, 127)

Both of these responses—to childlike innocence, on the one hand, and to "death made in a laboratory," on the other (127)—point in elemental ways beyond the narrow confines of the forms of life which Jack inhabits, either the narrowly familial or the contrived products of human mastery that derive from the modern project. These momentary epiphanies reveal a hunger on Jack's part for a meaning and a source of existence that underlies all the apparent simulacra. He searches for faith in the only places known to him, finding there incomplete manifestations, insufficient or inappropriate but suggestive receptacles for his misplaced belief.

Two other kinds of religious belief are manifested in this central section of the novel. In the first, Jack briefly encounters a "true-believing" millenarian who joyously and in tones of superiority awaits the coming kingdom of God. Jack finds his certainty troubling:

> I wondered about his eerie self-assurance, his freedom from doubt. Is this the point of Armageddon? No ambiguity, no more doubt. He was ready to run into the next world. He was forcing the next world to seep into my consciousness, stupendous events that seemed matter-of-fact to him, self-evident, reasonable, imminent, true. (*WN*, 137)

The one encounter with a person who believes in a transcendent God reveals such a person to be wholly lacking in introspection, doubt, or a sense of man's inferiority and imperfection in comparison to the God whom the believer professes to revere. Echoing aspects of the oldest heresies—Pelagianism or Arianism—the believer in the "two cities" lacks any Augustinian sense of humility or uncertainty and a sense of the human inability to effect or even predict the end of time. Faith is a means of overcoming doubt, as well as a simultaneous admission of human insufficiency. Millenarianism is, in this sense, simply a religious form of modern attempts at mastery.[35]

The other form of belief takes the form of stories of the afterlife that one finds in the supermarket tabloids that Babette reads to Mr. Treadwell and, during the toxic disaster, to any interested listener. Babette reads of the discovery of reincarnation and past lives irrefutably discovered by researchers at Princeton's Institute for Advanced Studies. The response to the story by Mr. Treadwell and the other listeners is less than overwhelming, but it evokes a form of belief nonetheless: "The story occupied some recess of passive belief. There it was, familiar and comforting in its own strange way, a set of statements no less real than our daily quota of observable household fact" (*WN*, 144–45). But to these familiar readers of the tabloids, these kinds of stories are akin to facts: they are the modern source of religious "information" for countless Americans who have no other spiritual life. As the final words of the novel relate, the alternative reality created every week by the tabloids provides a singular narrative into which our "unexpended" faith can flow:

> Everything we need that is not food or love is here in the tabloid racks. The tales of the supernatural and the extraterrestrial. The miracle vitamins, the cures for cancer, the remedies for obesity. The cults of the famous and the dead. (*WN*, 326)

Notably, it is Mr. Treadwell—blind, infirm, isolated, and without neighbors who notice his absence—who is addicted to the meaning that is provided by the tabloids. DeLillo describes a modern America in which alternative sources of belief are wholly desiccated, leaving only the epiphanic, the millennial, or the perverse.

Far from "secularized," the America of *White Noise* is replete with religiosity, but a religiosity manifested in forms of belief oriented in individualist, excessive, or aberrant directions. These characters are remarkably reminiscent of Tocqueville's analysis of the religious "enthusiasms" to which he believed democratic man would increasingly be prone. Because of the dominance of materialism in the lives of democratic people, religious beliefs will have been all but repressed. Nevertheless, Tocqueville believed that humans were incapable finally of religious forms of belief and that in such times, such belief would break out in excessive forms. "Although the desire to acquire the goods of the world may be the dominant passion of Americans, there are moments of respite when their souls seem to all at once break the material bonds that restrain them" (*DA*, 510). This "fierce spiritualism" gives rise to "bizarre sects" and innumerable "religious follies." Tocqueville describes a country of various religious manias, due not to excessive religiosity *per se*, but to a religious impulse that has been inadequately cultivated and improperly directed. The excess comes about as a result of the *absence* of healthy religious forms, not from a culture that is not yet sufficiently secularized. Tocqueville suggests that societies will be religious regardless of the attempts to create thoroughgoing materialism and that such attempts will only have the effect of fostering religious excesses:

> If the social state, circumstances, and laws did not restrain the American spirit so closely in the search for well-being, one might believe that when it came to be occupied with immaterial things, it would show more reserve and more experience and would moderate itself without trouble. But it feels itself imprisoned within limits from which it is seemingly not allowed to leave. As soon as it passes these limits, it does not know where to settle, and it often runs without stopping beyond the bounds of common sense. (*DA*, 511)

This implicit portrayal of belief that will find avenues of expression—most often in excessive and aberrant forms—informs the final conversation between Jack and the German nun. Jack's first impression of the nun is one of comforting piety: a picture of the Pope in heaven makes Jack "feel good, sentimentally refreshed" (*WN*, 317). Yet, upon asking the nun whether all the old verities are still observed, she responds, "Do you think we are stupid?" (*WN*, 317). Jack insists she must be mistaken—after all, she is a nun, and it is important that she believe. "This is true," she said. "The non-believers need the believers. They are desperate to have someone believe" (*WN*, 318). She reveals that their entire way of life is a pretense—that they simply pretend to believe in order to afford comfort to those who need to believe that some people believe:

> "It is for others. Not for us. . . . The others who spend their lives believing that *we* still believe. It is our task in the world to believe things no one else takes seriously. To abandon such beliefs completely, the human race would die. This is why we are here. A tiny minority. To embody old things, old beliefs. The devil, the angels, heaven, hell. If we did not pretend to believe these things, the world would collapse."
>
> "Your dedication is a pretense?"
>
> "Our pretense is a dedication." (*WN*, 318–19)

The nun appears to embrace the exact opposite of Luther's *sola fides*, instead manifesting an exaggeration of Catholicism: works without faith. At first, it seems their works consist of their willingness to minister to the sick and indigent in the inner city. But, Jack discovers that their good works actually consist of the pretense of belief.

Yet, the nun reveals that her pretense is undertaken for more fundamental reasons: without the pretense of religious belief, "the human race would die," "the world would collapse." In an echo of Dostoyevsky, she seems to imply that if the world knew of the death of God, all would be permitted. Yet, she refuses to allow this outcome: her life, until the moment of her death, will be committed to the appearance of belief. More revealingly, it is the apparent unbelievers who need this appearance of belief. Presumably, the nuns live, and could live well, without true belief; the unbelievers live with the need for true belief. It is as if the actual figures have been reversed: the nuns are the nihilists; the "unbelievers" are finally among the faithful, or at least those in need of the possibility for faith. The nuns' belief is a pretense; but equally, the unbelief of those who look to the nuns may also finally be something of a pretense, itself masking profound hunger for belief and a craving for faith that goes unfulfilled in a world of pretense and simulacra.

Yet, to keep alive even the possibility of faith, because civilization itself rests on belief, is to acknowledge that faith "is the permanent state of mankind." Faith will manifest itself, either "calmly" or perversely, but as Jack's own fears and epiphanies suggest, the human condition is finally one of alienation in which we cannot truly be at home. We think necessarily about a home and a condition that cannot be achieved either in the midst of our nuclear family, or through the material plenty assisted by the insecticides that also produce Nyodene D, or the salvation afforded by Dylar. *White Noise* is thus far from a celebration of the postmodern condition: it rather advances a searing critique of the emptiness of modernity and the shallowness of postmodernity and points to the possibility of post-postmodernity. Thus, through a long detour, democratic man may be led back to faith.

Notes

1. Don DeLillo, interview by Caryn James, *New York Times Book Review*, January 13, 1985, reprinted in Don DeLillo, *White Noise*, ed. Mark Osteen, Viking Critical Edition (New York: Penguin Books, 1998), 333–34; hereafter cited as *WN*.

2. DeLillo, *WN*, Critical Edition, 333.

3. On America's attraction to the mystery genre, and its connection to American democracy, see Wilson Carey McWilliams, "Democracy and Mystery: On Civic Education in America," *Halcyon* 11 (1989). Many of the great American authors were inexorably drawn to the mystery genre: see, for example, Mark Twain, "The Double-Barreled Detective Story" and the recently discovered "A Murder, a Mystery, and a Marriage," *Atlantic Monthly*, July/August 2001. Of course, among the best American authors wrote exclusively in the detective genre, notably Raymond Chandler.

4. Plots are also mentioned (e.g., DeLillo, *WN*, 291, 292).

5. Don DeLillo, "The Art of Fiction CXXXV," interview by Adam Begley, *Paris Review* 35, no. 128 (fall 1993): 275.

6. Don DeLillo, "Seven Seconds: An Interview," by Ann Arensberg, *Vogue* (August 1988): 338. Many critics have noted a change in DeLillo's fiction after 1980; DeLillo spent 1979 to 1982 living abroad, including time in Greece. His time abroad, in particular, helped him to see qualities about America that contributed to his concerns in writing *White Noise*:

> When I came back to this country in 1982, I began to notice something on television which I hadn't noticed before. This was the daily toxic spill—there was the news, the weather, and the toxic spill. This was a phenomenon no one even mentioned. It was simply a television reality. It's only the people themselves involved who seemed to be affected by them. No one even talked about them. This was one of the motivating forces of *White Noise*. [Quoted in John Duvall, *Don DeLillo's* Underworld: *A Reader's Guide* (New York: Continuum, 2002), 13].

7. In order to escape the "white noise" of America, Murray Siskind argues that we "have to learn to look as children again" (*WN*, 50). See Arnold Weinstein's discussion in *Nobody's Home: Speech, Self, and Place in American Fiction from Hawthorne to DeLillo* (New York: Oxford University Press, 1993), 298–99: "The capacity to be insider and outsider, 'to look as children again,' enables the author to depict the known world with the eye-opening vision of a Martian visitor, an anthropologist

seeking religious patterns in the daily routine of Americans" (298). The novel suggests how difficult this "insider/outsider" status is to achieve, since the children are perhaps more immersed in "white noise" than even the adults. Fiction—as DeLillo himself would acknowledge—continues to be surpassed by reality, since even the apparent innocence of Wilder is increasingly under assault by the extension of electronic media to the very young. See Tamar Lewin, "A Growing Number of Video Viewers Watch from the Crib," *New York Times*, October 29, 2003, A1, A21, which reveals that "a quarter of children under 2 have a television in their room" and "59 percent of children 6 months to 2 years watch television, and 42 percent watch a videotape or DVD."

8. See, e.g., Leonard Wilcox, "Baudrilliard, DeLillo's *White Noise*, and the End of the Heroic Narrative," *Contemporary Literature* 32 (1991): 346–65, and Michael Messmer, "'Thinking It Through Completely: The Interpretation of Nuclear Culture," *Centennial Review* 34 (1988): 397–413. For passing references to Baudrilliard and other French postmodern figures, see also Cornel Bonca, "Don DeLillo's *White Noise*: The Natural Language of the Species," in DeLillo, *WN*, Critical Edition, 456–79, and John N. Duvall, "The (Super) Marketplace of Images: Television as Unmediated Mediation in DeLillo's *White Noise*," in DeLillo, *WN*, Critical Edition, 432–55.

9. On "postmodernism rightly understood" (or even post-postmodernity) as a condition fundamentally antithetical to modernity, see Peter A. Lawler, *Postmodernism Rightly Understood* (Lanham, MD: Rowman & Littlefield, 1999). Lawler argues that "postmodernism" in its contemporary understanding is, in fact, a form of "hypermodernism," and that "postmodernism rightly understood" points instead to the rejection of corrosive forms of modernity, including atomism, aggressive atheism, and the attempt to overcome all natural limits.

10. I will discuss a fourth theme in a subsequent, revised version of this chapter: the inability of democratic man to make judgments and, thus, to distinguish between that which is praiseworthy and that which should be condemned. For a superb exploration of DeLillo's critical stance toward postmodern relativism, see Paul A. Cantor, "Adolf, We Hardly Knew You," in *New Essays on White Noise* (New York: Cambridge University Press, 1991), 39–62.

11. Alexis de Tocqueville, *Democracy in America*, trans. Harvey C. Mansfield and Delba Winthrop (Chicago: University of Chicago Press, 2000); hereafter cited as *DA*.

12. Judith Laurence Pastore, "Marriage American Style: Don DeLillo's Domestic Satire," *Voices in Italian Americana* 1 (fall, 1990): 1–19, has detected in the satirical portrayal of the Gladney family a subtle critique of the "postmodern" family and an endorsement of more "traditional" families that stems from his Italian American and Catholic heritage.

13. This aspect of television has been perceptively explored by Neal Postman in *Amusing Ourselves to Death: Public Discourse in the Age of Show Business* (New York: Penguin Books, 1985). A conversation among the Gladney family lacks even the nondescript transitional phrase that occurs frequently in television news programming, "Now this . . ." Postman stresses that television delivers a cascade of information without an accompanying context or history (99–113). The fact that Babette mentions her knowledge of camels in Utah as a result of a past history exam is, in this sense, profoundly ironic.

14. Among the more interesting statistical data about American family life is the declining frequency of dinner parties, card games, and other informal gatherings with friends and neighbors, which can be tracked from the 1950s to the present. See Robert D. Putnam, *Bowling Alone: The Collapse and Revival of American Community* (New York: Simon and Schuster, 2000), 93–115.

15. Hannah Arendt, *The Human Condition*, 2nd ed. (Chicago: University of Chicago Press, 1998), 198.

16. See Cantor, "Adolf, We Hardly Knew You." When Peter Singer was hired at Princeton University, several protest rallies against his views on euthanasia of young children and the mentally infirm were held on campus, although the protestors were almost exclusively nonlocal members of an organization called Not Dead Yet. Very few, if any, local citizens, students, or faculty objected to Singer's appointment.

17. It is interesting to note the long catalog of items that are accumulated in the station wagons. A first list includes "traditional" items like suitcases, clothing, blankets, books, bicycles, skis, and even "English and Western saddles." A list immediately following includes stereos, radios, computers, birth control pills, and junk food (*WN*, 3). The very first descriptions—from the combination of the first section's words "waves" (originally, water's natural motion) and "radiation" (the waste of modern science); to the juxtaposition of the station wagons and the "campus"; to the two lists of alternatively "traditional" and modern items—suggest that DeLillo seeks to draw an implicit comparison between the ancient and the modern.

18. See Wilfred McClay, *The Masterless: Self and Society in Modern America* (Chapel Hill: University of North Carolina Press, 1994), 24–26, on the transformative nationalizing effect of the railroads—including the significance of the need to introduce standardized time zones, a form of "technological" engineering that replaced time telling as the rough calculation based on the sun's position wherever one might happen to be standing.

19. See Thomas Peyser, "Globalization in America: The Case of Don DeLillo's *White Noise*," *Clio* 25, no. 3 (1996): 255–71. Peyser writes, "DeLillo suggests that national culture provides the vanished middle ground between global and local that the family needs in order to thrive" (268). While I share the view that DeLillo's characterization of "globalization" is critical, I don't conclude that DeLillo endorses the national, but rather recognizes the *loss* of the local, with the only alternatives careening between the severely atomistic and the vacuously global.

20. The only form of "entrance" that is opposed occurs during a scene in which Babette proposes to read erotica to Jack. "I don't want you to choose anything [to read] that has men inside women, quote-quote, or men entering women. 'I entered her.' 'He entered me.' We're not lobbies or elevators" (*WN*, 29).

21. It is worth noting that the Department of American Environments discusses almost exclusively topics centered on popular culture—especially film and television. "Environment" is not understood as connected to nature, but to human cultural inventions. This is, in fact, a more accurate understanding of "environment," inasmuch as that even in its more common usage in reference to the "natural" environment, humans are still the focus—the creature being "environed." Contrast the sense of the word "environment"—with its human-centered emphasis—with the implications of the word "nature." Rather than being at the center of nature, humans are best understood as part of nature's bounty and subject to nature's limits.

See Wilson Carey McWilliams, "Introduction," *Democracy and the Claims of Nature*, ed. Ben A. Minter and Bob Pepperman Taylor (Lanham, MD: Rowman & Littlefield, 2002).

22. The New York émigrés spend enormous amounts of time "remembering" irrelevant minutiae (such as where they were when they brushed their teeth with a finger) or where they were when crucial things happened on television or to media stars—such as what each was doing when James Dean died (*WN*, 67–69).

23. Tom LeClair, "Closing the Loop: *White Noise*," in DeLillo, *WN*, Critical Edition, 407.

24. Ernest Becker, *The Denial of Death* (New York: Free Press, 1973).

25. This singularity of the Old Burying Ground is also noted by Leonard Orr in *Don DeLillo's* White Noise*: A Reader's Guide* (New York: Continuum, 2003), 46: "The only place of silence in the entire novel, as Jack stands and listens, The Old Burying Ground of Blacksmith Village, out on the road, pre-twentieth century, forgotten, lost to the world, out of the loop, both comforting and disturbing."

26. Jack's momentary reflection upon the possible superiority of "life" after death perhaps not unintentionally recalls the reflections of Socrates in the moments before his death in the *Phaedo*. This resonant connection has been sensitively explored by J. Peter Euben in *Platonic Noise* (Princeton, NJ: Princeton University Press, 2003), 141–73.

27. I will further develop the "toxic" portrayal of German influences in the novel, but for the time being, a suggestion rather than a full-blown analysis will have to suffice. The role of German things in the novel appears to be sufficiently malevolent to suggest that DeLillo views German sources to be of decisive influence in the development of modernity and postmodernity. If this view contains, therefore, an implicit critique of the influence of German sources (and, in the deepest background, German philosophy), then DeLillo's view has an uncanny resemblance to the argument about the baleful influence of German philosophy advanced a few years later by Allan Bloom in *The Closing of the American Mind* (New York: Simon & Schuster, 1987). Bloom's own view of the unfortunate influence of Nietzschean and Heideggerian philosophy in the modern West echoed an argument first advanced by his teacher, Leo Strauss, particularly in his seminal essay, "Three Waves of Modernity," in *Political Philosophy: Six Essays*, ed. Hilail Gildin (Indianapolis: Pegasus, 1975). On the Heideggerian aspects of the novel, see especially Michael Valdez Moses, "Lust Removed from Nature," in *New Essays: White Noise*, ed. Frank Lentricchia (Cambridge, U.K.: Cambridge University Press, 1991): 64–86.

28. Serious scientific discussions about the possibility of functional immortality are ubiquitous; a recent example in the popular media is James Gorman's article, "High-Tech Dreamers Investing in Immortality," *The New York Times*, November 1, 2003, B7, B9.

29. This point has been forcefully made by Peter A. Lawler. See, for instance, Lawler's introduction to *Aliens in America: The Strange Truth about Our Souls* (Wilmington: I. S. I. Books, 2002), especially xxiii–xxix.

30. There are a number of failed "plots" in the novel: for example, Orestes Mercator's planned attempt to break a record of consecutive days with poisonous snakes also fails miserably. Willie Mink's plan to prove the efficacy of Dylar fails. More interestingly still, there have even been questions whether the "plot" of *White Noise* is finally successful, in particular because there is disagreement about

the success or failure of the conclusion of the novel. See Orr, *Don DeLillo's* White Noise, 27–28 (on the scholarly disagreement over the significance of Wilder's tricycle ride across the expressway in the last chapter) and 36 (on the "plotlessness" of the novel's structure).

31. Duvall, "The (Super) Market Place of Images," 442.

32. Not only are memory and generational transmission all but nonexistent in Blacksmith, but even the elderly must be taught—or retaught—what they might once have been expected to know and pass on to a recalcitrant younger generation. Babette later relates that she has been asked to teach a subsequent class on eating and drinking (*WN*, 27, 171).

33. Don DeLillo, *Mao II* (New York: Viking, 1991), 7.

34. Leonard Orr's comment is representative: he notes the singularity of the conversation between Jack and the German nun, inasmuch as "religion did not appear anywhere else in his thinking or activities during the book" (*Don DeLillo's* White Noise, 69). Not surprisingly, of the nine subject sections into which Orr divides the novel for purposes of discussion, none is devoted to an exploration of religion.

Among the authors DeLillo has pointed out as influential to his intellectual development is James Joyce, whose book *The Portrait of the Artist as a Young Man* features a character—Stephen Daedalus—who has a series of epiphanies during the course of the novel (Duvall, *Don DeLillo's* Underworld, 16–17).

35. DeLillo has written a fascinating essay in which he compares a secularized strain of millenarian religious belief with Nazism. He notes his own indebtedness to the study of Norman Cohn, *The Pursuit of the Millennium: Revolutionary Messianism in Medieval and Reformation Europe and Its Bearing on Modern Totalitarian Movements* (New York: Oxford University Press, 1970). See Don DeLillo, "Silhouette City: Hitler, Manson and the Millennium," in DeLillo, *WN*, Critical Edition, 344–52.

Index